KATEI
RYORI

FAMILY
COOKING

家庭料理

KIMIKO'S WORLD

Kimiko Sugano

Illustrations by
Tricia Sugano Grannis

Introduction by
ROBERT JOFFREY

Strawberry Hill Press
2594 15th Avenue
San Francisco, California 94127

Edited by Renee Renouf

Book design by Carlton C. Herrick and Nina Bredt

Typeset by Elan Graphic Resources

Cover by Ku, Fu-sheng

Printed by Abbey Press, Oakland, California

Library of Congress Cataloging in Publication Data

Sugano, Kimiko, 1927-
    Kimiko's world.

    Includes index.
    1. Cookery, Japanese.   2. Japan—Social life and customs.   I. Title.
TX724.5.J3S795   641.5952   82-5819
ISBN 0-89407-048-7   AACR2

To my daughters Arleen and Tricia
for helping me to share my world

Acknowledgments

October 4, 1980 is a date I will never forget. Feeling a bit as though I was a borrowed child, looking out at San Francisco Bay, I was riding to the Concord Pavilion to see the Peking Opera. I was totally absorbed in a personal heartache and nursing my sorrows, so I was not paying much attention to what was being discussed amongst the other passengers. The moon in front of our moving car was full and yellow, low on the horizon of the East Bay hills.

The man at the wheel, all of a sudden, directed his comments toward me. This man was Jean-Louis Brindamour, publisher of Strawberry Hill Press, and the man sitting next to him was his partner, Ku Fu-sheng. Jean-Louis was proposing I write a Japanese cookbook!

I looked, bewildered, at my friend, Renee Renouf, sharing the backseat with me. It was simultaneously exciting and scary, the book writing prospect, for the proposal was not for an ordinary cookbook of Japanese receipes, but would include my early life and the culture of my homeland.

I felt uncomfortable about my English competency. I looked at Renee again and realized she was responsible for creating the memorable, magical moment for me. *Kimiko's World* would never have been possible without her, and I am most grateful.

I would like to thank others for their time and assistance. Landonis Gettel assisted me in my poetry translations. Jane Garcia, Josephine Ventury and Cindy Gee helped type the manuscript. Besides dealing with their daily details, my daughters helped in a great way — Arleen Yoshiko for transcribing my tapes and Patricia Naomi for illustrating the text so beautifully.

Finally, I feel much gratitude to Jean-Louis Brindamour, Ku Fu-sheng and Carlton Herrick, who designed this book.

Portola Valley, California
September 1981

Contents

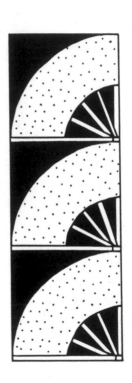

Introduction

It gives me pleasure to introduce Kimiko-san's book of family cooking and festival recipes, a pleasure second only to eating the results!

Dance is a universal language, and the popularity of ballet in Japan has grown continuously during the twentieth century. Now there is a yearly international ballet competition in Japan and some of the recent winners in other international ballet competitions have come from the Land of the Rising Sun.

Soon after Gerald Arpino and I met Kimiko Sugano in Hawaii, the Joffrey Company began to enjoy early summer seasons in the San Francisco Bay Area. Our annual visits were jointly sponsored by artistic institutions in the area and the Dance Touring Program of the National Endowment for the Arts. In a very real sense, our growth as a company has been very clearly connected with our Bay Area appearances where we always have been warmly and cordially received.

Mrs. Sugano and her two daughters have been faithful and enthusiastic supporters and members of the audience during these Bay Area engagements. Kimiko-san's graciousness rapidly expanded from the flowers given to the company and crew members to dinners at local Japanese restaurants where she diligently explained the subtleties and rationale of Japanese cuisine to Mr. Arpino and me. When the company started appearing at the San Francisco Opera House, Kimiko-san expanded her practice to *obentos*, or lunches. More recently, Mr. Arpino and I had designated two special *obento* boxes which Kimiko-san reserves especially for our San Francisco visits.

Kimiko-san's collection of youthful memories, festival and domestic recipes very clearly reflects the thoughtful, traditional schooling and sensitivity to which Kimiko's flowers and *obento* boxes have been such personal testimony over the seasons.

Another audience member, *Dance News* correspondent for the Bay Area, Renee Renouf, should be acknowledged for having persuaded Strawberry Hill Press to provide the dance and eating worlds with a glimpse of Kimiko-san's rare and unique art of living.

Robert Joffrey
Artistic Director, Joffrey Ballet
Member, National Council on the Arts

Kimiko's World

May I invite you to open this book as you would a door, leading you to explore the fascinating traditions of *Katei-Ryori*, Japanese family cooking.

Let me confess my Japanese heritage did not confer special competence in the kitchen. My parents sent me to Tomi Egami, Japan's most famous cooking teacher as part of my post-university "finishing" experience. Like many other pampered young persons, however, I was not expected to practice my learned skill in the kitchen.

After I was married and moved to Hawaii, I found that people there *expected* me to cook. I was ashamed to admit *I did not know how*. Getting out my cooking school notebooks and taking one menu at a time, I taught myself each dish, step by step, repeating each menu until I had mastered it. (The notebooks were spattered with *shoyu!*) The final results were so enthusiastically received by my guests that I was persuaded to share this knowledge.

I undertake being your guide with pleasure and confidence. The opportunity to teach many Americans in person, as well as through television, has provided me with valuable experience in anticipating your questions. Each recipe in this collection has been carefully selected for the availability of ingredients in local markets. I have attempted to present directions in a clear, concise manner so that you soon will approach the challenge of cooking the Japanese way with confidence.

Although my book is contemporary in its approach, I wish to mention with respect and love the remarkable heritage of *Katei-Ryori*. Mealtime in Japan has always been considered an art, a labor of love, and not a swiftly concluded necessity.

The flow of influence from China, commencing in the seventh century, A.D., came to a nearly complete end in the ninth. As the Japanese moved into a long era of isolation, my ancestors created a refined, exquisite way of life, blending the best of both cultures. The art, literature, architecture as well as the preparation and serving of food, are the offspring of this union.

What came to be developed were methods of cooking which can be divided into five broad groups, having minor differences among them. Some methods are rarely used, and one should bear in mind that it is nearly impossible to make a generalization.

1. Katei Ryori — family cooking, is an everyday meal meant to be prepared for family members. The dishes are rich in nutrition and are eaten with boiled white rice.

2. Kaiseki Ryori — tea ceremony dishes, were developed by Sen Rikyu in the sixteenth century and derived from the tea ceremony or *Cha-No-Yu*. It is said the right materials, flavoring and seasoning — and, most importantly, the right heart — are the most important ingredients of *Kaiseki*.

3. Gishiki Ryori — ceremonial dishes, are served for either celebration or mourning. Dishes carry the symbolic meaning of the event. For instance, lobster is a very important food for festival days and its body is bent to resemble that of many old people's backs. Those partaking of the lobster hope to achieve the ripe old age which it symbolizes.

4. Kaiseki Ryori — party dishes, have a different *kanji,* or Chinese character, than that of the tea ceremony dishes, even though the pronunciation is the same. This cooking is intended to enhance sake drinking and is most often served at teahouse-style restaurants. In good establishments, ten courses usually are served and enjoyed by Japanese as well as visitors to Japan. Sushi is a part of this cooking style.

5. Yushiki Ryori — court dishes, date back to the Nara period, 645-794 A.D. This style was served at the Imperial Court and practiced among courtiers. It is not now practiced except for very special occasions.

To return to *Katei Ryori,* this cooking has a tradition of long-standing knowledge, passed from grandmother to mother, mother to daughter. It is thought everyday meals for the family should be varied, nourishing and delectable, emphasizing the natural tastes of the ingredients. *Katei Ryori* history starts in the Heian period, about 830 A.D. when the nobleman, Sanin Chunagon ran the Imperial Household. He had to provide meals for the Emperor, his consort, the Empress, and 45 princes and princesses! This cultivated nobleman learned to delight his imperial diners with offerings of an astonishing creation, but from simple ingredients. The Imperial Household was living in impoverished conditions at the time, under the power of Fujiwara Kampaku, the regent.

Sanin Chunagon's style of cooking became *shiji-ryu.* Most methods of Japanese vegetable cutting were evolved from his methods.

Essential to Japanese tradition is bringing to the table meals reflecting the seasons. Spring dishes are adorned with sprigs of pine or crisp, green leaves. Autumn selections are cushioned on several freshly washed maple or chrysanthemum leaves. Visual excitement is created, using dishes and bowls whose shape displays the food to advantage. Sometimes the shells of fruit and seashells are selected, together with the careful arrangement of contrasting textures, colors and shapes. Tables are throughtfully arranged rather than "set." Thus, the Japanese meal is organized to achieve a synthesis to please sight and taste. In attaining this harmony, Japanese food is internationally recognized as a superb aesthetic dining experience.

Several small notes should be made here. There is strict procedure of types of dishes to be served at festivals and on festive occasions. Variations do exist, but here is the principle of the type of food and the order of its service:

Zensai — hors d'oeuvres	*Aemono* — salad
Suimono — a clear soup	*Shiizakana* — fried things
Mukozuke — raw fish	*Gohan* — rice
Hachizakana — broiled fish	*Bancha* — tea
Nimono — boiled things	

TABLE SETTING

I thought it would be of interest to chart the progression and positioning of courses for a formal Japanese dinner. My daughter Tricia devised the accompanying chart to indicate where the dishes go. The numbers conform to the following list:

1. **Sakazuki** — wine cup
2. **Zatsuki** — hors d'oeuvres
3. **Suimono** — clear soup
4. **Mukozuke** — raw fish
5. **Kachitori** — special dish
6. **Hachizakana** — broiled fish
7. **Nimono** — boiled dish
8. **Sunomono** — salad
9. **Shiizakana** — entree
10. **Gohan** — rice
11. **Miso Shiru** — miso soup
12. **Konomono** — pickle

It looks like a lot, doesn't it? But when you realize that such a dinner is pre-served and habitually Japanese food portions are small and carefully arranged to conform with the plate or bowl in which it is served, the length will not seem quite so gargantuan!

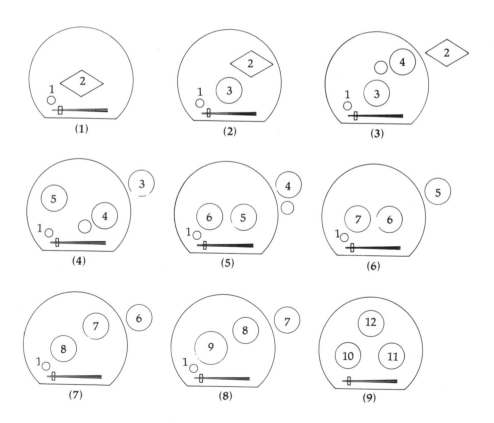

At Japanese dinners and other meals this order usually is followed, omitting one or two dishes in the sequence for informal dining.

Most of my recipes will be grouped around special menus relating to festivals, but there are some which are *simply* seasonal. These dishes are grouped according to their place in the order of a meal and start with the simple recipes and proceed to the more complex. Each of the recipes is designed to serve five or six persons, depending upon appetite!

One might assume Japanese cooking is too difficult to attempt at home. However, many dishes are relatively simple and uncomplicated, allowing the cook to experiment and be imaginative. The same holds true in the method of serving, whether the food is served on leaves, in bowls, or on oblong dishes. Except for obvious requirements like bowls for sauces, soups and a liquid vegetable or meat dish, one's eye and feeling for the appropriate frame for the food is the measuring stick.

We Japanese have much folklore in our life which permeates our way of doing things. Numbers are included. Five, for instance, is a magical number in Japan — sets of older ceramics come in fives — five cups, five plates, etc. There are five colors and five flavors as well. The five flavors, particularly *shoyu* and the uses of vinegars, you will find discussed in the Introduction. Ingredients discussed will follow the Japanese order for a meal and you will find this in festival dishes in sections on the four seasons.

The five flavors are: *shoyu*, salt, sugar, vinegar and hot spices. Hot spices are considered mustard, ginger root or *shoga* and *wasabi*.

Dave Brubeck composed a popular tune called "Take Five." In Japan, five is not just a tune, it's a way of life!

ETIQUETTE

The biggest adjustment to eating Japanese-style relates to the knees, for if you eat in the traditional Japanese manner you will be sitting with your legs jackknifed underneath you. Japanese restaurants, however, have learned to cheat, providing a well underneath the table so that you can sit at a low table but still not have to fold your legs beneath you. Japanese tables are low, perhaps fifteen inches high, because of our tradition of sitting on *tatami* without our street shoes on. Those we leave at the door upon entering the home and in traditional Japanese homes one sleeps with *futons* or blanket-like pallets which we pick up and fold away during the day.

Most of our meals are eaten with *hashi* or chopsticks. The dishes are pre-served and brought in separate portions to each member of the family dining. Wherever possible, meals are presented on separate table-like trays or *ozen*. One-pot cooking is either "country style" or has connection with the Japanese desire to "Westernize" — such as *sukiyaki*.

When offered sake at the beginning of the meal, one reciprocates by pouring sake for someone else. It is considered impolite either to pour one's own sake or to drink before the host gives the signal for everyone to raise one's cup. Turn the cup upside down if you do not wish a refill. (It's a new interpretation of the phrase "bottoms up!")

Rice is served at practically every meal and it should be uncovered first. The bowl is held in the left hand with the middle three fingers underneath, the thumb pressing down on the upper rim. The procedure is reversed for the left-handed. It may be brought close to the face when using chopsticks, but one never empties the bowl if one is having another helping, only at the end of the meal.

Soup is drunk directly from the bowl without a spoon. Garnish is removed with *hashi*.

We also have a pleasant habit of providing hot towels in individual trays before and after meals. We believe in instant refreshment!

SPECIAL EQUIPMENT

The Japanese have developed many special cooking utensils. Some have equivalents in Western and American cooking ware, but some are unique. While I have included their names in the Glossary, I mention several now, for I refer to them in recipes by their Japanese names. Most Japanese household and hardware stores carry these items.

I might also mention that the dream of every Japanese cook is to own a set of knives tempered by a swordmaker. They are, of course, very expensive now, but as you can imagine highly prized and carefully handled by generations of cooks whose families had them made during the times when samaurai were active swordsmen. A few swordmakers are still alive. I remember my teacher, Tomi Egami, telling me about one who was very temperamental about for whom he would make a set of these knives. So, the privilege of having a set made these days means that the maker likes you as much as it says your pocketbook can afford it! It is an interesting distinction, but then you will find this form of elitism is not uncommon in Japan!

Benrina — Slicer, the Japanese precursor of the Cuisinart! It is a "must" for slicing, grating and shredding.

Bocho, Hocho — Knives, by themselves are called *hocho*. It is only when they are modified by a special usage that they become *bocho* — the character remains the same.

Traditionally Japanese knives are made of tempered steel with single cutting edges. Today, stainless steel and other metals are available, but none can match the finely honed iron knives, which I personally prefer and use whenever I can. Since iron knives rust easily, they must be kept dry when not in use. A light scrub with cleansing powder removes the rust. The Japanese often use ashes. The various knives are known as: **deba bocho** — for fish and meat, a heavy-duty, tapered knife; **ko deba bocho** — for preparing shellfish; **sashimi bocho** — for slicing fillets of raw fish; **usuba bocho** — for cutting vegetables and soft materials, a broad bladed knife.

Donabe — Earthenware pots used for cooking one-pot dishes. These pots have a glaze inside, but are earthenware outside. When the outside is wet, one needs to avoid placing it directly on the heat for it might crack and then the stove gets the stew and not your guests!

Hashi — Chopsticks. We have long bamboo ones for cooking, short ones for eating and serving.

Kana-gushi — Metal skewers.

Katsuo-bushi-Kezuri — Box used for dried bonito shavings.

Makuno-uchi-kata — For pressing small rice balls for *bento*, made of cedar wood.

Miso-Koshi — A strainer made of bamboo in a basket shape. The miso-koshi is placed over the *dashi* and one strains the *miso* through the bamboo *koshi* into the *dashi*. An ordinary medium sized wire sieve will substitute. Japanese prefer bamboo or wood in most things since it avoids any metallic taste.

Mushi-ki — A food steamer, usually two tiers in height. Can be purchased round or square in shape and originally was made of bamboo. Steaming is an economical way of cooking since little heat is required to generate a great deal of moist heat. Moisture and heat makes for the maximum of flavor and tenderness in steamed food. Most food prepared this way is placed in a special container so that the metallic surfaces of the *mushi-ki* does not touch it.

Nagashi-bako — A metal mold used for gelatin and custard. It possesses a removable inner tray. *Nagashi-bako* is convenient for it has many uses.

Oshi-waku — Square in shape and made of cedar wood, *oshi-waku* is used for pressing rice and other ingredients together.

Shamoji or **Hera** — Rice spoon. A wooden, spatula-shaped spoon or paddle for mixing and serving rice. Used with the *uragoshi* to press ingredients through it.

Sudare — Bamboo slats lashed together to form mats. Used for rolling foods, such as *sushi*.

Sukiyaki-nabe — Heavy skillet made of cast iron. After use one must wash and dry it immediately over high heat. Inner surface is then coated lightly with oil after each cleaning before the skillet cools.

Suribachi — A stone or earthenware bowl with rough inner surface — the Japanese version of the mortar — used for grinding and mashing various ingredients into fine particles or a puree.

Suri-kogi — Used to crush and grind ingredients against the inside wall and bottom of the *suribachi*. The stick is made of fragrant cedar wood.

Sushi-oke — Used for preparing *sushi* rice, and is made of cedar wood.

Take-gushi — Bamboo skewers.

Tamago-yaki-nabe — Omelet pans, rectangular in shape, with wooden handle. The very best are made of copper.

Togi-ishi — Stone for sharpening knives.

Uchiwa — Flat fan to cool *sushi* rice while seasoning.

Uragoshi — Strainer used for soft ingredients and sifting flour or draining liquids.

SHOYU

Shoyu, or Japanese soy sauce, is perhaps the most important seasoning in Japanese cooking, and is one of the five traditional flavors, which are: *shoyu*, salt, sugar, vinegar and hot spices. The taste of many dishes, in fact, depends on

Sukiyaki-nabe (heavy skillet)

Donabe (earthenware casserole)

Wok

Suribachi (mortar and pestle)

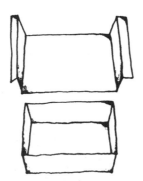
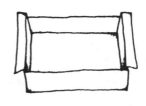

Nagashi-bako (metal mold)

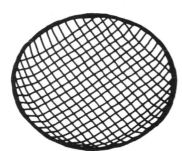

Uragoshi (sieves)

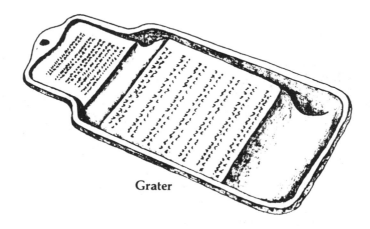

Grater

Deba Bocho

Sachimi Bocho

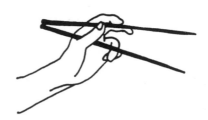

Hashi (chopsticks/how to use)

the amount and quality of *shoyu* used. *Shoyu* is more necessary to Japanese cooking than any sauce to any other cuisine I know.

The origin or date of the invention of *shoyu* is not certain. Japanese tradition has it that Gakushin, a Chinese Buddhist priest, taught the people in Wakayama the method of making *shoyu* in 1228. It is first mentioned in the records found in the *Shoshoin* of the *Todaiji* Temple where Emperor Shomu's (the forty-fifth emperor) personal belongings are preserved along with those of other emperors.

Chinese *shoyu* was imported during the early years of the Ashika regime in the 1300's. During the Yoshiharu Ashigaka's shogunate in the 1500's, large quantities of *shoyu* were manufactured in Kyoto. *Shoyu* was known to be made at Choshi, another village in Chiba Prefecture in 1616 and in 1645 when a *shoyu* maker from Wakayama came to Choshi to coax others into making *shoyu*. Noda, also in Chiba Prefecture, began manufacturing *shoyu* during the late 1600's in the Genroku era and is now one of the largest centers of *shoyu* manufacture in Japan.

Shoyu was widely used during the Tokugawa shogunate. Earlier it is certain that *shoyu* was not in liquid form. Only during the early period of the Tokugawa shogunate was *shoyu* first made in liquid form. During the Meiji Era, 1868-1912, *shoyu* was greatly improved. Now Japan produces millions of liters of *shoyu*, a share of which is made in Choshi and Noda, Chiba Prefecture.

Shoyu is manufactured from wheat or barley, soy beans, salt, malt and water. The quality of *shoyu* depends greatly upon the quality of the wheat. The wheat is grilled in a large iron pan until toasted brown, then crushed. Soy beans are next boiled in a large kettle, a heavy weight being placed on the kettle cover to prevent steam from escaping.

When the soy beans have boiled three or four hours, the fire is put out and the beans left overnight in the same kettle. (Alternatively, soy beans can be steamed five or six hours.) Grilled wheat and boiled soy beans are then mixed and placed in the malt room where malt seeds are added, turning the combination into malt in a few days. Salted water or brine is poured over the malt which is kept for several days. Stirring occurs occasionally until the mixture matures through fermentation.

This combination is next placed into a press and the liquid extracted is *shoyu*.

KATSUO BUSHI

Katsuo-bushi, dried bonito, is one of the basic flavors of Japanese cuisine whether used by a restaurant chef or the housewife in a family kitchen. One of the most essential ingredients to Japanese cooking, *Katsuo-bushi* looks like a mouldy piece of driftwood. Actually, it is dried bonito fillet.

Products of the sea for the Japanese have been highly esteemed since ancient times. Perhaps it is no accident that *Katsuo-bushi* in calligraphy also means "victorious samurai — *katsuo* = victory, *bushi* = samurai. Traditionally, it is presented as a token on any felicitous occasion. The habit of giving *katsuo-bushi*, *kombu* or *awabi* all convey the meaning of joy and happiness.

Four pieces of *Katsuo-bushi* can be made from one bonito.

To identify the best quality dried bonito, hit two dried pieces together. The sound should be very high-pitched. A dull sound usually indicates a crumbly inside. To insure the best flavor, dried bonito is shaved while the *dashi* water is boiling.

Labelled *kezuri-bushi*, or shaved bonito, *Katsuo-bushi* flakes can be purchased packaged.

MENRUI

One finds many *soba* and *udon* — noodles — shops in Japan. One can see rope-braided curtains under the eaves of the shop front marked with characters denoting *soba* and *udon*, two of the most common noodles in Japan. One also can enjoy *demae-service* (delivery service) from such shops. One places an order for noodles over the telephone and within a half hour's wait, the delivery can be expected. I call this "instant noodles."

Noodles can be served hot or cold with an endless variety of ingredients. An acquaintance of mine starts the day with *zarusoba*, noodles made of buckwheat flour, served with a dipping sauce. *Udon*, the thick noodles with hot broth, are for lunch. Another type of noodle is eaten for the evening meal. Certainly not everyone can survive solely on noodles, but in Japan they are popular with old and young at all times of the year.

Noodle eating in Japan is a noisy affair. Slurping sounds and blowing are perfectly acceptable. These noises are signs of appreciation to the chef and one mustn't hesitate to show one's delight!

The following are the most common forms of noodles in Japan:

Udon — commonly 3 mm in diameter. *Udon* is most often served in a hot broth, topped with fried things, fish cakes, vegetables and eggs. *Udon* makes a wonderful party snack and is used in *nabemono* or *sukiyaki*.

Kishimen — flat, ribbon-like noodles, 1 cm in width. *Kishimen* are sometimes called *himokawa in the Tokyo area.*

Hiya-mugi — made of wheat flour, 1 mm in thickness. *Hiya-mugi* is served mostly in the summertime with a cold broth or dipping sauce.

Somen — are very thin, thinner than *hiya-mugi* and pure white in color. *Somen* are most often served in large crystal bowls of iced water with a cold dipping sauce — a summertime favorite.

Soba — made of buckwheat grain, slightly coarse in texture and beige or a slightly darker color. *Soba* is eaten the year around and served hot in broth.

Ramen — Chinese-style soup noodles made from wheat flour, served hot in a slightly lard-flavored soup with roast pork. Sapporo, the city in Hokkaido, Japan's northernmost island is famous for *ramen*. I was told *ramen* would warm you inside and out on bitter winter nights. *Ramen*, of course, is now packaged commercially as a snack with a variety of flavors for the broth.

Unless one is making noodles, I suggest using *menrui* in a dry, packaged form. Fresh *menrui* frozen or refrigerated, and called *nama*, are more perishable. Packaged *menrui* are brittle and resemble dried egg noodles and come intended for a single portion serving, perhaps 3 to 5 ounces.

Cooking Soba and Udon

Fill a large pot 3/4 full with water and bring to boil. Scattering the dried noodles over the boiling water, stir occasionally to prevent sticking. When water starts boiling the second time, add 1 cup cold water. This is called *sashimizu*.

Continue cooking over high flame until water boils a third time. Repeat *sashimizu*, and allow water to boil again. *Menrui*, when tested, should be translucent and not gummy. If *menrui* is not cooked, *sashimizu!*

When *menrui* is cooked, place in colander, run under cold water at the sink and drain.

MISO

Miso, or soy bean paste, is indispensable in Japanese cuisine. Although it is used at the table, it is not used as Westerners use butter. The Japanese believe that *miso* is partially responsible for their sound physical health. The Japanese have *miso* soup at breakfast with vegetables and boiled rice the way Americans eat bacon and eggs. *Miso* also is used in preserving vegetables which will keep years without rotting if the *miso* is good.

Miso is made from soy beans which may be yellow, blue or white in color. Actually there are many kinds of *miso: aka-miso*, red; *shiro-miso*, white; *inaka-miso*, local; *sendai-miso*, Northern Japanese miso; *Edio-miso* and *Hatcho-miso*.

According to the kind of *miso* being made, the beans are soaked overnight and then boiled so soft the following day that they can be pounded into a paste. This paste is thoroughly mixed with quantities of salt and *aoji*, a mold prepared from wheat or rice. After being stirred several times, the *miso* mixture is packed into a tub for a long time — sometimes for several years — until it matures and ferments. One often finds *miso* in a local farmer's house which has been kept for several decades. The belief is that the longer *miso* is kept, the better it tastes.

Every farmer makes *miso* for his own use in the rural districts. In the urban areas, however, *miso* is supplied by commercial *miso* companies.

MIRO SHIRU

As a child living in Japan, I would awaken each morning to a breakfast which included *miso* soup whether I had bacon, eggs, toast, oatmeal or broiled fish. It never failed to be there. Many a time I was surprised by the various ingredients used in the soup.

Miso is made in several varieties. Perhaps the most commonly used soy bean pastes are white and red *miso*. The soup stock generally used for breakfast soups is prepared from dried. bonito and *nitoshi*, or *katsuobushi*. Vegetables usually are added. Foods such as *tofu* (bean curd), shellfish and some kinds of seaweed, however, are used. A more hearty protein soup may be desired at the evening meal, using pork, chicken and fish.

Even when served three times a day no one seems to tire of *miso shiru*. In fact, some Japanese feel that meals are not complete when *miso shiru* is omitted from the menu. This every-day-three-times-a-day soup can really test one's creativity and imagination to invent combinations of ingredients to enhance the *miso* flavor.

Note the importance of timing in adding *miso* paste to the *dashi*. The rule for successful *miso shiru* making is not to overcook after *miso* paste is added to the *dashi*. A small amount of *dashi* is used to dissolve *miso* paste. This mixture is returned to the *dashi* and brought to boil. One can also use a silk screen strainer, *kinu goshi,* for the same purpose.

Miso shiru is at its prime when first brought to boil after adding *miso* paste to *dashi.*

OCHA

Tea, or *ocha,* was brought to Japan by Japanese monks returning from religious training in China. At first it was used as medicine and a stimulant. Through the centuries it has become the national beverage of Japan.

Tenth century literature notes that court nobles and ladies chewed chizzled tea bits — tea leaves crushed and pressed into brick-like form — to stay awake while serving in the night-long poetry parties of the Imperial Court. Zen monks engaging in all-night prayers or meditation used them to stay awake.

In the late sixteenth century, townsmen in the Osaka region started to make powdered tea for simpler and more economical tea drinking. One of the tea-makers, Sen Rikyu, was a friend of Hideyoshi. Another of the later tea-masters of the early Tokugawa shogunate, in the Takagamine artists' colony outside Kyoto was Honnami Koetsu who was noted for his calligraphy. They all helped evolve the ritual cultural institution *Cha-no-yu,* or The Way of Tea, which is regarded as essential cultural training for refined and aristocratic Japanese. To the Japanese, this ceremony is not just a pastime, but an experience of harmony and spiritual communion with one's natural environment.

There is, of course, a human side to the tea ceremony. I personally found the ceremony a knee-breaking and boring experience. This may imply my lack of spiritual mastery. I hope sometime to re-engage myself as a student.

Tea in Japan is served without milk or lemon as it is in the West. Tea further is divided into many varieties, with types for every activity: office or factory, restaurant, family, mealtime, guest and ceremonial teas. Growing up in Japan, one of my responsibilities was to place frehly made *ocha* on my ancestors' altar each morning. Before the breakfast began, warm covered tea cups awaited me and my morning task.

Some types of tea are:

Gyokuro — "Jewel Dew," is the best leaf tea. The extra tender young shoots of old tea bushes are hand-picked in early spring and set to dry. The fragrance of *gyokuro* cannot be compared to other tea leaves. When dried, they are long, thin and deep green in color.

Sencha — in fused tea, is a medium grade green tea. The leaf-picking has been done with care so that there are no twigs and stems in the tea.

Bancha — will contain more mature leaves and sometimes even stems. Lower grades will have dried stems, even twigs in the tea. *Bancha,* nonetheless, is the most consumed of Japanese teas because of its economical price. As soon as one is seated in a restaurant, the *yunomi* is brought to the table filled with fresh *bancha* so that one has something to sip while reading the menu. *Bancha* is poured again when the meal is underway. *Bancha* enjoys popularity also at office, factory and in the home.

Hojicha — is *Bancha* roasted to heighten the flavor.

Genmaicha — is *Bancha* mixed with grain of roasted, popped rice.

Hikicha or **Matcha** — is powered or pulverized tea, ground from the same tender leaves cultivated for *gyokuro*. The freshly-picked leaves are dried into small curls, then ground to a very fine powder with a special mortar and pestle.

The method of serving *matcha* differs from other teas because it is made by the portion, not by the pot. This tea may be made thick and frothy, or thin and liquid by the bamboo tea whisk, according to one's desire.

Such loose and/or powdered tea should be purchased in small amounts, stored in air-tight containers in a cool, dark and dry place. The freezer is also a good storage place for loose tea.

Mugicha — is roasted barley without any tea leaves. When chilled, it is a very refreshing summer drink.

Kobucha — is powdered *konbu*, occasionally made and combined with plum flavor. The taste is like a light broth.

Sakura — is tea made by pouring hot water over salted cherry blossoms. Because of the auspicious symbolism, it is served for betrothals or simply to honor the spring.

CHA-NO-YU or SA-DO

Tea Ceremony, or Way of Tea, was fully formulated and an independent art during the Ashikaga shogunate, and particularly under the patronage of Ashikaga Yoshimasa, 1449-1473. As we know the practice today, the tea ceremony was perfected by Sen-no-Rikyu, 1518-1591, a one-time friend of Taiko Hideyoshi. Hideyoshi was responsible for bringing many Korean potters back to Japan after his invasion of Korea and the particular aesthetic associated with *Cha-no-Yu* derives from this time.

Sen-no-Rikyu prescribed how the delicate performance of each act teaches precision, poise and tranquility, producing a natural harmony and tranquility.

Cha-no-Yu usually follows a meal called *kaiseki* which is served on *kozen*, or individual trays. When the meal is ended, guests retire into the waiting room, re-maining there until the host summons them with gentle strokes on a brass gong. At the sound of the gong, the guests re-enter the room for the *koi-cha*, or thick tea, the real tea ceremony.

Prescribed etiquette not only outlines the sipping of the tea, but insists that the privilege of inspecting the tea bowl closely for an appreciation of its qualities is a part of the entire ceremony.

Koi-cha is prepared from powdered tea. Two or three spoonsful are placed in a large cup-like bowl. Hot water is poured on it and the tea is then whisked with a delicate bamboo whisk to a creamy froth. When the preparation is ready, the host places the bowl in front of the principal guest. With a bow to fellow guests, the principal guest holds the bowl in the palm of his left hand, steadies it with his right, takes a sip and compliments the host on its excellent flavor. He takes two or more sips before passing the bowl on to the second guest. The procedure is repeated and the bowl passed around until each guest has tasted *koi-cha*.

There also are instances of special rooms and small houses reserved exclusively for the tea ceremony.

Cha-no-Yu requires years of training to master its etiquette. It is said that one can attain enlightenment and mental composure through its practice. Alas, my exposure has been very shallow and my main memory is that it hurt my knees!

MENU PLANNING

One basic idea of *Katei Ryori* menu planning is that Japanese do not divide meals like Westerners do, especially for family meals. Japanese serve soup near the end of the meal at a formal dinner, but for the family the day begins with *miso-shiru* for breakfast. The recipes for these menus are all in these pages.

Typical breakfast menus:

Miso-shiru of season	*Miso-shiru* of season
Dashi-maki-tamago	*Maguro-no-mizozuke-yaki*
and *Oroshi-daikon*	*Gohan*
Gohan	*Shiozuke*
Nukazuke	*Umeboshi*
Nori	

Standard lunch menus:

Tonkatsu and finely	*Temaki-zushi*
shredded cabbage	*Hamaguri-Ushio-jiru*
Gohan	*Nara-zuke*
Nameko miso-shiru	
Tsukemono	

Ika no-kimizu-ae
Oyako donburi
Aburage to wakame no
miso-shiru

Dinner menus by season:

WINTER

Ishikari-nabe	*Karei no yuburi*
Ra Pai Tsuai	*Buta bara-niku to*
Sekihan	*daikon no nikomi*
Kokabu no yakumi-zuke	*Chigusa-ae*
	Hamaguri gohan
	Hakusai no Shiozuke

SPRING

Ikano tataki age	*Butaniku-no-miso-yaki*
Tori-niku no tomato-zume	*Age-tofu-no-ankake*
Asparagus no goma-	*Horenso-no-peanut-ae*
karashi-ae	*Miso-shiru*
Sumashi-jiru	*Gohan*
Takenoko-gohan	*Takuan*
Tsukemono	

SUMMER

Katsuo-no-yaki-tataki
Nasu-no-Hasami-age
Tori to Kyori no
  peanute-Shogu
Katsuo nagashi-jiru
Gohan
Tsukemono

Hiyashi bachis
Gomoko-ni
Ingon no gomamiso ae
Botan-obi to somen no
Sumashi-jiru
Kyuri no Shiozuke

AUTUMN

Karei no Oroshi-ni
Nasu no shigi-yaki
Kabu to aburage no sunomono
Miso-shiru
Gohan
Hasami zuke

Sakana no shio-yaki
Hakusai to gomodoki
  no nimono
Momiji-ae
Dobin-mushi
Yamaji gohan
Osaka-zuke

TIPS ON FISH AND MEAT

When serving whole fish whether steamed, deep fried or broiled, place head to your left on serving dish, belly opening toward you, and tail to the right.

In broiling fish fillet and chicken meat give great concern to the appearance of the final result. The skin side is considered the "face side." The "underside" is the flesh near to the bone. Always start cooking with "face side" first, turning to the underside second.

COOKING TIME

Cooking time depends very much on the kind of stove a cook habitually uses. Most Japanese kitches are equipped with merely one or two gas burners. Until recently, ovens were very uncommon means of cooking in Japan. Steaming was the common means to cook the Japanese equivalent of cake or sweets. Space, as you may have read, is at a premium in Japan and the kitchen is no exception. Therefore, my timing is based solely on my own experience with stoves, usually gas.

GOHAN

Rice is so important to the Japanese that its name also means "a meal." Like the majority of Asians from India to Korea, nothing eaten is quite complete without this domesticated grass. First believed to have been domesticated in India, evidence recently has been found in archeological diggings in India that rice culture existed in this delta-rich country of southeast Asia as early as 3500 B.C.

As you can imagine, this important staple in the Asian diet is surrounded by much folklore throughout Asia. In Japan, *Jizo*, the guardian of children and caretaker of departed souls, enjoys many stories about his intervention in the rice fields during a farmer's crisis. The tales are numerous enough so that Jizo is shown in images with muddy feet. When rice has been transplanted there is the practice in some parts of Japan of throwing mud at the image to insure a good yield at harvest time. Mud even is thrown at each other.

Seeing farmers engaged in transplanting fresh shoots to the paddy, or rice fields, is a lesson in closed rank coordination. The fields themselves, when the planting is completed, are an unforgettable brightly-minted green. Sun or rain catching the water in the paddy fields adds to the lustre of this Asian-wide agricultural phenomenon. It is even said that rice is responsible for the population density of the lands where it is grown!

While Japan still grows a great deal of rice, the United States also exports rice to Japan. Favorite among the Japanese is a round, pearl-shaped variety, which has a glistening quality when steamed. Some manufacturers of this form of rice have coated it with talc to preserve the pearl-like quality and the shelf life of the rice. Although directions are given for washing this rice, care must be exercised in purchase and use to ensure thorough washing before cooking.

The rice straw in Japan has acquired many practical uses over the centuries. While much of it is fed to cattle, rice straw is woven into bales to contain the harvested rice grains. One of the symbolic uses rice straw has enjoyed is being woven into the *shimenawa*, or "sacred rope," placed before Shinto shrines and around a sacred spot or article. Rice ears should be properly a part of it.

Rice straw also is used for footgear in the country. *Zoris* are made with strips to tie over *tabis* and also for snow boots and snow shoes. Perhaps the most evocative use of rice straw can be seen in Japanese woodblock prints, however. When depicting rain and storm in a country scene, you will often see a solitary figure in the landscape trudging along in a thick, shaggy-looking cape. The figure is wearing a raincoat called *mino*, another use for woven rice straw.

GOHAN NO TAKIKATA *basic rice*

    4 cups uncooked rice
    4-3/4 cups water

One hour before cooking, wash rice until rinsing water becomes clear. Drain. Place rice and water in deep pot and mix well. Cover, bringing to boil over strong flame. When rice boils, turn flame as low as possible, simmering 3 minutes. Bring rice again to boil over slightly stronger flame. As water diminishes, turn flame to low. When water is nealy gone, 20 minutes later, turn flame strong 1-2 seconds, then remove from fire, still covered. Let stand 7 minutes before serving. When removing lid to serve, if rice has risen, you can be assured of delicious rice.

Note: In all following recipes 4 cups of rice are used unless otherwise mentioned. The Japanese prefer a small pearly toned white rice. When purchasing, be careful to read instructions on sack or package since many domestic brands of this rice have been coated with talc to preserve both the pearly tone and the rice. Other forms of white rice are equally good.

SUSHI MESHI *basic vinegar rice*

    4 cups rice   *Seasoning:*
    4 cups water   1/2 cup rice vinegar
    1/2 cup mirin   3 tbsp sugar
    1/2 oz konbu   1 tsp salt

    Special equipment:
    fan for cooling rice   wooden paddle for mixing

Wash and drain rice one hour before cooking. In large heavy pot with lid, bring to boil water, mirin, konbu. Remove konbu before adding rice. Mix well and bring rice to boil over medium flame. When rice and water boils, reduce flame to very low. Let stand a few minutes, then turn flame up. As cooking water evaporates, lower flame to simmer. When water has disappeared, turn off flame and let stand 5 minutes. Remove hot rice to pan the size of dishpan. Pour seasoning mixture over hot rice quickly. Fan to cool while mixing. Use wooden rice paddle with cutting motion to mix rice and seasoning.

Sushi rice seasoning differs depending upon the region in Japan. The further south, the sweeter sushi becomes.

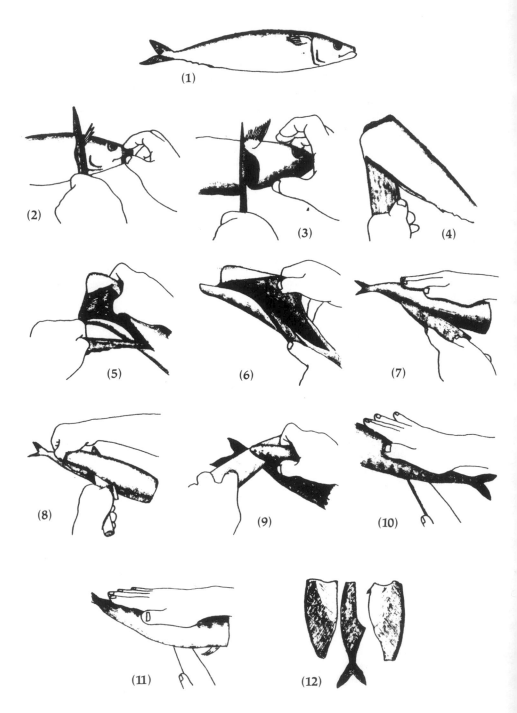

Sashimi Cutting

OCHA ZUKE *tea-flavored rice*

Ocha zuke has been served as a snack as well as the ending of a beautiful meal, sometimes with tea only, often with various condiments. Many households have their special combination.

Rice and tea must be absolutely hot. Ingredients commonly eaten are uneboshi, broiled fish, tempura, the roe of fish, sashimi, with broiled, salted salmon topping the list.

During Heian times, court nobles invented this particular method of eating rice, and called it water rice or *Sui Han* in the summer. Dried, steamed rice was soaked in cold water and eaten when it became soft. During the Kamakura Period, the custom changed gradually when cold water was poured over freshly steamed hot rice. Samurai then started eating rice with hot water poured over. As the tea ceremony became more common, tea was substituted for hot water.

SASHIMI NO TSUKURI KATA *raw fish cutting*

1 lb fresh fillet of sea bass,	*Dipping sauce*
striped bass, red snapper,	
squid, abalone or tuna	4 tbsp shoyu or tosa joyu
1/4 lb daikon or red radish	(see recipe)
1 med.-sized carrot	
1 stalk celery	

There are four sashimi cutting methods. For each, a very sharp knife is required. *Hiragiri* or flat cut. This is most popular shape and is suited for any filleted fish. Hold fish firmly, cutting straight down to board in slices 1/4 to 1/2-inch thick and 1 inch wide, depending on fillet size.

Kaku giri or cubic cut. The style is most often used in cutting tuna. Flat cut tuna before slicing into 1/2-inch cubes.

Ito zukuri or thread shape. This method is suited for all small fish and most suited for squid. Cut squid straight down into 1/4-inch slices, then cut lengthwise into 1/4-inch-wide strips.

Usu zukuri or paper-thin slices. Place fillet on flat surface, holding fish firmly with one hand. Slice on angle into almost transparent sheets.

Peel daikon or radish and shred. Soak in cold water until ready for use. Daikon should resemble white hair and is therefore called *hakuhatsu* daikon. When using red radish, cut into matchstick size. Slice and cut carrot in same manner as daikon. Cut celery lengthwise in half. Shred and soak in cold water until ready.

Many Westerners who delight in raw clams and oysters should be able to enjoy certain types of sashimi.

The most important rule to follow is that first of all, sashimi must be *absolutly fresh! Frozen fish is definitely out!* Fresh water fish is seldom used because of the possible parasites they might contain. After buying the fish, keep it refrigerated, wrapped in a dish towel until ready for use. Handle fish as little as possible.

SHIKI NO MISU SHIRU *miso soup combinations for the four seasons*

HARU (spring):
   hard-shelled clams and minced green onion
   potatoes and cabbage
   bamboo shoots and wakame
   tofu cubes and minced green onion
   turnips and aburage
   kiriboshi daikon and *kinu zaya* (Chinese peas)

NATSU (summer):
   green beans and wakame
   eggplant and aburage
   tomato and pork fillets
   kampyo and cucumber

AKI (autumn):
   yam and fishcake
   beef slices, tofu and onion
   tofu and chrysanthemum flowers
   daikon, carrots, gobo and ground sesame seeds
   mushrooms and grated daikon oroshi
   fish fillet and mitsuba

FUYU (winter):
   sato-imo and carrots
   frozen tofu and green onion
   moyashi and wakame
   turnips and spinach
   aburage and shredded daikon
   shijini clams and green onion

ICHIBAN DASHI *basic cooking stock*

Ichiban dashi is a cornerstone of Japanese cooking. The Western equivalent would be chicken or beef stock. Used as cooking stock for many meat, poultry and fish dishes, with the adding of various garnishes and ingredients, dashi becomes a meal in itself.

When I was learning to cook we had to make our dashi from scratch. Often called *dashi no moto*, ichiban dashi is easily made in these modern times from packages. The packages make cooking much easier and the kitchen counter less cluttered. However, there is a marked difference between instant and freshly prepared dashi. The freshly prepared dashi possesses a subtle, smoked flavor.

The main ingredients of ichiban dashi are katsuobushi flakes and konbu, which resembles dusty black leather. The art of good dashi making is in the timing of how long the kelp, or konbu, should be boiled and how much in advance the bonito should be shaved before adding konbu stock. Konbu should not be boiled for the first stock. The bonito or katsuobushi flakes are brought just to the boiling point, then strained through silk cloth strainer or *kingushi*, placed over a colander inside a large bowl. Katsuobushi flakes should be caught and allowed to drain into the bowl naturally, not squeezed in the cloth. For anyone wishing to attempt making a basic dashi, the directions follow:

> 1/3 oz konbu
> 1/3 oz katsuoboshi
> 4 cups water

Rinse konbu slightly. Freshly shave or use packaged katsuobushi shavings. Boil water and add konbu, stirring around several times in water. Remove konbu and continue boiling hot water. Add katsuobushi shavings and remove pot from burner immediately. Let stand for a minute. Skim and save materials for Niban dashi.

NIBAN DASHI *cooking stock for vegetables*

> Skimmed ingredients from Ichiban dashi
> 2 cups water

Niban dashi is an economical way to use leftover ingredients of Ichiban dashi for a weaker, but equally good stock. Niban dashi is used instead of water for cooking vegetables.

As you can guess, Ichiban refers to ichi or one, and Niban refers to ni or two, first and second dashis!

NIBOSHI DASHI *dried fish dashi*

    1/3 oz konbu
    1-1/2 oz *Niboshi*
    4 cups water

Rinse konbu slightly. Remove innards from Niboshi, breaking into half lengthwise. Soak Niboshi overnight in 4 cups water. Bring to boil but remove konbu before boiling point is reached. Continue cooking 5 minutes. Strain.

Niboshi is an ingredient commonly used for misoshiru. Niboshi are small fish which have been parboiled and dried, purchased as whole-bodied fish. Niboshi intestines must be removed to avoid a bitter and fishy taste in the dashi. When cooking do not cover with a lid because doing so creates a fishy taste.

SHOJIN DASHI *meatless cooking broth*

    10 inches konbu
    1 cup daizu
    1-1/2 oz kampyo
    1-1/2 oz shiitake
    8 cups water

Wipe off dust and clean konbu. Wash and drain daizu. Wash and clean kanpyo and shiitake, squeezing out any excess water. In large pot or bowl combine water and listed ingredients and let stand 8 hours or more. Mix and turn over, top to bottom. Strain. Dashi is ready for Shojin-ryori.

TORI GARA NO DASHI *chicken bones stock*

    1/2 lb chicken bones
    3 1/4-inch thick slices of ginger
      root, fresh
    2 green onions
    6 cups water
    2 egg shells

Using very large pot bring ingredients except egg shells to boil rapidly. Skim any residue, reduce to simmer, cook 60 minutes and drain through colander. Discard bones and vegetables. Return dashi to pot, add 2 crushed egg shells, bring to boil again, then strain through cheesecloth.

BUTA TO HORENSO NO MISO SHIRU *pork and spinach soup*

    5 oz miso
    4 cups water
    1 lb spinach
    1/2 lb pork shoulder
    1 green onion, minced
    2/3 oz ginger, grated

Dissolve miso in water. Add spinach cut in 1-inch lengths and bring to boil. Cube pork in 2-inch pieces and cook in soup until well done. Remove from burner, add minced onion and grated ginger. Serve immediately.

ABURAGE TO WAKAME NO MISOSHIRU *fried aburage and wakame miso soup*

    2 aburage
    2 oz dried wakame
    3 cups dashi
    young shoots of konbu
    2 stalks green onion, minced
    4 tbsp miso
    1/4 tsp salt

Pour boiling water over aburage to remove excess oil, then cut into 1-inch long sided triangles. Soften wakame in cold water, drain and cut into 1/2-inch long pieces. Bring to boil dashi, aburage and wakame. Place miso on bamboo strainer, or misokoshi, then dip into dashi and strain miso. Add salt and stir. Remove from heat after boiling, serve in soup bowls and garnish with minced green onion.

SATSUMA JIRU *chicken and vegetable miso soup*

    6 cups water
    3/4 lb chopped chicken meat
    3/4 lb yams
    1/3 lb carrots
    1/2 lb radish
    a few shiitake
    5 oz miso
    crushed Japanese pepper
    1 green onion, minced

Bring water to boil and drop in chicken. Simmer 50 minutes until very tender. Skin and bones should separate easily. Peel vegetables and cube to 1/4 inch. Soften shiitake in enough cold water to cover, then cut into pieces when soft. Add chopped ingredients to chicken. Continue to boil until all are tender. Using a little broth, dissolve miso paste, add to soup. Bring to boil, add minced onion and serve immediately, sprinkling with crushed Japanese pepper.

TOFU TO ABURAGE NO MISO SHIRU *soybean curd and fried soybean curd miso soup*

    2 square aburage
    3 cups dashi
    4 tbsp miso
    1/4 tsp salt
    1/2 cake tofu
    2 tbsp nori flakes
    Special equipment: misokoshi

Pour boiling water over aburage to remove excess oil, then cut into 2-inch by 1-inch rectangles. Bring dashi to boil, add cut aburage when it is boiling. Strain in miso and salt with misokoshi. Cut tofu into 1-inch squares, drop into dashi. Bring to boil and serve with nori flakes floating on top of dashi.

TOFU EBI OKRA NO MISO SHIRU *tofu, shrimp and okra soup*

>   10 shrimp, fresh or frozen
>   10 medium size okra
>   1/4 cake tofu, if whole
>   3 cups dashi
>   3/4 tbsp miso
>   4 tbsp miso

> Special equipment: *Misokoshi*

Devein shrimp. Cook in water with 1/2 tsp salt 5 minutes. Drain, shell, leaving tail. Wash okra, cut in 1/4-inch slices, then in 2-inch strips. Bring dashi to boil and add okra. Add miso and 1/4 tsp salt through misokoshi. Add tofu and shrimp. Dividing ingredients evenly, serve in individual bowls.

KYABETSU TO TOFU NO MISO SHIRU *cabbage and tofu miso soup*

>   *3 cups dashi*
>   1-1/2 cups shredded cabbage
>   1/2 square tofu
>   1/4 cup miso

Save 1/4 cup dashi to mix with miso. Cook shredded cabbage with remaining dashi. Add miso paste and cubed tofu, being careful not to overcook. Add wakame for variation.

This is a breakfast soup.

WAKAME JIRU *young seaweed and bamboo shoot soup*

>   1/2 oz dried wakame
>   1 small bamboo shoot
>   4 cups dashi
>   1-1/2 tsp salt
>   2 tsp shoyu
>   5 umeboshi, pickled

Soften wakame in cold water and cut in 1/2-inch square pieces. Slice bamboo shoot thinly. Boil dashi with sliced bamboo shoot. Add salt and shoyu. Add wakame and reheat. To serve place single umeboshi in each soup bowl. Divide sliced bamboo shoot equally and add to each bowl. Add dashi and serve.

KASU NO MISO SHIRU *turnip miso soup*

>   5 oz miso
>   3/4 lb turnips with leaves
>   4 cups dashi

Peel and quarter turnips, slicing each quarter into 1/4-inch slices. Cut leaves into 1-inch lengths. Bring dashi to boil, add turnips with leaves and cook until tender. Dissolve miso in a little dashi and add. Bring dashi to boil and serve.

BOTAN EBI NO OSUIMONO *peony shrimp and snowpeas*

10 uncooked medium size prawns
2-1/2 tsp cornstarch
10 snowpeas
4 cups dashi

Special equipment: 10 toothpicks, 5 soupbowls with lids

Devein prawns by inserting skewer and shell except for tail. Arrange 2 prawns, fastening together at center with toothpick (see illustration). Coat center of shrimps with cornstarch. Drop into boiling salted water, cook until tender. Drain, cool and remove toothpicks carefully. Clean snowpeas, sprinkle with 1 tsp salt and drop into pan of boiling water for 15 seconds. Remove and place immediately under cold running water to retain bright green color. Bring to boil Ichiban dashi, 1-1/2 tsp salt and shoyu, then remove from burner. Arrange prawn peony and 2 parboiled snowpeas in bottom of each soup bowl. Fill the bowls 3/4 full with dashi. Top with lemon peel cut into strips 1/2-inch long, 1/3-inch wide. To make a pine sprig, cut slit from each end, leaving 1/8 inch. Crisscross ends. Place lids on bowls and serve.

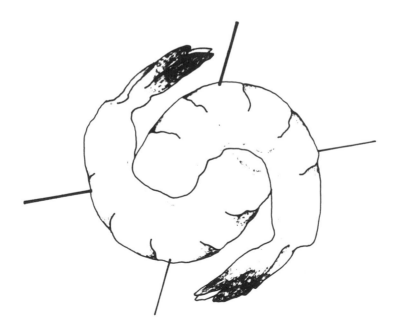

TORINIKU TO SHIITAKE NO SUIMONO *clear chicken mushroom*

1/2 lb chicken breast meat
2 tsp salt
cornstarch
boiling water
3 medium shiitake
4 cups Ichiban dashi
1/2 tsp shoyu
peel of 1 lemon

Special equipment: 5 soup bowls with lids

Discard chicken skin and slice meat into long pieces, salt and let stand 30 minutes. Coat with cornstarch, drop into water salted with 1/2 tsp salt and cook until tender. Do not overcook. Drain. Soak shiitake in cup of cold water, remove and discard stems, slice each mushroom in 4 pieces. Cook a few minutes over low flame in clear dashi. Remove shiitake, save dashi. Arrange two pieces of chicken and 2 slices of shiitake in each soup bowl. Fill with heated Ichiban dashi flavored with 1 tsp salt and shoyu, adding a slice of lemon peel for flavor. Place lids on bowls and serve.

SOBORO JIRU* *pork and vegetable stew*

1/4 lb pork
1 small bamboo shoot
1 onion
a few shiitake
1 cup soybean sprouts
a few string beans
4 cups pork or chicken stock
salt

Slice meat into 2-inch thick pieces and salt. In enough cold water to cover, soak shiitake 15 minutes to soften. Slice onion, shiitake, and bamboo shoot thinly about 1-1/2 inches long. Clean bean sprouts and green beans, slicing the latter very fine. Bring the soup stock to boil. Add ingredients except onion and bring to a second boil. Season with 1 tsp salt, skimming any residue which forms. Add onion, remove from burner and serve.

Sumashi Jiru refers to stews in general.

KENCHIN JIRU *vegetable stew*

1 square tofu
2/3 lb radishes
1/3 lb carrots
a few dried shiitake
1 green onion
1 tbsp sesame oil
4 cups dashi
2 tbsp salt
shoyu

Remove water from tofu by squeezing in cheesecloth. Slice radishes and carrots into 1-1/4 by 1/4 inch strips. Soften shiitake in enough cold water to cover, then slice as thin as possible. Cut green onion into 1-1/2-inch lengths, then slice lengthwise as thin as possible. In sesame oil, saute sliced radishes, carrots and mushrooms until tender. Mash tofu with fingers, add to vegetables and saute again. Add dashi. When hot, and ingredients are tender, add green onion. Without further boiling remove from burner and serve immediately.

YASAI *vegetables*

According to recipes from the Edo Period, Irish potatoes and carrots were already cultivated in Japan and had Japanese seasoning in cooking as though they were native produce. Corn, lima beans, lettuce, turnips, watermelon, eggplant and squash were considered native. After the Meiji Restoration, however, the government imported a variety of seeds from China, Europe and the United States and made vast improvements in cross-pollination. Whatever vegetable may be served in a Japanese home must, at one time or another, have been crossed with a foreign vegetable.

During the Twenties, tomatoes, asparagus and lettuce were relatively unknown in Japan. My investigations led me to interesting documents about foodstuffs and vegetables imported to Japan at that time.

Cucumber was good for stomach ailments, asparagus for kidneys, lettuce for insomnia and nervousness. Tomatoes were called red eggplants. People would not think of eating tomatoes for they believed them to cause fiery indigestion. Cabbage was called "green ball," cauliflower" the "flower vegetable."

Lettuce, cauliflower and celery have been cultivated in Japan only since 1946. When American occupation troops came to Japan after World War II, they had fresh produce shipped from California. Due to the length of travel time by ship, the produce lost its freshness. Pragmatic military advisors decided to ask Japanese farmers to try producing these much-desired fresh vegetables, since they were not common to the corner market or the wholesaler. These vegetables had only been cultivated by the small farmer to fill requests by French restaurant owners or the needs of a few foreign residents in Japan.

OKASHI TO KANMI *desserts*

Japanese sweets, or *wagashi*, traditionally have taken a big place at the end of a Japanese meal. Fruits of the season are most frequently served at the end of a meal in Japan.

Our sweets are quite different from Western style pies and cakes since most of them are made from sweet bean paste. Cakes from sweet bean paste are served with green tea in mid-afternoon, for evening snacks and are considered an essential part of the tea ceremony, or *cha no yu.*

SAKE / NIHON SHU *Japanese spirits*

This rice wine is Japan's national alcoholic beverage.

The earliest brew which can be called *sake (sah'kee)* was a thick drink of milky yellow and in the ninth and tenth centuries was reserved for use by the nobility and priests. Sake had a special role in the practice of Shinto rites. At festival times, small bottles of sake, together with cups, were set before household shrines. In Shinto wedding rites, the couple seals their marriage by the exchanging of cups and drinking of sake. This tradition is to Japanese weddings what the exchange of rings is to Christian ceremonies.

Sake is not a vintage drink, nor does it age well, but is best drunk within the year it is bottled. Sake has various grades: *Tokkyu* — special class, *Ikkyu* — first class, *Nikkyu* — second class. Most sake is 15 to 17 percent alcohol, and while it can be drunk cool, it is most often served warm and in a special serving bottle called *Tokkuri,* a vase-like shaped bottle of porcelain or stoneware. The sake-filled Tokkuri, or *O-choshi,* is placed in a small pot with hot water over a low flame, heated to 115 degrees F. Heating sake releases the lovely rice aroma.

Masuzake is a very popular way to serve cold sake. Using a small square cedarwood liquid measuring box, sake comes with a small mound of salt at one corner or edge of the box when served in this manner. The taste of salt before drinking brings out the sweetness of the sake.

When sake is offered, one holds one's cup to receive the sake. It is considered common courtesy to return the pouring of sake to the other party after receiving a cup of sake from them.

SHOCHU

Shochu* is a fiery, distilled spirit made from sweet potatoes, rice or millet. The alcoholic content is usually higher than *sake,* being 20, 25 or even 35 percent. Some local brews can go as high as 90 proof! *Shochu* was used to make fruit liqueurs in my mother's kitchen. One such recipe follows:

UME SHU *plum liqueur*

> 2 *lbs green ume* or apricots
> 1-1/4 lb *zarame,* rock crystal sugar
> 2 quarts *Shochu*

Remove stems of *ume* or apricots and wash well. Turning *ume* or apricots occasionally, let stand in the sun to dry. In alternate layers, place *ume* or apricots in a large glass or porcelain jar and add *shochu.* Seal tightly and store in a dark, cool place for 2 to 3 months. With crushed ice in the summer time this is a very refreshing drink.

Ume-shu was dispensed by my grandmother as an aid to stomach disorders! In various seasons we also had a strawberry liqueur, ichigo-shu, and a lemon liqueur, lemon-shu.

*Shochu is available in Japanese food stores.

AE MONO *Basic Dressings*
GOMA AE *(sesame seed dressing)*

> 5 tbsp sesame seeds
> 2 tbsp sugar
> 2 tbsp shoyu
> 4 tbsp dashi

Wash sesame seeds, patting dry to remove moisture. Toast, then grind either in *suribachi* or food processor until seeds become paste. Add remaining ingredients and blend until creamy in texture.

SHIRA AE *(tofu dressing)*

> 1 tofu
> 5 tbsp white sesame seeds
> 4 tbsp sugar
> 1 tsp salt
> 1/2 tsp shoyu

Place tofu in pot with enough water to cover. Allow to boil 2 minutes, then place in colander and drain. Press through uragoshi and set aside. Wash, dry and then toast sesame seeds. Grind in suribachi or food processor until seeds become paste. Add seasonings and pureed tofu. Blend until thick and creamy.

MISO AE *(bean paste dressing)*

> 1 egg yolk
> 2-1/2 tbsp sugar
> 1/2 cup white miso
> 1 tbsp red miso
> 1 tbsp sake
> 1/2 cup dashi

Beat egg yolk lightly. Add miso and blend until smooth. Add sugar and mix well. Add sake and dashi, place mixture in top of double boiler over medium heat. Stir well and then cool. Miso ae is a useful dressing for many things, such as coating grilled tofu and eggplant, tomato, fish, meat dishes.

OROSHI AE *(radish dressing)*

> 1 cup grated daikon
> 1-1/2 tbsp vinegar
> 2 tbsp shoyu

Combine the ingredients. Dressing is ideal for mushrooms.

UNI AE *(sea urchin dressing)*

> 1 egg yolk
> 1/3 cup sea urchins, bottled
> 1 tsp mirin
> 1 tbsp sake

Beat egg yolk and blend with sea urchin. Add mirin, sake and blend until smooth. Use immediately and do not plan to keep it longer than twenty-four hours.

Tsukejiru Dipping Sauce for Sashimi

Style	Sake	Mirin	Shoyu	Tamari Shoyu	Others
Shoyu Tosa Joyu Bai	2 tbsp	3 tbsp	1 cup	3 tbsp	2-inch konbu, 1/4 oz bonito flakes
Bai niju joyu					2 tbsp pickled plum meat, 1/2 cup tosa joyu
Wasabi shoyu			1/2 cup		1 tbsp wasabi
Goma joyu		1 tbsp	1/2 cup		2 tbsp sesame seeds
Shoyu joyu		1 tbsp	1/2 cup		1 tbsp grated ginger
Ponzu		3 tbsp	1 cup	2 tbsp	1 cup lemon juice, 1/3 cup vingar, 1/2 cup bonito flakes, 2-inches konbu
Karashi-sumiso	2 tbsp				3/4 cup miso, 2 egg yolks, 2 tbsp sugar, 1/2 cup water, 1 tbsp vinegar, 1 tbsp mustard

AE GROMO AND AWASEZU TABLES

These two tables, like the *Ae-Mono* dressings, may not now seem very clear to your. As you read, however, you will understand that the finishing part of a dish rests very much with the taste and the imagination of the cook. As you read the recipes, you will understand more clearly the possible usages outlined in these tables, so that you can suit your fancy and that of your diners!

Awasezu Dressings with vinegar

Style	Vinegar	Salt	Shoyu	Sugar	Other Ingred.	Appropriate Food
Nihaizu	1 part		1 part			clam, fish
Sanbaizu 1*	2 parts		3 parts	1 part	dashi for tartness	fish, clams, vegetables
Sanbaizu 2*	3 parts		2 parts	2 parts	dashi for tartness	fish, clam, vegetables
Amazu†	3 parts			3 parts	2 tbsp sake 2-inch konbu	ginger, turnip, renkon
Chuka-fu	1 part		2 parts	1 tsp		
Kakezu, Chinese style						
Kimizu	3 tbsp	1/3 tsp	1 tsp	1 tbsp	2 egg yolks, 2 tbsp dashi 2 tsp mirin	clam, prawn, white meat fish, crab, chicken, cucumber

* *These two dressing are the most commonly used of the vinegared dressing.*

† *When added to thinly-sliced ginger, the ginger is known as* **gari** *and is the popular accompaniment to sushi.*

AE GOROMO Literally: Dressing of Outer Garments

Type	Salt	Shoyu	Sugar	Other Ingred.	Appropriate Food
Shiro ae	1 tsp	1/2 tsp	4 tbsp	1 tofu, 4-1/3 tbsp sesame seeds	carrots, konnyaku, hijiki, sweet potato, green vegetables, mushrooms
Shirozu ae	1 tsp		3tbsp	1 tofu, 4 tbsp sesame seeds, 2 tbsp vinegar	prawn, squid, clams, jelly fish, chicken, cucumber, bamboo shoots, oysters, daikon, renkon
Goma ae		2 tbsp	2 tbsp	5 tbsp sesame seeds, 4 tbsp dashi	green vegetables, chinese cabbage, green beans, bean sprouts, egg plant, konnyaku, watercress, daikon, cabbage
Gomazu ae	1 tsp		3 tbsp	4 tbsp goma, 2 tbsp vinegar	oyster, jelly fish, konnyaku
Miso ae			2-1/2 tbsp	6 tbsp white miso, 1 egg yolk, 1 tbsp sake, 1/2 cup dashi	clam, tuna, squid, mackerel, tofu
Su miso ae			3 tbsp	5 tbsp red miso, 1 egg yolk, 1 tbsp sake, 1/2 cup dashi, 2-1/2 tbsp vinegar	clam, tuna, squid, mackerel, bamboo shoots, green onion, lettuce, tofu
Uni ae				1 egg yolk, 1/3 cup sea urchin, 1 tsp mirin, 1 tbsp sake	bamboo shoot, wakame, rock cod
Oroshi ae		2 tbsp		1 cup grated daikon, 1-1/2 tbsp vinegar	clams, scallops, sea cucumber, chicken, mushroom, cucumber, spinach, peas

List of basic ingredients and suggested quantities for the kitchen

Japanese name	English name	Suggested Size/Quantity
Miso	soybean paste	1 pint
Shoyu	soy sauce	5-16 oz bottle
Mirin	sweet wine	12 oz bottle
Sake	rice wine	12 oz bottle
Su	rice vinegar	12 zo bottle
Gohan	rice	5 lbs
Mochi-gome	glutinous rice	1 lb
Dashi-no-moto	soup stock essence	1 box, 5-6 packets
Shoga, fresh	fresh ginger	3 oz
Daikon	fresh radish	1-1/2 lb
Tofu	soy bean curd	10-1/2 - 16 oz
Shiitake	mushrooms, dried	8 oz
Kamaboko	fish cake	13 oz can/package
Wasabi	horseradish	1 oz can, 1 packet
Karashi	mustard, powdered	1 oz
Nori	seaweed sheets	1 oz
Konbu	kelp	.5 oz
Katsuobuchi	bonito, dried	1.75, 2, 4 oz
Aburage	soybean curd pouches	2-4/package
Takenoko	bamboo shoots	5 oz can
Kona sansho	Japanese style pepper	.5 oz
Gobo	burdock	1 root 4-8 oz
Renkon	lotus root	
Konnyaku	gelatin cake made from root	8 oz package
Gin-nan	ginkyo nuts	2 oz cans
Harusame	noodles, white transparent	2-8 oz package
Goma, white	sesame seeds	3-4 oz
Goma-abura	sesame seed oil	6-12 oz
Moyashi	bean sprouts	
Sato-imo	taro potatoes	1 lb
Umeboshi	pickled plums	5-12 oz jar
Kanten	gelatin base stock	.5 oz
Shirataki	konnyaku, cut in strips	6 oz
Beni shoyu	pickled ginger	12 oz jar

Winter

GANJITSU or OSHOGATSU— New Year

Ganjitsu, or original day, new month and new year, are refered to as Osho-gatsu. What happens during the first few days will regulate one's fortunes the rest of the year. People all are in the highest spirits. All ill feeling, all disagreeable recollections and ill luck are left behind with the old year. Life opens at Ganjitsu.

To people in Japan, the New Year is not simply a date set for the new year on the calendar but possesses deep mystic significance. Each New Year brings new hope. What is past has no bearing on the future. Whatever the calamities of the year gone by, the New Year begins with a clean slate and the best prospects. The past indeed has died with the stroke of 108 bells.

Preparations for Oshogatsu begin in mid-December. Two Kadomatsu are placed in front of the main gate of the house. They are very elaborate ornamental arrangements of pine with bamboo intermingled with the longer bamboo upright section in the middle. The Kadomatsu stand on the ground like gate guardians. Because of its hardiness, the pine tree stands for long life, and the bamboo for constancy and virtue — a pun on its name. Shimenawa, or rice straw rope, hangs from the lintel of the entry door, a sacred rope from which hang wisps of gohei, white paper. Another arrangement of pine branches and bamboo adorns the main room within the house to which blossoming plum is added.

Mochi makers come to the house the last few days in December, bringing their wooden mortars and a portable fire box with rice steamer. Mochi is the glutinous kind of rice, much enjoyed in certain parts of Asia. When steamed and pounded it becomes a very rubbery dough. It then is shaped in sometimes round, kagami mochi, or a flat sheetcake-like shape. When it is cold, the mochi is cut in small squares for serving. Kagami mochi, a large one surrounded by small ones, is placed on the stand in the main room's tokonoma, or alcove, next to the pine, bamboo and blossoming plum arrangement. Everyone must eat mochi during Oshogatsu. I remember as a child we had a contest amongst us about how many mochi one of us children could eat!

To receive the New Year properly, each household must have susu barai, or cleaning day. It was formerly hearth exorcism. Though I have lived away from my homeland for many years, I still practice this ritual at each year's end so that I can have a very fresh start at the beginning of the new year. It is one of those old habits I can not and do not want to discard!

After the exhaustion of preparing the food and the Oshogatsu decorations, the susu barai and so on, Toshikoshi soba is prepared. These are the noodles to bridge the year and to insure wealth as long as the noodle's string. While eating toshikoshi soba, the gods permit humanity a fresh start. This, too, is a childhood habit I still practice. I feel I cannot make the bridge to the New Year without soba!

Our New Year's food is served in the main room on footed individual lacquer trays or ozen. The children find on their individual tray a special monetary gift, *otashi dama,* or "jewel of the year." As principal beneficiaries of this custom, we children looked forward to this *otashi dama!* On a lucky year when visiting adult relatives were numerous, children often have a dozen or more envelopes.

Otso, or sweetened sake is served, then various foods. This was perhaps the only time of the year I wore *kimono* without feeling uncomfortable. I was born in New York City and spent part of my early years in Europe where I got used to wearing Western dress and sportswear. Especially since I was concentrating on learning classical ballet, I was used to the physical freedom. My grandmother, however, painstakingly ordered a silk *kimono* each year from Kyoto and I felt a certain obligation to look pretty in it.

Also, I received a *hago-ita,* the battledore and shuttlecock, as a New Year's gift. You can occasionally see a dance about this in a classical *buyo,* or Japanese dance recital, the girls moving pigeon-toed with their festive *geta* and white *tabi* underneath their *kimono,* complete with *obi* and the many layers underneath which take so long to arrange properly!

Boys are given enormous-sized kites. I often thought, "Why don't I get a kite?" When I visited home with my younger daughter, Tricia, a few years ago, I had an opportunity to go kite-flying at the foot of Mt. Fuji. The weather was cold, but it was great fun, and since the occasion occurred on the third day of *Oshogatsu,* I finally had fulfilled my long-cherished wish — to have a kite and go kite-flying.

On the second day of *Oshogatsu,* artists and poets take their brushes, or *fude,* in hand for the first time in the new year. Dancers and musicians have their *hat-sugeiko,* or first practice. It is very important for children to write a few lucky characters or some famous verse on clean white paper with new brushes. I still treasure the second day of *Oshogatsu,* for it is then I, also, bring out fresh paper and brush and practice calligraphy.

Many games are played by old and young alike. One of the most traditional is *Hyaku-nin-isshu,* a game with a collection of one-hundred thirty-one syllable poems. This hundred poem game usually is only played during *Oshogatsu.* The poems reputedly were chosen in the twelfth century by Teika Fujiwara, a scholar of the time. The selections include those written by emperors (7), an empress, court ladies (20), courtesans (57) and priests (15).

The thirty-one syllable poem form is the Japanese *waka* with the upper portion possessing syllables of five-seven-five and the lower portion of seven-seven syllables. The game divides the *waka* into two parts, one for the reader which has the upper portion, the lower portion for the players with the final sets of seven-seven syllables.

Players gather on two opposing teams. Fifty cards for each team are placed in full view, face up, on the *tatami.* The reader recites the first half of each poem, which, incidentally, has the *haiku* poetic form of five-seven-five syllables, making a *haiku* like one half of the game and suggesting the other half! The corresponding card with the second half of the same poem is picked up. The team eliminating its cards first wins the game. Cards may be picked up by either side. Part of the goal of the game is to have players so familiar with the hundred poems that one or two words can suggest the entire poem.

One of the activities in preparation for *Oshogatsu* is a reviewing exercise for the hundred poems. Most of us had a few invitations to *Karuta-Kai* or the hundred poem game party planned for *Oshogatsu*. We carried flash cards of upper and lower halves, taking turns reading upper half and struggling with the lower half.

Osaki Koyo the major Japanese novelist of the Meiji Era, and other literary figures, have written many romantic stories based on the *Karuta-Kai*. This was one of the few ways proper young Japanese men and women could meet socially and exchange a few words without feeling improper or embarrassed. The world I grew up and lived in was no exception. I practiced memorizing the whole hundred poems fiercely. To me this was an absolutely necessary task in my tender youth. I could not afford to lose the game in the presence of so many young men!

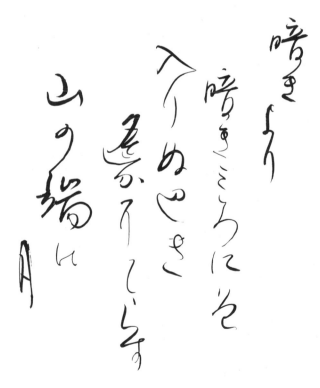

The author of this *waka* was Shikibu Izumi, a late tenth century lady of the court, and an attendant for the Empress Akiko, wife of the Emperor Ichijo.

A prayer, the Lady Izumi awaits the full-moon's rising. She thinks the landscape is like her life and that she is stumbling blindly along a dark path. The Lady Izumi prays for understanding of the Buddha's truth to provide her life meaning and direction just as the moonlight makes the path before her clear. She prays for Enlightenment.

OSECHI RYORI — *New Year's Cooking*

The Japanese Imperial Court in the tenth century designated certain days for celebration. They were January 1 and 7, March 3, May 5, July 7 and September 9. Tracing food history in Japan, offerings of foodstuffs would be made to the gods on these occasions and very elaborate party dishes prepared. Each party was called *Osechiku. Osechi* is the abbreviation.

During the Edo Period of the Tokugawa Shogunate the merchant class acquired and accumulated wealth. It began to follow the Imperial Court tradition. They started to make party foodstuffs stored and served in lacquer boxes and containers. The merchant class started calling the first three days of the year *Osechi*, and so it is known today.

Traditionally, the Japanese household does not prepare any meals for the first three days of the year. There is the very practical tradition that women should not start working from the first of the year. Prior to New Year's Day, however, the women of any Japanese household are kept extremely busy preparing for those forthcoming three days!

Unfortunately, modern lifestyles do not make this tradition convenient. Houses heated in the wintertime are not conducive to much of the traditional food which does not keep well without the cold or refrigeration. In traditional times, there usually were tiered lacquer boxes containing cold hors d'oeuvres — braised and simmered meat, fish and vegetables. Family members as well as guests were served both *sake* and the food from the lacquered boxes, somewhat like a boxed buffet!

What is prepared for *Oshogatsu* possesses significance in each name or in the ingredients used. The origins of many of the foods derives from superstitious practices. I can appreciate the many dreams and wishes sent through the New Year's food by my ancestors to insure prosperity, longevity and good luck to the grain harvest. *Dai Dai*, for instance, means 'forever.' This also is a green Japanese lime. *Kushigaki* means "it is a persimmon tree" for the persimmon tree has a long life. Therefore, the dried fruit of the persimmon is used.

Taro potatoes, or *sato-imo*, are included because they are very small potatoes and they stand for prosperity. Herring eggs, or *kazu-no-ko* signify fertility because like many newborn children, the eggs are packed in a sac. When we are so worried about overpopulation in this modern day, I wonder if we should eat *kazu-no-ko* during *Oshogatsu!*

As a child, I looked forward to *Osechi Ryori.* While I was not too keen about everything prepared, it all looked so pretty! My favorite foods were always in the first box, the one at the top of the tier. The boxes came in five tiers with the first one containing all the sweets, beans and fishcake. The second box usually displayed oiled things. The third box possessed braised and simmered dishes, or *onishime.* Box number four contained vinegared and pickled vegetables and smoked fish. On the bottom, box number five held all the surplus.

The lacquered boxes were set with the lacquered service for the *Oshogatsu* drink, or *otoso*, and lacquered *sake* cups on the *tokonoma* of the main room.

Continued on next page

Most *Oshogatsu* visitors stayed only a very short time, but were all taken to the main room after exchanging New Year's greetings. There they were invited to help themselves to the contents of the lacquered boxes, accompanied with hot *sake*. I remember seeing mostly men, not very many women guests. Where were they?

SOBA-ZUYU *sending-out-the-old year-noodles*

6 cups water	1/4 lb green beans
3/4 cup bonito shavings	1 egg
2/3 cup shoyu	2/3 cup cold water
4 tbsps mirin	1 cup flour
1-1/2 tbsps sugar	1 egg yolk
1 lb soba, dried	oil for deep frying
3/4 lb shelled shrimp	2 stalks green onion for garnish

Soba-zuyu: Bring to boil water, bonito shavings, shoyu, mirin and sugar. Strain and set aside.

Cook soba noodles with sashimizu method. Rinse well and set aside. Cut shrimp in ½-inch pieces. Remove strings from green beans and cut in size similar to shrimp. Beat egg in bowl, adding cold water and stir. Add flour, stirring gently. Add shrimp, beans and egg yolk, stirring quickly. While preparing egg batter, heat cooking oil to 365 degrees. Using a small sauce dish to scoop tempura batter, slip in from frying pan side. Turn. When dough becomes crisp, remove from oil. Drain off oil on rack of paper towel.

Dip serving bowl in hot water to warm. Rinse soba with hot water. Drain well. Pour hot soba-zuyo topped with a few tempura and garnish with minced green onion. *This is a must in sending out the old year.*

Cooking soba: Fill large pot with water. Bring to boil. Shake excess flour off noodles, add to boiling water and cook. When noodles and water come to boil, stir gently. Cook 1 minute, drain and rinse with cold water. Drain again. Serve either hot or cold. Recipes follow.

GO NO JIU *Five Tiered Box*

Ichi No Jiu — First layer: Sweets, beans and fishcake

Kuri Kinton	Anzu No Kanro Ni	Ebi Shinjyo
Mame Kinton	Tori Kurumi	Ume Tamago
Sarasa Kan	Baika Kan,	Awayuki Kan
Masago Dake		

Ni No Jiu — Second layer: Oiled things

Kajiki Maguro Mizo Zuke	Shofu Yaki
Gyuuniku No Miso Yahata	Kuruma Ebi Sake Shio Yaki

San No Jiu — Third layer: Braised and Simmered dishes or *onishime.*

Sato Imo	Saya Endo	Koori Dogu
Shiitake	Ninjin	Gin Nan
Kuai	Renkon	Fuku Bukuro
Gobo	Konnyaku	
Niku Dango To Renkon No amakari Ni		
Tori Niku To Kuri Umani		

Yo No Jiu — Fourth layer: vinegared and pickled vegetables.

Ko Haku Namasu	Sake No Hoso Maki	Tataki gobo
Temari Renkon	Kiku No Hitashi	Ra Pai Tsuai

Go No Jiu — Fifth layer: contains surpluses of any of the above.

ICHI NO JIU *Assortment of Kuchitori*

First box mostly sweet things and cold hors d'oeuvres sweet chestnuts with sweet potatoes

KURI KINTON *sweet chestnuts with sweet potatoes.*

3/4 lb sweet potatoes	1 cup liquid from canned
3 cups water	chestnut syrup plus water
1/2 cup sugar	1 (8 oz) can sweet chestnut
dash of salt	in syrup
1-1/2 tbsps mirin	

Peel sweet potatoes and cut in 1-inch rounds. Rinse well, soaking in water 30 minutes to blanch. Bring 3 cups water to boil, then cook sweet potatoes for 15 minutes. When tender, drain.

Add 1/4 cup sugar and stir well, using blender to whip. Return whipped mixture to pot, add dash of salt and 1/4 cup sugar to syrup/water combination.

Heat pot over slow flame, bringing mixture to boil. Remove any scum that surfaces and reduce heat to simmer.

When texture consistency thickens, add chestnuts and mirin. Simmer additional 2-3 minutes. Cool.

MAME KINTON *sweet lima beans*

2 cups white lima beans, dried	1/5 tsp salt
8 cups water	2 tbsps mirin
2 cups sugar	1/8 tsp red food coloring (opt.)

Wash and rinse lima beans 2-3 times and then soak overnight in 8 cups of water. Bring beans to boil in soaking water. Boil 5-6 minutes. Drain. Repeat procedure 4-5 times.

Add equal amount of water and simmer until beans are tender.

Sieve one-third portion of cooked beans and set aside. Place remaining beans in saucepan with sugar and salt and simmer 20 minutes. Add sieved beans and mirin. Stir quickly.

If you desire color, add red food coloring.

SARASA KAN *batik gelatin*

1/2 lb chicken thigh meat	1/2 tsp oil
4 cups water	3 tbsps gelatin powder
4 oz ham, cooked	3 cups chicken stock
4 oz green beans	1 tbsp sake
1 egg	1-1/2 tsps salt
dash of salt	1 tsp sugar

Special equipment: *nagashi bako*

Cut chicken thigh meat in 1/2 for easy cooking. Bring to boil 4 cups water. Cook chicken meat 20 minutes. Drain and reserve cooking broth for later use.

Cool chicken meat until easily handled with fingers. Shred with fingers into fine strips and set aside.

Shred ham in very fine strips.

Remove strings from green beans. Dip beans in boiling water 3-4 minutes. Drain, rinse with cold water and shred fine.

Beat egg with dash of salt. Heat skillet and coat with oil. Make 2 thin crepes, cool. Cut ito-giri, or thread-cutting style.

Using chicken broth, add gelatin. When gelatin is dissolved, cook over slow flame, adding sake, salt and sugar. Set in shallow pot of iced water. When gelatin starts to thicken, add chicken, ham, beans and egg. Fold into gelatin mixture.

Pour into nagashi-bako, or rectangular Japanese gelatin mold, or shallow pan. Cover with plastic wrap and chill. Cut into desired shapes.

The romantic name for this dish comes from the delicate similarity of gelatin squares and batik designs.

BAIKA KAN *plum blossom gelatin*

BENI KAN *red plum gelatin*

1 stick kanten, agar-agar	1 cup orange juice
2 cups water	2 tbsps red wine
3/4 cup sugar	
Special equipment: *nagashi bako*	

Soak kanten in water for 30 minutes. Squeeze out water and shred into cooking pot with 2 cups water. Heat until kanten dissolves. Add sugar. When it dissolves, strain into another pot and cook 3-4 minutes. Remove from stove. Cool slightly. Add orange juice and red wine. Pour into *nagashi-bako* or rectangular gelatin mold. Let sit to gel at room temperature.

AWAYUKI KAN *first snow-covered blossoms*

1 stick kanten	1-1/2 cups sugar
3 cups water	2 egg whites
Special equipment: *nagashi bako*	

Follow direction for cooking kanten in red plum gelatin, but cook kanten with 3 cups water and sugar. While kanten is cooking with sugar, beat egg whites until stiff. Place beaten egg whites in container set in shallow pan with iced water. Pour hot kanten mixture in egg whites while mixing with whisking motion. Mix until frothy. Place into nagashi bako.

Cut red plum and first snow fallen gelatin with plum flower cutter or cut into desired shapes.

My eyes always went to these pretty condiments. One is called Beni Kan, made to resemble a red plum flower. The other is called Awayuki Kan, and created to resemble the first snow-covered blossom, white in color.

UME TAMAGO *plum blossom-shaped quail eggs*

8 quail eggs	1/4 tsp vinegar
1/2 cup water	10 bamboo shewers
red food coloring	2 pcs carrots cut into 1 inch rounds

Hard boil quail eggs, while cooking turn eggs to insure yolk settling in center. When cooked, dip in cold water and peel under running water. Mix water and food coloring. Add 4 hard-boiled quail eggs and bring to boil. Pour in vinegar and simmer 20 minutes. Rinse with water and drain. On carrot pieces, place 3 bamboo skewers evenly, insert colored quail eggs, add 2 more skewers to form 5 petals of plum blossom. Secure top with rubberband. Repeat with four uncolored quail eggs.

When eggs are shaped in plum blossom petals, remove skewers. Cut off ends and slice in half. Makes total of 16 tiny plum blossoms to adorn New Year's box.

MASAGO DAKE *bamboo look-alike stuffed fishcakes*

4 small chikuwa	1/2 tbsp butter
2 oz fresh cod roe	1 tsp lime juice

Chikuwa is steamed and grilled fishcake and has a center hole. When cut diagonally, it resembles bamboo adorning the house entrance at Oshagatsu.

Place chikuwa in colander and pour boiling water over it. Slit open cod roe, scrape out pink roe and discard sac. Mix roe with butter and lime juice.

Cut chikuwa in 1-inch long diagonal pieces. Stuff with cod roe mixture and refrigerate.

NI NO JIU *second box - assortment of yaki-mono, mostly marinated and broiled things.*

KAJIKI MAGURO MISO ZUKE *miso marinated broiled tunafish*

1-1/2 lbs tuna, fresh or frozen	3-1/2 tbsps shoyu
1 tsp salt	2 tbsps sake
3/4 cup miso paste	

Slice fish fillet in 1/2-inch thick, 2-inch square pieces. Salt evenly all pieces and let stand two minutes. Mix miso, shoyu and sake. Place on bottom of 8-inch square glass dish. Wipe moisture off fish.

Bury tuna in miso bed 12 hours. Take tuna from miso bed, removing miso with hands. Do not wash with water. Broil both sides of tuna taking care not to burn.

GYUUNIKU NO MISO YAHATA *miso-flavored beef rolls*

1/2 lb gobo	2 tbsp sake
4 cups water	1-1/2 tbsp sugar
1 tbsp vinegar	1 lb beef, sliced bacon-thin
2/3 cup red miso paste	

Scrape gobo skin off with knife. Cut in 3-inch long pieces. Cook in 4 cups water and vinegar 10 minutes. Drain and place cooked gobo onto cutting board, pounding with bottom of jar to soften. It takes 3 sharp pounding movements to soften. Combine miso, sesame oil, sake and sugar. Spread beef and gobo on bottom of baking dish and marinate 24 hours.

Remove excess miso paste mixture from beef and gobo.

Place gobo onto sheet of beef then roll to 1-1/2 inch diameter. Wrap with aluminum foil twisting both ends. Broil 8 minutes.

Remove from wrap, cut in bite-size pieces to serve. Total of 12 to 15 rolls can be made from recipe.

SAWARA YUAN YAKI *broiled white meat fish with lime fragrance*

3 tbsps shoyu
1-1/2 tbsps sake
1-1/2 tbsps mirin

4 slices lime
8 fillets, 1-1/2 lbs snapper or
other white meat fish

Combine shoyu, sake, mirin and 3 lime slices in shallow, wide-bottomed dish. Add snapper fillet and marinate 15 hours. Insert metal skewers in fish fillet fan apart with twirling motion so skewer does not pierce other side. Broil 7-8 minutes one side, turn, then broil other side. Make sure broiling does not burn fillets. Intense heat will burn fish.

When cooked, remove skewers with twirling motion, without breaking fish texture. Place lime slice immediately for fragrance. Cool.

SHOFU YAKI *pine-breeze broil — broiled ground chicken meat*

1/2 cup red miso
5 tbsps sugar
1 tbsp mirin
2 tbsps sake
1-1/2 lbs chicken meat, ground

4 egg whites
1 cup bread crumbs
1 tsp oil
1/4 tbsp poppy seeds
aluminum foil, 12-inch square

Bring to boil miso, sugar, mirin, sake. Simmer until smooth and slightly thick in consistency. Set aside to cool. Using food processor or Japanese hand mortar, suribachi, work chicken meat until it is a paste. Lay flat a 12-inch square aluminum foil on baking sheet. Brush with oil. Turn chicken mixture onto foil, spread evenly, 1 inch high, 8-9 inches square. Bring edges of aluminum foil up on all sides to build ridge for chicken mixture. Over chicken mixture sprinkle poppy seeds evenly. Preheat oven to 375 degrees F. Bake 20 minutes. When cooled, cut in small fan shapes.

KURUMA EBI SAKE SHIO YAKI *broiled large prawns*

5 large prawns
2 tbsps sake
1/2 tsp salt

Devein and wash prawns. Sprinkle with salt and sake. Let stand 10 minutes. Pat prawns with paper towel to remove excess moisture. Insert metal skewer between shell and meat of prawn, except for last ridge of shell and tail. Tail should have curved look. This hunchbacked shape of prawn represents an elderly person, symbolizing long-lasting life. The prawn must have that curled look! Broil each side slowly 4-5 minutes. Remove skewers with twirling motion. Leave shell on when arranging prawns.

SAN NO JIU *third box — assortment of nishime, braised and simmered things*

FUKI YOSE *blown together simmered vegetables*

This dish involves a number of seasoned and cooked vegetables. Prepare each vegetable individually, keeping each in individual containers until serving time. Arrange in third section of tiered boxes.

SATO IMO *taro potatoes*

> 10 small sato imo (approx 2 lbs)
> 1-1/2 tsps salt
> 4 cups water
> 1-1/2 cups dashi
> 4-1/2 tbsps sugar
> 2 tsps shoyu

Peel sato imo and remove both ends. Boil in 1 tsp salt and 4 cups water 3-4 minutes. Drain. Rinse in cold water until glutinous substance is removed. Drain. Bring to boil dashi and boiled potatoes. Reduce to simmer. Add sugar and 1/2 tsp salt. Cook 7-8 minutes before adding shoyu. Simmer 10 more minutes and set aside.

SHIITAKE *dried mushrooms*

> 10 large shiitake
> 1-1/2 cups dashi
> 1-1/2 tbsps sugar
> 1 tbsp shoyu

Soak shiitake in warm water to soften. When soft, cut edges off to make a hexagonal shape. This resembles shape of turtle shell (In Japan, the turtle is believed to live a thousand years symbolizing longevity.) Combine dashi, mushrooms, sugar, shoyu. Simmer approximately 30 minutes or until cooking broth is reduced to 1 tbsp. and set aside.

KUWAI *arrowhead*

> 10 medium kuwai
> 1 cup dashi
> 1-1/2 tbsps sugar
> 1/2 tsp salt
> 1 tsp shoyu

Peel and cut stem ends off arrowheads, keeping 1/2 inch of stem. To blanch, soak peeled arrowheads 10 minutes in bowl of cold water. Bring arrowheads to boil and cook 4-5 minutes. Drain and rinse with cold water. In saucepan, boil 3 minutes. 1 cup dashi with arrowheads. Reduce heat and add sugar and salt. Simmer 10 minutes with dropped lid. Add shoyu and simmer another 7-8 minutes and set aside.

Renkon—Lotus Root

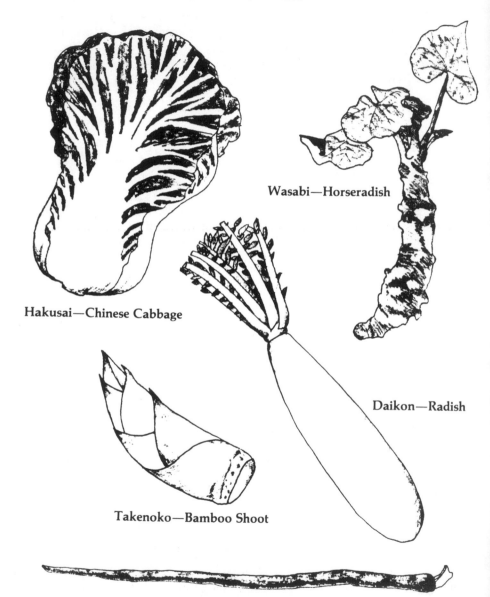

Hakusai—Chinese Cabbage

Wasabi—Horseradish

Daikon—Radish

Takenoko—Bamboo Shoot

Gobo—Burdock Root

GOBO *Burdock root*

> 1/2 lb gobo
> 2 tsp oil
> 1 cup dashi
> 1 tbsp shoyu
> 1/2 mirin

Scrap gobo and cut diagonally 5/8-inch pieces. Wash and soak 10 minutes in cold water to blanch. Drain and dry well with paper towel. Heat skillet with 2 tsp oil and saute gobo 3 minutes. Add dashi, boil at once, then add shoyu and mirin. Simmer 20 minutes or until gobo becomes tender.

SAYA ENDO *green beans*

> 1/3 lb green beans
> 4 cups water
> 1 tsp salt
> 1/2 cup dashi

> 2/3 tbsp sugar
> 2/5 tsp salt
> 1/4 shoyu

Remove string from beans and wash. Sprinkle with salt and let stand 3 minutes. Bring water to boil, dipping salted green beans in water 30 seconds. Remove, rinse with cold water and drain. Bring to boil dashi, sugar, salt. Add green beans, cooking 2 minutes, stirring constantly. Add shoyu. Turn onto plate to cool and retain bright green color.

NINJIN *carrots*

> 2 large carrots
> 1 cup dashi
> 1-1/3 tbsp sugar
> Special equipment: *ume gata*

> 3/5 tsp salt
> 1 tsp shoyu
> 1 tsp salad oil

Cut carrots into 3/4 inch thick rounds and then cut in plum blossom shapes using flower cutter *ume gata*. Combine dashi, salad oil and carrots in large enough saucepan. Cook over medium flame 5 minutes. Add sugar, salt and cook 10 minutes. Add shoyu, cooking 5 minutes.

RENKON *lotus root*

> 2 joints renkon (approx 2/3 lb)
> 6 tbsps vinegar
> 6 cups water

> 1/2 cup dashi
> 3 tbsps sugar
> 1 tsp salt

Peel renkon and cut 3/8-inch thick rounds. To avoid discoloration, soak immediately in 2 tbsp vinegar and 3 cups water 10 minutes. Drain, rinse and bring 3 cups water and 1 tbsp vinegar to boil. Add renkon and cook 2 minutes before rinsing in cold water. In enameled pan or glass saucepan, place dashi, sugar, salt and 3 tbsp vinegar. Bring to boil. Add renkon and cook 2 minutes. While stirring with chopsticks, turn onto plate to cool.

KONNYAKU *devil's tongue — tuber vegetable cake*

1-1/2 lbs konnyaku (2 cakes)	3 tbsps sugar
1 tbsp salad oil	3 tbsps shoyu
1 cup dashi	

Slice konnyaku in 2 x 1 x 1/2-inch rectangles. Make inch slit through center of piece parallel to long side. Pull one end through slit. This decorative cut is called *tazuna-giri,* braided straw rope. Heat skillet with salad oil. Saute konnyaku 3 minutes. Bring to boil dashi, sugar, shoyu. Add konnyaku, simmering 20 minutes.

KOORI DOFU *freeze-dried tofu*

2 lbs freeze dried tofu	2 tsps salt
4 cups dashi	2 tbsps mirin
1 cup bonito flakes	1 tbsp shoyu
7-1/2 tbsps sugar	

To large bowl filled with boiling water, add freeze-dried tofu cakes. Place drop lid on and let stand until water is completely cooled off. Place soaked, freeze-dried tofu between palms of hands. Squeeze out water gently. Dip in water and squeeze. Repeat procedure two times with each piece. Using wide-bottomed pot, pour dashi, line freeze-dried tofu overlapping each other. In corner of pot, place bonito flakes wrapped in gauze. Bring to boil immediately, reduce to simmer, then add sugar, salt. Place drop lid on simmering 15 minutes. Add mirin and shoyu and simmer 15 minutes. Keep cooked freeze-dried tofu in cooking broth 30 minutes or until serving time. Before serving, cut in bite-size triangles.

GIN NAN *ginkyo nuts*

1 cup water
1/2 tsp salt
8 oz ginkyo nuts

Bring to boil 1 cup water. Add salt, dipping ginkyo nuts in and out. Drain.

FUKU BUKURO *treasure pouch — stuffed, fried soybean curd*

3 shiitake	3/4 lb ground chicken meat
10 aburage pouches	2 tbsps sugar
3-inches kanpyo	3 tbsps shoyu
1-1/2 tsp salt	
1 medium carrot	
1/2 medium onion	**Cooking broth:**
4 oz shirataki canned	3 cups dashi
24 ginkyo nuts	1 tbsp shoyu
1-1/2 tbsp oil	1-1/2 tbsps sugar

Soak shiitake in warm water to soften. Dip aburage in and out of boiling water to remove excess oil. Drain. Cut each aburage in half across width. Place half

Continued on next page

aburage in palm of hand, slapping air out. Gently open cut pouch edge. Do this to all beancurd pouches. Rub kanpyo with 1 tsp salt. Rinse and cook in boiling water 4-5 minutes. Drain, divide and cut in 12 even lengths. Peel and cut carrot in 1/2-inch long, very thin strips. Cut shiitake and onion in same manner as carrot. Pour boiling water over shirataki and cut in 2 inch long pieces. Rinse gingko nuts in water. Heat skillet with oil and saute ground chicken 3 minutes. Then add carrot, shiitake, onions, shirataki, stirring and sauteing another 2 minutes. Add sugar, 1/2 tsp salt and shoyu, simmer 3 minutes and cool. Divide cooked ingredients 12 ways. Stuff into aburage pouches with 2 ginkyo nuts, tie closed with gourd ribbon. Combine cooking broth ingredients in deep, wide bottomed saucepan and place treasure pouches in single layer. Cover with drop lid. After cooking broth boils, reduce to simmer 30 minutes. Store in cooking broth.

One does not easily forget *fuku bukuro* from the New Year's menu. Although the ingredients in the pouch may differ from household to household, it is one of those on the *must* list. The exterior appearance will be similar in size, however, all hoping for prosperity for the forthcoming year. Two or three treasure pouches make a very generous portion for a meal with soup, rice and pickled ingredients.

NIKU DANGO TO RENKON NO AMAKARIA NI *pork balls and lotus roots*

1 lb ground pork	oil for deep-frying and for
1 tsp ginger juice	hands
1 tsp sake	2 joints renkon, (approx 3/4 lb)
1/5 tsp salt	1 can konnyaku (8 oz)
2 tsp shoyu	2 dried peppers
2 tsp cornstarch	1 tbsp oil
1 small egg	4 tbsps sugar
1-1/2 tsps salt	2 tbsps shoyu

Combine gound pork, ginger juice, sake, salt, 2 tsp shoyu, cornstarch and egg. Mix until texture is sticky. Oil palms of hands and make balls with 1 tbsp of mixture. Heat cooking oil to 370 degrees F. Cook each meatball 3 minutes. Drain and set aside. Peel lotus root and cut in bite-size pieces. Dip in and out of boiling water. Remove seeds from red peppers, slice thin. Heat skillet with oil, add red peppers, konnyaku, renkon and saute. Add sugar, dashi, salt, 2 tbsps shoyu and cook 10 minutes. Add meatballs and simmer 15 minutes.

TORI NIKU TO KURI NO UMANI *braised chicken and chestnut*

1-1/2 lbs chicken thigh meat	1 inch cube ginger
5-1/3 tbsps shoyu	3 tbsps oil
3 tbsps sake	1 can, 8 oz cooked chestnuts
10 plums, dried	1 cup water
1/4 lb green beans	1-1/3 tbsps sugar

Wash and wipe chicken thigh meat, then cut in bite-size chunks. Place chicken on platter and sprinkle with 1-1/3 tbsps shoyu and 1 tbsp sake. Let stand 15 minutes. Remove seeds from plums. Cut ginger in 10 pieces. Remove strings from green beans. Heat deep skillet with oil and saute green beans 3 minutes. Remove. In the same skillet, place slice ginger, marinated chicken and stir-fry until slightly brown in color. Add chestnuts, water, 4 tbsps shoyu, sugar, 2 tbsps sake. Stir from bottom to prevent sticking. When boiling point is reached, reduce heat to medium and cook 20 minutes. Add plums and simmer 10 minutes. Add green beans and remove from stove.

YO NO JIU *fourth box — namasu, fresh things with vinegar*

The fourth box contains an assortment of fresh vegetables and fish cured with vinegar or mainly vinegared things.

KO HAKU NAMASU *vinegared red and white*

1-1/2 lbs daikon	1 tbsp lime peel, shredded
2 large carrots	3 tbsps vinegar
2-1/2 tsps salt	2 tbsps sugar

Peel daikon, slice and cut sengiri style shredded. Peel and cut carrots into finer *sengiri* than daikon. In bowl, combine daikon and carrot, sprinkle with 2 tsps salt and let stand 20 minutes. Mix shredded lime peel with vinegar, sugar and 1/2 tsp salt. When vegetables are wilted, squeeze out water and marinate in vinegar mixture. Store covered, in refrigerator.

Red and white are colors of happiness in Japan and are thought of as being particularly festive. This color combination is used at weddings, graduations, birthdays and is even used in rice cake offerings at shrines. The arrival of the New Year cannot exclude these happy colors. Here it is with white of daikon and red of carrot.

Kohaku — Red and white

You will see many things in Japan wrapped in red and white. While purple is symbolic of royalty, we also prize white and red, or *kohaku,* and use it frequently in wrapping gifts. The cord of three or five gift-giving, is governed by the Chinese ideograph five, which represents the origin of everything in the universe. The cord represents a stream of purifying water, and ritual purification is very important to the traditional Japanese.   *Continued on next page*

Red and white in Japanese prehistory also has significance. White refers to Prince Ninigi, founder of the Imperial dynasty in Yamato. Red was the court color of the Izumo tribe, so that the double territory-color records the union of the two prehistoric courts of Izumo and Yamato.

There also is a feudal history of the two colors in Japan which is not unlike the dynasty struggle of the houses of York and Lancaster for the English monarchy, ultimately united under the red rose of the Tudors. The Japanese struggle, however, was symbolized by flags of the clans of Minamoto and Taira. Minimoto was identified by a white flag in the twelfth century, Taira by the red flag. It is even said that the white flag of surrender, introduced into Europe by Gengis Khan, has its origin in the Minamoto flag.

TAMARI RENKON *mustard flavored handball lotus root salad*

3 joints renkon, approx 3/4 lb	2 tbsps sugar
3 tbsps vinegar	2 tbsps water
Tamari sauce:	1/2 tsp salt
4 tbsps vinegar	2 tsps mustard paste

Peel renkon and slice in 1/4-inch rounds. Soak in 2 tbsps vinegar and 3 cups water 10 minutes to blanch. Drain. Bring to boil 3 cups water with 1 tbsp vinegar and cook renkon in it 1 minute. Rinse with cold water and drain.

Tamari sauce: Combine vinegar, sugar, water, salt and mustard paste. Marinate renkon in sauce until serving.

SAKE NO HOSHO MAKI *salmon-wrapped turnip*

1 large turnip	**Amazu sauce:**
3 cups water	3 tbsps vinegar
1 tsp salt	1-1/2 tbsp water
1/3 lb salmon fillet, fresh	1 tbsp sugar
6 inch konbu (kelp) sheet	1/2 tsp salt
1 tbsp vinegar	

Peel turnip and slice in very thin rounds. Soak in 3 cups water and 1 tsp salt 15 minutes and drain. Slice and cut salmon fillets in length of turnip and 1/4-inch in thickness. Line plate with konbu sheet and place salmon strips on it. Sprinkle with 1 tbsp vinegar. Let stand 30 minutes. Squeeze water out of wilted turnip. Place salmon strip, turnip and roll in small tube shape. Slice kelp sheets in 1/4-inch strips to tie rolled turnips.

Amazu sauce: Combine vinegar, water, sugar and salt in glass or ceramic container. Add rolled turnips to marinate. Let stand 10 hours or more before serving.

KIKU NO HITASHI *chrysthanemum and green salad*

        2 lbs spinach
        2 cups water
        1 tsp vinegar
        4 oz yellow chrysanthemum petals
        3 tbsps shoyu
        6 tbsps dashi

Wash spinach and cook in boiling water 2 minutes. Drain. Rinse in cold water and drain. Squeeze out all water and cut into 2-inch long pieces. Bring to boil 2 cups water and 1 tsp vinegar. Add yellow chrysanthemum petals and stir with chopsticks. Cook for 1 minute. Drain and rinse in cold water. Drain again and squeeze out water. Combine spinach and chrysanthemum in a bowl. Mix shoyu and dashi. Add 1/3 portion to vegetables and toss together. Squeeze out liquid and arrange in serving dish. Pour remaining 2/3 shoyu mixture over before serving.

TATAKI-GOBO *pounded burdock root*

        3/4 lb gobo
        3 cups water   **Sesame sauce:**
        1 tbsp vinegar   2 tbsps white sesame seeds,
        1/2 tsp sugar   ground
        1 tsp shoyu   1 tbsp sugar
        1/5 tsp salt   1 tbsp shoyu
        1/2 cup dashi   1 tbsp vinegar

Scrape gobo. Boil in water and vinegar 4 minutes. Drain. Wrap gobo in a dishcloth. Pound with bottom of soda bottle. Cut gobo in 2-1/2-inch long pieces. Combine sugar, shoyu, salt and dashi. Add gobo and cook 10 minutes.

Sesame sauce: Combine sesame seeds, sugar, shoyu and vinegar and mix well. Arrange cooked gobo. Spoon sauce over gobo and serve.

RA PAI TSUAI *Chinese cabbage with spiced vinegar sauce*

        1-1/2 lbs Chinese cabbage,   3 tbsps vinegar
            without leaf tips   2 tbsps sugar
        1 red pepper   1-1/2 tsps salt
        1 cucumber
        2 tbsp oil

Cut off crinkly leaf tips from Chinese cabbage, saving leaf tips for soup or another dish. Cut cabbage 4 inches long, 1/2-inch wide. Remove seeds from red pepper and cut into very thin round pieces. Heat skillet with oil. Saute red pepper and cabbage 2 minutes and remove from heat. Combine with vinegar, sugar and salt and let stand. Wash and cut cucumber ends and cut in 1/2-inch round pieces. Remove seeds and insert 3 or 4 pieces cabbage in cucumber ring and serve.

OZONI *rice cake dumpling soup for New Year's*

Ozoni is a must the first three days of the New Year. Depending on the different regions of Japan, Ozoni has many variations of ingredients and seasonings. I have provided three variations. All contain rice-cakes. I was told one would develop perserverance and maintain strong lower backs like wrestlers from eating rice cakes. I often muse I have never suffered from lower back aches.

TOKYO FU *Tokyo style*

1/3 lb chicken meat	1-1/2 tsp salt
4 tsps + 1 tbsp shoyu	3 oz kamaboko
1 tsp sake	12 oz mochi rice cakes, 4 pieces
1/2 lb spinach	3-1/2 cups dashi
1/4 lb daikon	bonito flakes
2 medium satoimo	lime peel

Cut chicken in bite-size pieces. Marinate in 1 tsp shoyu and sake. Let stand 15 minutes. Wash spinach, then dip in boiling water 1 minute. Remove, rinse in cold water, drain and cut in 2-1/2-inch lengths. Peel and cut daikon into 3/8-inch thick pieces. Cook 10 minutes in water or until tender. Peel and cut satoimo in 3/4-inch thick pieces. Rub with 1 tsp salt. Rinse and cook in water until tender. Slice kamaboko in 3/4-inch thick pieces. Pour boiling water over. Broil mochi rice cakes. Combine 3 cups dashi, 1/2 tsp salt, 1/2 tsp shoyu and bring to boil. Cook marinated chicken. When cooked, add cooked radish, satoimo, kamaboko and last spinach. In small saucepan, simmer 1/2 cup dashi. Warm broiled mochi rice cakes in simmering dashi and then place in soup bowl. Serve other ingredients in mochi cake-filled soup bowl. Garnish with lime peel.

NIIGATA FU *Northern Japan style*

8 oz salmon, fresh	3 cups dashi
8 oz daikon	1/2 tsp salt
4 oz carrot	1 tbsp shoyu
1/2 cake konnyaku (devil's tongue)	12 oz mochi rice cakes, 4 pieces
3 oz gobo	12 ginkyo nuts, canned
8 oz kamaboko	

Cut salmon in large bite-size pieces. Peel and cut daikon and carrot into 1-1/2 x 3/4 x 1/8-inch rectangles. Cut konyaku in same manner. Scrape gobo skin and cut in thin pieces 2 inch long. Soak in water 10 minutes to blanch and drain. Cut kamaboko in 1/2-inch cubes. Lay blanched gobo, daikon, carrots, konyaku in large pot with salmon pieces on top, adding 3 cups dashi. Bring to boil, then simmer until carrot is tender, 5 minutes. Season with salt and shoyu. Broil rice cakes and place in serving soup bowl. Fill bowl with cooked vegetables and salmon. Sprinkle with kamaboko and ginkyo nuts and serve.

INAKA FU *country style*

12 oz daikon	3 oz watercress
4 oz carrot	12 oz mochi cakes, 4 pieces
3 satoimo	5 cups dashi
1/2 cake yaki tofu, grilled	6 oz miso

Peel and cut daikon, carrots, satoimo in half and then into 1/2-inch thick, half-moon shaped pieces. Cut grilled tofu in 1/2-inch lengthwise, then slice 1/2 inch in thickness. Wash watercress, dip into boiling water 2 minutes and remove. Rinse in cold water and drain. Broil rice cakes and set aside. Bring dashi to boil before adding daikon and carrot. When dashi starts to boil, add half miso paste, add satoimo and simmer until vegetables become soft. Add remaining tofu, grilled tofu and watercress. Simmer additional 2 minutes. Add broiled mochi rice cakes and divide evenly in soup bowls.

DAIZU TO ABURAGE NO SANBAIZU *soybean and fried soybean curd with vinegar sauce*

1 cup dry soybeans	1 tbsp shoyu
2 squares fried soybean curds	2 tbsps mirin
1 tbsp vinegar	1/4 cup dashi

Wash and soak dried soybeans in water 3 hours. Drain and using pot large enough for cooking, place beans in pot, fill with boiling water and let stand 30 minutes. Drain and fill again with boiling water. Let simmer 20 minutes. When cooked, one cup of dried soybeans yields 5 cups of cooked soybeans. Broil fried beancurd without burning. Cut in 1/2-inch wide strips. Combine vinegar, shoyu, mirin and dashi and mix well. Add cooked soybeans and fried bean curd. Toss and serve right away.

KOKABU NO PEANUTS AE *turnips with peanut sauce*

6 small turnips	1/2 cup peanuts
1 tsp salt	2 tbsps vinegar
1 oz coriander	1 tsp shoyu

Wash and slice turnips lengthwise in very thin sheets. Sprinkle with salt and mix well until wilted. Wash coriander and separate stems and leaves, mincing stem portion. Grind peanuts. Then add vinegar and shoyu. Rinse salted turnips, squeeze out moisture. Combine with peanut sauce and minced coriander stems. Garnish with coriander leaves.

CHIGUSA AE *lettuce salad*

1 head medium iceberg lettuce	**Sauce:**
8 oz daikon	2 tbsps vinegar
1 medium carrot	2 tbsps shoyu
2 medium cucumbers	2 tbsps mirin
1/2 medium onion	
1 stalk celery	
1-1/2 tbsp white sesame seeds, roasted	

Wash and shred lettuce in very thin strips. Peel and cut daikon and carrot in 4 inch long strips. Cut cucumber diagonally, then cut in strips. Slice onion in 1/8-inch thick pieces. Remove strings from celery and cut as other vegetable. In large bowl filled with cold water and a few ice cubes, soak vegetables 60 minutes. When crisp, turn in colander and drain. Extract any excess moisture by gently squeezing. In salad bowl, place crisp salad vegetables and sprinkle with roasted sesame seeds.

Sauce: Combine vinegar, shoyu and mirin and pour over salad.

SU BASU *vinegared lotus root*

1 joint medium renkon, lotus root	**Sauce:**
	1/2 cup vinegar
2 tbsps vinegar	2 tbsps dashi
	1-1/2 tbsps sugar
	1 red pepper

Peel and cut lotus root in 1/4-inch thick rounds. Drop in 3 cups water with vinegar 10-15 minutes. In saucepan, bring to boil 2 cups water and 1 tbsp vinegar cook lotus roots 3-4 minutes in it. Drain. Cook vinegar, dashi and sugar. Using a ceramic or glass container place cooked lotus root in sauce. Remove seeds from red pepper and cut in thin strips. Mix with lotus roots. Marinate 60 minutes before serving.

TAMAGO NO SHINODA NI *fried bean curd stuffed with egg*

3 aburage, fried bean curd	2-1/2 tbsps shoyu
6 eggs	2-1/2 tbsps sugar
2 cups dashi	2-1/2 tbsps mirin

Dip aburage in boiling water to remove excess oil. Drain. Cut in half and gently open cut edge. Break egg in each pouch without breaking yolk. Seal opening of the pouch with a toothpick. Fill small saucepan with dashi, shoyu, sugar and mirin and bring to boil. Place egg-filled aburage in sauce and simmer 8-10 minutes. Serve hot or cold.

BUTA TO AGE NO MISO AE *pork and fried tofu, bean curd with miso sauce*

1-1/4 lb pork
3 aburage *fried bean curd*
1 or 2 cabbage leaves
1 green pepper
2 cups soybean sprouts
2 tsps oil
1 finger fresh ginger root, minced
1 clove garlic, minced

Miso sauce:
1 tbsp miso paste
1 tbsp sake (rice wine)
1/2 tsp sugar
1-1/2 tbsps shoyu
1/2 tsp sesame oil

Slice pork in 1-inch strips. Also cut aburage in thin strips. Cut cabbage in 2-inch squares. Remove seeds from green pepper. Cut in 8 pieces. Clean bean sprouts and pinch off hairlike roots. Heat oil, saute ginger, garlic, red pepper. Add pork, stir and cook until done. Add aburage and miso sauce mixture and toss few times. Add vegetables and stir until vegetables are done but crisp. Serve family style in large bowl.

KANI TO KYURI NO MISO AE *crab meat in vinegared miso dressing*

1 large cucumber
4 tbsps rice vinegar
1 tsp salt
2 tbsps vinegar
12 oz fresh or canned crab meat or abalone
1 medium finger fresh ginger

Su Miso sauce:
5 oz miso paste (soy bean paste)
2 tbsps sake or dry sherry
2-1/2 tbsps sugar
4 tbsps rice vinegar

Peel cucumber partially, leaving occasional 1/4-inch strips of green peel to add color to finished dish. Cut cucumber lengthwise in quarters. Scoop out seeds with small spoon and slice each quarter crosswise in thin pieces. Salt. When cucumbers are soft, squeeze out water gently. Place cucumber in bowl and mix well with rice vinegar. Remember, this is vinegar wash. Squeeze out liquid gently. Using crab meat, discard any cartilage and bits of bone. Shred finely with fingers. If using abalone, slice thinly to match cucumber size. Peel ginger. Slice lengthwise in paperthin pieces and cut in needle-like pieces. Soak 1 hour in 1 cup water. The needle-like ginger pieces will turn very white. This is called *"hari shoga"* needle-like. Drain. Pat excess moisture with paper towel.

Su miso sauce: Mix first 3 ingredients in small saucepan. Place on very slow fire, stirring constantly to avoid burning bottom of pan. Pour onto flat plate to cool. When cooled, add rice vinegar and mix well. Place cucumber and crab meat in small, individual bowls and pour sauce over. Garnish top with *hari-shoga.*

HORENSO NO GOMAAE *spinach with toasted sesame seeds*

1 tsp salt	1/4 cup niban dashi
2 cups water	1/2 tsp sugar
1-1/2 lbs fresh spinach, washed	1 tsp shoyu
1 tbsp black sesame seeds	

In deep 2-quart pot, bring 2 cups water to boil, adding salt. Gather spinach into large bunch, setting stemside down in pan, covering tightly. Cook 5 minutes over high heat, or until upper leaves begin to wilt. Drain spinach immediately in colander and immerse in cold water to stop cooking and retain green color. Cut away stems and discard. With hands squeeze leaves as dry as possible. Cut leaves in 1-inch pieces and squeeze dry again. Set spinach aside in bowl.

Heat heavy skillet over high heat until a drop of water immediately evaporates in the skillet. Lower heat to medium. Add sesame seeds lightly toasting 3-4 minutes, shaking pan constantly. Combine niban dashi, sugar, shoyu in a small saucepan, stir and bring to boil. Remove from heat and cool to room temperature. Pour sauce over spinach and toss together to coat leaves thoroughly. Divide spinach among 6 bowls, sprinkling each with sesame seeds. Serve *horenso no gomaae* at room temperature as first course or vegetable.

KANI TAMA SANBAIZU *crab ball with vinegar sauce and ginger*

1 lb potatoes	**Sauce:**
2 eggs	2 tbsps vinegar
1/2 tsp salt	3 tbsps shoyu
1 tbsp cornstarch	2 tbsps dashi
10 ginkyo nuts	1-1/3 tsps sugar

8 oz crabmeat, fresh, frozen or canned
1 tbsp ginger, grated for garnish

Peel, cut potatoes in small pieces and cook until soft. Drain and put through sieve. Add eggs, salt and cornstarch. Cut ginkyo nuts in half. Combine crabmeat, ginkyo nuts and potato mixture. Mix well. Heat cooking oil to 365 degrees F. Spoon crab and potato mixture into oill. When golden brown, remove and drain on towel.

Sanbaizu dipping sauce: Combine vinegar, shoyu, dashi and sugar. Serve garnished with grated ginger, and dipping sauce on the side.

CABBAGE NO TATAMI ZUKE *pickled cabbage fold*

2 cucumbers	3 oz dried apricots, raisins or
3 oz dried shrimp	plums
2 inch ginger	8 cabbage leaves
1 clove garlic	1-1/2 tsp salt
1 stalk green onion	1 tbsp crystal consomme
	essence
	3 tbsp sake

Wash and cut cucumbers in 1/4-inch thick rounds. Mince dried shrimp, ginger, garlic, green onion and dried fruit. Cut cabbage in glass loaf baking dish on bottom and fold over once. Arrange evenly sliced cucumber and 1/3 portion minced ingredients. Sprinkle over 1/3 portion salt and crystal consomme essence. Repeat arrangement 3 times. Finish with cabbage leaves layer on top. Pour sake from all sides. Press overnight with twice weight of ingredients. Cut and serve without disturbing arrangement.

KOKABU NO YAKUMI ZUKE *small turnip pickled with lime flavor*

1 lb small white turnips	1 lime
4 oz ginger	1 tsp salt

Wash turnips under running water. Drain and cut in 1/4-inch rounds. Peel and shred ginger. Soak in water 10 minutes. Drain. Squeeze lime juice and save for later use. Shred lime peel. In pickling container, combine turnips , ginger and lime peel. Sprinkle salt. Place weight twice that of ingredients. After 4-5 hours, drain water. Sprinkle with reserved lime juice. Mix well and serve.

TSUBO ZUKE *kiriboshi daikon pickle*

8 oz kiriboshi daikon	4 tbsps shoyu
2 red peppers	2 tbsps sugar
1/3 cup vinegar	1/2 cup dashi

Wash kiriboshi daikon in warm water and drain. Remove seeds from peppers. In pickling container, combine vinegar, shoyu, sugar and dashi and stir well. Add washed kiriboshi daikon, red peppers and mix well. Let stand 10 hours or more and mix again. Place weight 3 times ingredients and press for week. This pickle will keep months without refrigeration.

Very often sold in cellophane packages, kiriboshi daikon, sun-dried shredded radish, is very low in calories, rich in minerals and looks very much like short straws.

YUKIMI *Snow Viewing Party*

A snow-viewing poetry party often was held in February. We hoped, of course, that the weather was cooperative, covering lanterns in the garden with a mound of cold snow to view.

Early, the room was heated by the tea kettle, making a ra-ta-ta noise, on the gas burner. I recall an arrangement of budding red and white plum branches, *fukuji-so*, adorned the *tokonoma* for the occasion. Often by evening, the gentle warmth had caused one or two plum blossoms to open.

On party nights, a fire box with charcoal brazier, a small handwarming, *hiyoke*, was placed between each guest. The main room did not enjoy central heating and these *hiyoke* were necessary to warm one's hands for using the brush.

Soon after the greetings were accomplished, hot tea and towels were served. Everyone settled on his proper cushion to view the snow through the glass panel of the *shoji*. The guests quietly started grinding the ink stick for the calligraphy against the ink stone, a practice which can be meditative and conducive to concentration. My very honored responsibility was to pass the poem-writing paper, *shikishi*; a paper sheet narrow and long in shape like a scroll for painting, *to tan-zaku*, the felt-padded writing area where the ink stones were set. It was fun to watch the expression of guests engaged in poetic composition. When everyone was finished composing, they transposed the *waka* poem on to the *shikishi*. I then collected them with great reverence.

When the teacups were removed — the teacups are an indispensable accompaniment to composition — critizing of the poetry started. Hot sake and *zenzai* were brought in by my mother or grandmother. Cold h'ors d'oeuvres prepared ahead of time, *zensai* were served to increase the pleasure of drinking sake. It was a pleasant experience to view the *zensai*. Beside the food, something of the season always would be artistically displayed on the tray.

First served was the fresh fish *sashimi*, *mukozuke*, which came in various sizes and shapes. Then came the red bean rice, *sekihan*, a dish commonly prepared for such occasions, served alone with cooked vegetables, fish or meat, *taki-awase*. Next was the steamed food — steamed turnip with *yuzu-miso*, the most elegant, warming dish I remember from those winter gatherings. Last, one of my favorite soups, a clam soup, *tome-one*, the subtle signal of the end of the meal. You can imagine by the time the *tome-one* had arrived, many cups of sake had been emptied!

I remember vividly one particular February evening. It was soon after World War II when we did not have much of anything in Japan, particularly foodstuffs. Snow had fallen thickly everywhere. The outside was so bright and cold as if the stars were frozen in the sky. The moon reflected silver blue on everything. Nothing possessed a definite shape or form and yet everything was joined with endless gentle nuances. When I have steaming turnip cup with miso sauce I remember warmly that silver-silhouetted February night so long ago.

ZENSAI *cold hors d'oeuvres*

KIKUKA MAKI *chrysanthemum wrap*

3/4 lb cooked crab,
   canned or frozen
1 tsp ginger juice
1 tbsp vinegar
1-1/2 tbsps shoyu
1 tbsps dashi

2/3 tsp sugar
4 oz smoked salmon
1 cucumber
2 eggs
2 nori sheets

Special equipment: *Sudare* square egg pan

Combine crabmeat with ginger juice, vinegar, shoyu, dashi and sugar. Mix well and let stand. Cut salmon in 1/4-inch strips. Cut off ends of cucumbers, wash and cut in half, then in strips 1/4-inch thick. Beat eggs and make 2 very thin crepes in square egg pan. Place crepe on *sudare* or bamboo mat and spread crabmeat mixture on 2/3 of crepe, leaving 1/2-inch space nearest you. On middle of crabmeat, lay strip of cucumber and salmon horizontally. Roll in sushi rolling manner, then wrap with sheet of nori. Wet edge of seaweed to close. Roll seaweed wrapped crab gently 2 minutes in heated unoiled skillet. This toasts nori wrapping. Cut in bite-size pieces and serve.

KURUMA EBI HAKATA OSHI *Hakata-style sandwich with shrimp*

4 large prawns
1-1/2 tsp salt
2 cups water
4 eggs, yolks and whites separated
3-1/2 tbsp sugar
1/2 tsp green nori flakes

Special Equipment: *sushi meshi mold*

Devein prawns. Insert bamboo skewer or toothpick lengthwise in back between shell and meat to maintain straight shape rather than curled and hunched look as in New Year's shrimp. Boil in 1 tsp salt and 2 cups water 5 minutes until tender. Chill, shell and remove skewer and split in half lengthwise via underside of prawn. Top should remain intact. Using double boiler, combine 4 egg yolks, 1-1/2 tbsps sugar, 1/4 tsp salt. Stir until crumbly but not dry and hard. Set aside. In small bowl, mix egg whites, 2 tbsps sugar, 1/4 tsp salt. Place in steamer until mixture becomes firm. Wrap eggwhite mixture with cheesecloth, press between boards and squeeze out moisture. Using fine mesh strainer to sieve, add green nori flakes. Wipe small, square sushi press mold with wet towel. Line bottom of mold with egg white and press. Place egg yolk and smooth it out, press again. Arrange prawns evenly on top. Press down firmly, let stand 60 minutes. Remove from mold, cut in desired shape.

UZURA TERIYAKI *teriyaki quail or chicken*

4 quails, deboned
Sauce:
1/4 cup sake
1/2 cup mirin
1/4 cup shoyu
1 tbsp sugar
1 tbsp honey

Combine sauce ingredients in pot and simmer until only 10% of liquid remains. Broil quail while turning, brushing frequently with sauce on all sides, 3-4 minutes required for both sides. Arrange kiku k a maki, kuruma ebi, hakata oshi, uzura teriyaki onto zensai serving dish.

SEKIHAN *red rice with chestnuts*

4 cups mochi rice	dash of red coloring
12 cups water	1-1/2 tsp salt
1/2 cup azuki or red beans	1 tbsp black sesame seeds
8 oz chestnuts	

Wash and soak mochi rice in 8 cups water overnight. Wash and soak red beans in 2 cups water overnight. Soak chestnuts in water overnight, peeled and quartered. Mix red food coloring with soaked rice. Let stand 60 minutes and drain. Boil red beans, continue cooking 10 minutes, then lower flame. Simmer red beans until tender and then drain. Cooking beans this way will keep beans whole. Mix rice, cooked red beans, and chestnuts. Place in steamer and steam with 1 tsp salt in 2 cups water over high heat 40-50 minutes. While steaming, make small holes in rice so that steam gets through, spray with hot salt water over rice 3 or 4 times. Mix 1/2 tsp salt and black sesame seeds well and roast over low heat. Sprinkle over rice when serving. Serve hot or cold.

In Japan, sekihan is a festive dish, served at weddings or birthdays.

My fondest memories of my mother come alive when I prepare Sekihan or happy-day rice. Chewing each grain of mochi rice, brushed pink, colored with azuki beans, I realize that manifestations of my mother's human, beautiful, feeling did not come in spoken form, but rather softly brushed with Sekihan. My mother transmitted the essence of Japan through her serving of Sekihan abroad.

My memory eye gazes back to my childhood long ago. Wherever we happened to be residing my mother promptly would learn the festival and celebration days of the country where my father's assignment as a diplomat with the Japanese Foreign Ministry took us. My mother would prepare Sekihan honoring the holidays of the country we visited as well as the traditional Japanese festivals. My mother's Sekihan became quite a habit amongst the diplomatic circle for when they came to call on a holiday they always know they would be offered Sekihan.

I remember, sometimes she ran out of the azuki beans she brought with us and we had to find foreign beans as a substitute. She brought renewal, excitement and the pleasure of homeland to share with the other Japanese abroad. I am so touched by her gentle memory and her heart of delicacy and compassion. I have kept this tradition alive in cooking and serving Sekihan and my friends are quite familiar with my happy-day rice, Sekihan!

ATSU-MONO *something warm — steamed things*

KABURA FUROFU *steamed turnip*

4 large turnips	1 egg yolk
7 inch square konbu	1/2 cup sugar
1 tsp salt	1/4 cup sake
4 cups water	1/2 cup dashi
2/3 cup miso	1 tsp lime peel, grated

Wash and clean turnips. Slice off upper third with stem to use as lid. Spoon out insides of bottom two-thirds of turnips, being careful edges are thick enough to hold up while cooking. Place bottom portion of turnip in large pot filled with water. Place drop lid on turnip. Bring to boil, reduce heat to simmer and continue cooking 30-40 minutes. Cook top of turnip separately. To test for doneness, a bamboo skewer should easily go through turnip. Bring pot under running water without water force directly hitting turnip, the gentle force of water blanching turnip 30 minutes. Let stand in water 2 hours, changing water every 30 minutes. Drain. Line bottom of pot with kelp sheet, add salt and water. Place blanched turnips and simmer 10 minutes until soft. Combine miso, egg yolk, sauce, sake, dashi in double boiler cooking until slightly thickened. Add grated lime peel. On serving plate or bowl, place turnip, spoon in miso sauce and replace turnip cover. Serve with spoon.

TOME-MAN *meal ending soup*

HAMAGURI USHIO NI *clear clam soup*

8 cherrystone clams	dashi stock
2 tsp salt	2 oz enoki dake mushrooms
7 cups water	1/4 tsp shoyu
4-inch square konbu	lime peel
1/2 cup sake	

Soak clams one hour in 1 tsp salt and 2 cups water to clean out sand. Place in 5 cups water, konbu, sake and clams and bring to boil. Discard konbu just as water comes to boil. Remove clams as soon as shells open. Set aside. Add 1 tsp salt to dashi stock and strain using very fine mesh strainer. Wash mushrooms and dip in and out of boiling water. Drain and remove clam meat from shell. Discard one side of shell. Place meat back into shell. In each soup bowl, arrange 2 clams in shells with mushrooms. Bring dashi to boil, drop shoyu, fill each soup bowl with broth and garnish with lime peel, *matsuba yuzu,* or pine-needle-cut style lime peel.

BURI TERIYAKI *glazed yellow-tail broil*

1-1/2 lbs yellow-tail, fresh or frozen	**Tare sauce:** 4 tbsp mirin
1/2 tsp salt	4 tbsp shoyu
	1 tsp sugar

Slice yellow-tail fillet in 4-5 pieces and sprinkle with salt. Let stand for few minutes then wipe off moisture with paper towel. Insert metal skewers in fan shape. Broil each side 3-4 minutes. Remove from broiler and brush both sides with tare sauce. Return to broiler, dry tare sauce, remove and brush again with tare sauce and return to broiler to dry. This is repeated 3 times. Remove the metal skewers with twirling motion while fish is still warm.

Tari Sauce: In small sauce pan boil mirin. Ignite with match to burn off alcohol. Add shoyu, sugar and simmer 4-5 minutes. This makes glaze sauce or *tare.*

SAKE NO KOBU JIME *vinegared kelp-salmon sashimi*

2 lbs salmon fillet, fresh	1 daikon
1 tbsp salt	1 cucumber
4 pieces 10-inch long dashi konbu	bunch fresh coriander shoyu
4 tbsps vinegar	1 tbsp wasabi paste

Cut fresh salmon fillet 10-inches long. Sprinkle with salt and let stand 7-8 minutes. Rinse with cold water and pat dry. Brush konbu, rinse with cold water and wipe clean. Sprinkle vinegar on 1 side of each piece of konbu. Wrap each fish fillet with konbu, vinegared side facing fish fillet. Wrap fish fillet and konbu sandwiches tightly in plastic wrap. Store in refrigerator overnight with weight on top. Cut radish and cucumber into very thin *sengiri.* To crisp soak in cold water. Unwrap fish after being refrigerated overnight. Place knife between skin and meat, pull away skin, cutting straight down, slice in bite-size pieces. Garnish with drained segiri radish, cucumbers and coriander sprigs. Serve with shoyu and wasabi paste.

A favorite snack for drop-in guests at busy New Year's time.

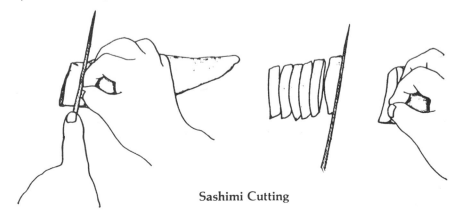

Sashimi Cutting

IKA NO KIMI SOBORO AE KODAI NO SASHIMI

squid with crumbly egg yolk, fresh porgy or small snapper sashimi

1/3 lb squid, 6 fillets only	4 oz red radishes
1 egg	4 leaves chiso
1-1/2 lbs (approx) fresh porgy	1 tbsp washi paste
or snapper	5-6 tbsps shoyu
1/4 tsp salt	

Remove 2 layers of skin from squid fillets. Cut in 3-inch lengths, and slice in thin strips. Make hard-boiled egg. Using just yolk, put through fine mesh sieve and allow to cool. Dust squid slices with crumbly egg yolk. Cut porgy in 3-fillet manner. Sprinkle with salt and let stand 6-7 minutes. Pat moisture away. Slice fish thin, diagonal pieces. Wash red radishes, slice very thin and then cut in matchstick-like pieces. Soak in water to crisp. Wash and wipe chiso leaves. Slap between palms of hands to release fragrance of leaves. Arrange in serving bowl, chiso leaves, porgy slices on top divided in 4 equal portions. On side place squid with crumbly eggyolk, also divided in 4 equal portions. Make mound of shredded red radish with wasabi paste. Serve with shoyu.

KAREI NO YUBURI *partially-cooked flounder sashimi*

1 to 1-1/2 lbs flounder	*Miso Sauce:*
1 cucumber	4 oz miso
8 chiso leaves	3 tbsps sake
2 tbsps wasabi paste	2 tbsps sugar
	1-1/2 tbsps vinegar

Prepare flounder in five-fillet manner. Cut fillet in 1-1/4-inch cubes. Bring water to rapid boil and have bowl of cold water ready next to boiling pot. Dip flounder cubes, few at a time, in boiling water 30 seconds and then dip in cold water. Drain. Wash cucumber, shred in thin strips. Shred chiso leaves in thread-like strips. In small saucepan, combine miso, sake and sugar. Cook over medium flame. When smooth in texture, remove from heat, cool, add vinegar and mix well. Divide all ingredients in individual serving dishes. Arrange cucumbers, chiso leaves and partially cooked flounder, some with dark skin side up, some with white flesh side up to make an interesting black and white design, Garnish with wasabi paste, serve with 1/4 portion of miso sauce poured in small container.

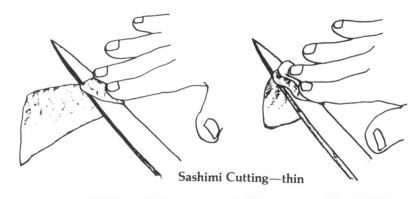

Sashimi Cutting—thin

SHIROMI ZAKANA NO KABŪRA MUSHI *steamed fish fillet and turnips*

5 white fish fillets	**Sauce:**
1/2 lb spinach	1 cup dashi
2/3 lb turnips	1/3 tsp salt
1-1/2 tbsps egg white	1 tbsp shoyu
2/3 tsp salt	1 tbsp cornstarch
1 oz fresh ginger root	1 tbsp water

Salt fish and allow to stand 2 hours. Wash and wipe dry. Boil spinach in boiling, salted water until tender. Immediately rinse in cold water and drain. Cut in 1-1/2-inch lengths to form clumps. Peel and grate turnips, add egg white, salt and mix well. Place 1 piece of fish topped with one clump of spinach and 1/5 turnip sauce on shallow individual dishes. Steam 20 minutes. Serve while hot. In small saucepan, mix dashi, shoyu, salt and bring to boil. Add mixture of cornstarch and water to cooking sauce. Heat until thickened and pour over steamed fish. If desired, add grated ginger for garnish.

BUTTER FISH MISO ZUKE YAKI *broiled butterfish in miso marinade*

1/2 cup miso	1 lb fillet, fresh butterfish, cut
5 tbsps sugar	in 3-inch pieces
3 tbsps mirin	hajikami or bottled pickled
	ginger sprouts

Place miso in small bowl and stir in sugar and mirin. Arrange fish in baking dish large enough to make one layer. With rubber spatula, spread marinade evenly over fish. Cover with plastic wrap and refrigerate 2 days. Preheat broiler or light hibachi or charcoal broiler. With rubber spatula and paper towels, remove marinade carefully and discard. Place fish 4 inches from heat and broil 7-8 minutes or until golden brown. Carefully turning fish, broil 1 minute more. Serve at once with pickled ginger sprouts. This dish can be served as part of Japanese meal, as first course or luncheon dish. Fillet of mackeral is equally tasty.

ISE EBI NO NITSUKE *broiled lobster*

1-1/2 lbs fresh lobster	2-1/2 tbsps shoyu
3/4 cup mirin	2 tbsps sugar
1/3 cup sake	

Wash lobster. After cutting head off lobster, save it. Cut each segment apart and cut off tail. Cut legs off at first joint. Cut head lengthwise in symmetrical pieces. Each piece of head should be cut again crosswise into 3 sections. Mix mirin, sake, shoyu and sugar in deep saucepan and bring to boil. Add lobster pieces to mixture starting with head. Place shell side against pan. Continue to add pieces from head to legs. Boil 4-5 minutes over strong flame. While boiling, turn pieces not covered by sauce. While hot, remove pieces to plate. Pour remaining sauce over lobster pieces.

TORI FUKUMI NI *ground chicken balls and satoimo*

1 lb chicken meat
1/4 cup onion, minced
2 tsps shoyu
1 tsp sake
1/2 tsp ginger juice
1/2 cup bread crumbs
1 egg
1 lb satoimo
1 lb spinach

Sauce A:
2-1/2 tbsps sake
1 tbsp sugar
1 tbsp shoyu
1/2 cup dashi

Sauce B:
2 tbsps sugar
2 tbsps mirin
1 tsp salt
2 tsps shoyu

Sauce C:
1/2 cup dashi
1 tbsp shoyu
1/2 tbsp mirin
1 oz ginger, haro shoga style

Combine ground chicken meat, minced onion, shoyu, sake, ginger juice, bread-crubs, egg and mix well. Divide mixture in 10 even-sized balls. Bring to boil Sauce A ingredients. Add chicken balls and reduce heat to medium. Cook 7-8 minutes and remove from heat. Let chicken mixture steam itself, tight-lidded 10 minutes. Peel satoimo and rub with salt. Cook in hot water, bring to boil then cook 5 minutes. Drain and rinse with cold water. Combine Sauce B ingredients. Bring to boil and add satoimo. Simmer 10 minutes. Wash and boil spinach. Drain and cut in 2-inch long pieces. Cook with Sauce C 3 minutes. Arrange cooked chicken balls, satoimo and spinach in serving bowls. Garnish with ginger haro shoga style.

KO GAREI NO FUKUSA MUSHI *steamed small flounder*

4 small flounder
1 tsp salt
4 oz carrot
4 dried shiitake
2 oz green beans
1 oz ginger
2 stalks green onion
8 tbsps sake

Ume Shoyu:
2 large umeboshi, pickled plums
1/2 tbsp shoyu
1 tbsp mirin

Clean flounder. Sprinkle salt on both sides and let sit 10 minutes. Wipe off moisture. Peel and cut carrots in 1-inch strips. Place shiitake in warm water to soften. Remove stems and cut in strips. Remove strings from green beans and cut in 1-1/2-inch long pieces, julienne style. Peel and cut ginger into very thin strips. Cut green onion in 1-1/2 inch long pieces, julienne. Place flounder on plate for steaming in steamer. Sprinkle 2 tbsp sake on each flounder. Arrange vegetables over flounder and steam 15 minutes in steamer over high heat. Remove from steamer and discard liquid from steaming. Serve with *ume shoyu*.

Ume shoyu: Remove seeds from umeboshi. Sieve through mesh, mix with shoyu and mirin.

MOCHI NO SHINODA NO BUKURO *fried beancurd pouch*

4 fried beancurds
2 cups water
1 kanpyo
1/2 tsp salt
8 small rice cakes

3 cups dashi
2 tbsps shoyu
1 tbsp mirin
1 bunch coriander
1/2 cup daikon, grated

Pat fried beancurd between palms of hands a few times and cut in half. Open to make pouch and cook in 2 cups water 5 minutes. Drain. Soak kanpyo in water and salt 30 minutes. Drain and cook in salted water until soft. Fill fried beancurd pouch with rice cake cut in quarters. Tie with softened kanpyo. Bring dashi to boil with shoyu and mirin. Add pouches simmering until rice cakes are tender, about 7-8 minutes. Use soupbowls to serve with broth. Garnish with coriander and grated daikon.

DAIZU TO GAN MODOKI NO NIMONO *soybean and fried tofu stew*

1/3 cup hijiki, dried black
  sea vegetable
2 carrots
1/2 cup beansprouts
2 cups dashi

1/2 tsp salt
1 tbsp shoyu
2 tsps sugar
8 gan modoki fried
1 cup cooked soybeans

Soak dried hijiki in water. It will swell many times its dried volume. Rinse and drain. Cut carrots in sengiri strips. Clean, wash beansprouts and drain. Using fairly large heavy pot, bring to boil dashi, salt, shoyu and sugar. Add gan modoki, hijiki, carrots, beansprouts and cooked soybeans. Cook until liquid has been reduced. Makes lovely, nutritious accompaniment for riceballs.

BUTA BARA NIKU TO DAIKON NO NIKOMI *pork spareribs in radish*

2-1/2 lbs pork rib meat,
  deboned
4 lbs daikon
2 cups sake

2 tbsps ginger juice
6-8 cups water
1 cup shoyu

Cut pork meat in approximately 4-inch square pieces. Fill large pot with water and bring to boil. Cook pork ribs 2-3 minutes until scum appears on cooking water surface. Drain, rinse clean with water and set aside. Wash daikon and cut in 2-inch thick pieces. Fill large pot with cold water and daikon and cook 4-5 minutes. After reaching boiling point, drain and rinse with cold water. In heavy skillet, combine 2 cups sake and pork. Stir, add 1 tbsp ginger juice and 6-8 cups water to cover meat. Bring to boil, cover and reduce to simmer. After 40-50 minutes, remove scum or fat that rises to surface. Add sugar and daikon and cover partially with lid. Simmer 40-50 minutes. Add 1/2 cup shoyu, cover and simmer another hour. Add remaining 1/2 cup shoyu and simmer until liquid is reduced approximately 1 cup. Add 1 tbsp ginger juice. Serve individually or on large platter. A warming dish for cold winter nights.

GOBO IRI SATSUMA AGE *deep-fried fishcake with burdock root*

3-inch daikon, lemon or
lime peel
1/3 lb gobo
/4 lb fresh fish fillet
2/3 tsp salt
1 egg

4 tbsps flour
2 tbsps black sesame seeds
1 tbsp mustard paste
1 tbsp shoyu

Slice daikon in very thin pieces and shred very fine. Peel and shred lemon or lime. Soak in water to crisp. Drain. Scrape gobo skin with back of knife, wash and shave in small cut bamboo leaf, as you would sharpen pencil with pocket knife. Soak in water to blanch. Cut fish fillet in small pieces, then work in food processor 1 minute. Add salt, egg, flour and work another minute. Combine mixture with shaved gobo, black sesame seeds and mix well. Divide mixture in 12 parts and shape into flat ovals. Heat cooking oil to 370 degrees F. deep fry. When fish patty starts to surface, turn over and fry until color is golden brown. Garnish with shredded daikon and lime or lemon peel. Serve hot with mustard paste mixed with shoyu.

TORI NIKU NO KARASHI AGE *deep-fried chicken with mustard batter*

1 lb chicken breast meat
1/4 tsp salt
2 tbsps plus 1 tsp sake
2 tbsps mustard paste

2 tbsps shoyu
oil for deep-frying
1 cup cornstarch

Lay chicken meat flat on cutting board. Using wooden mallet or soda bottle, pound and flatten meat. Two or three heavy strokes should do. Place flattened chicken on plate. Sprinkle evenly with salt and 1 tsp sake. Combine 2 tbsps mustard paste and shoyu. Mix well with whisk, adding sake to complete mustard batter. Batter must be well-mixed. Heat the cooking oil to 365 degrees. Dip marinated chicken in mustard batter, dust well with cornstarch, shaking off any excess. Deep-fry 2 minutes and turn. When golden brown, remove and drain. Delicious hot or cold, one can pack it for lunch for a tasty treat and a delightful change.

EBI SURIMI NOSE *deep-fried lotus root and shrimp paste*

1 large joint renkon	1/4 tsp salt
3 cups water	1 cup flour
1 tbsp vinegar	1 egg yolk
2/3 lb shrimp meat,	1 cup iced water
frozen or fresh	oil for deep-frying
1 tbsp sake	1/4 head lettuce
1 tsp plus 1/4 cup cornstarch	mustard sauce

Peel and cut lotus root in 1/2-inch thick pieces. Soak 15 minutes in 3 cups water with vinegar. Work shrimp meat 1 minute in food processor. Add sake, 1 tsp cornstarch, salt. Work 1 minute. Drain lotus root, wipe off water with paper towel. Dust with cornstarch. Apply shrimp mixture on one side like open-faced sandwich. For batter combine flour, egg yolk, iced water and mix well. Heat oil to 365 degrees F. Dip lotus root open-faced sandwich in batter. Then fry until it surfaces above oil. Serve with mustard sauce on bed of shredded lettuce.

TAI NO OKASHIRA TSUKI AGE MONO *whole snapper in its deep-fried meat*

1 whole snapper,	1/2 cup cornstarch
approx 2-1/2 lbs	1 bunch parsley
3 tbsps salt	lemon wedges
oil for deep-frying	small pine branches

Remove scales and clean fish. Rinse in water, drain and pat dry with paper towel. Cut fish fillet according to following instructions. Sprinkle with salt and let stand 2 hours. Insert 2 metal skewers to partially-filleted, removed fish body, now mostly fish head, backbone and tail end. Using *odori zushi*, as though fish is alive and swimming or dancing style, with slight waving motion, head and tail should be up. Rub *salt onto* bone joints of head and tail. Broil fish without burning skin. Heat cooking oil to 365 degrees F. Cut salted fillets in 1-inch cubes, dust with cornstarch and deep-fry. Wash parsley, dry well and break into small clusters of sprigs. Dip into *tempura batter* (see index) and deep-fry. Garnish with lemon wedges and pine branches. This particular dish can be served at New Year's, birthdays, graduations and weddings.

BUTA NO DANGO AGE *fried pork balls*

1/3 oz shiitake	**Sauce:**
1 bunch green onions	4 tbsps shoyu
1 lb ground pork	3 tbsps vinegar
2/3 tsp shoyu	1 tbsp sugar
1/2 tsp salt	2 dried red peppers
1 tsp sugar	1/3 oz katsuobushi, dried
1 egg	1/3 oz konbu
1 tbsp sake or dry sherry	
frying oil	

Soften shiitake in enough cold water to cover, squeeze and mince. Mince green onions. Mix well pork, shiitake, onions, shoyu, salt, sugar, egg and sake. Form 1/2-inch balls and deep fry.

Mix sauce ingredients, bring to boil and skim off residue. Place meat balls in sauce. Marinate 6 hours, then remove and serve.

RINGO TO BUTANIKU NO AWASE AGE *fried pork balls with apples*

2 large shiitake	2 cups cooking oil
1 apple	1 head lettuce
1 lb ground pork	1/4 cup vinegar
1 tbsp green onion, minced	mustard
1 egg	1/4 cup sake or dry sherry
2/3 tbsp sake or dry sherry	1/4 cup shoyu

Soften shiitake in enough cold water to cover. Squeeze out water and cut into about 1/6-inch pieces. Peel and cut apple same size as shiitake. In large bowl, combine ground pork, chopped mushroom, apple and minced onion. Add egg, sake or dry sherry, salt. Mix well together. Make 16 patties. Fry in deep fat and drain. Cushion meat patties on shredded lettuce bed. Serve with mixture of vinegar, 1/4 cup sake or dry sherry, 1/4 cup shoyu, and add bit of mustard.

SHIRO GOME IRI CHAMESHI *shoyu flavored rice with sesame seeds*

3 cups rice	2 tbsps sake
3 cups water	2 tbsps mirin
3 tbsps shoyu	4 tbsps white sesame seeds,
3/4 tsp salt	roasted

Wash and drain rice. Combine all ingredients except sesame seeds in heavy, metal pot and let stand for 30 minutes. Bring to boil. When it reaches boiling, reduce heat to medium, cook 5 minutes. Reduce to simmer for 15 minutes. Let stand another 10 minutes. Mix with white sesame seeds.

KANI ZOSUI *soft rice stew with oyster*

3/4 lb oysters
3 tsps salt
2 cups water
1 medium carrot
2 oz mushrooms

4 oz watercress
1 sheet nori
3 cups cooked rice
5 cups dashi
1 tbsp shoyu

Rinse oysters with 1 tsp salt and water. Drain. Peel and cut carrots in 2-inch long strips. Wash and cut mushrooms in half. Wash and cut watercress in 2-inch long pieces. Cut nori in 2-inch strips and set aside. Wash cooked rice with water to rinse off glutinous substance. In large ceramic pot, combine dashi, carrots, mushrooms and cook 2 minutes. Add 2 tsp salt, shoyu and oysters. Cook 2 minutes. Add cooked rice. When it starts to bubble, add watercress. Remove from heat and serve warm in donburi bowl. Sprinkle with nori strips.

KANI ZOSUI *soft rice stew with crab*

2 cups cooked rice
3 cups dashi
1/2 tsp salt
1 tsp shoyu
1 tbsp sake

4 oz crab meat, fresh, frozen
   or canned
1 tbsp green onion, minced
1/4 green peas
1 tbsp ginger juice

Combine cooked rice, dashi and bring to boil. Add salt, shoyu and sake. Reduce to simmer 5 minutes. Add crab meat, minced green oinon, green peas. Bring to boil once more and remove from heat. Mix in ginger juice and serve hot.

HAMAGURI GOHAN *clams with flavored rice*

3 cups rice
3 cups water
12 cherrystone clams, medium
1/2 lb shrimp
1 medium onion
1 medium carrot
3 shiitake

1/4 cup green peas,
   frozen or fresh
1-1/2 tbsps oil
2 bouillon cubes
1 tsp salt
1 tbsp shoyu

Wash rice few times and drain. In large bowl, place rice and 3 cups water. Let stand 30-60 minutes. Brush off clam shells holding clam in each hand rubbing against each other's shell. Wash, clean, devein and shell shrimp. Mince onion. Peel carrot and cut in 1/2-inch square cubes. Soak shiitake in warm water to soften. Squeeze. Remove stems and cut in 1/2-inch squares. Dip green peas into salted boiling water, rinse in cold water and drain. Drain rice from bowl but reserve water for cooking. Heat large heavy metal pot with oil. Add onion and saute 2-3 minutes and add drained rice. Stir, add reserved water, bouillon cubes, salt, shoyu and carrot, shiitake in that order. Bring to boil and then add clams and shrimp. Cook with medium flame until liquid is absorbed. Add green peas. Turn off heat, cover tight and let stand 15 minutes. Toss ingredients lightly before serving.

KAYAKU GOHAN *vegetable in flavored rice*

3 cups rice	3 shiitake
3-1/3 cups water	4 oz konyaku
3 tbsps sake	4 oz green beans
1 aburage	1 tsp salt
6 oz gobo	2 tbsps shoyu
6 oz carrot	

Wash rice several times and drain well. After final rinsing, place washed rice in heavy metal pot and measure in water and sake. Let stand 30 minutes to 1 hour before cooking. Dip aburage in boiling water to remove excess oil. Slice open 3 edges to make flat sheet. Cut in four lengthwise, then in thin strips. Wash and scrape skin off burdock root with knife blade. Cut into *sasagiri,* as though sharpening a pencil with knife. Cover with water to soak 5-8 minutes for *aku-nuki,* to remove bitter taste of certain vegetables. Peel and cut carrot in 1-inch strips. To soften, soak shiitake in warm water. Squeeze. Remove stems and cut in strips. Cut konyaku in julienne strips and blanch 1 minute in boiling water. Drain. Remove strings from green beans and blanch 2 minutes in boiling water. Cut into diagonal strips. Add salt, shoyu and all vegetables except green beans to cooking rice pot. Bring to boil, stirring gently, making sure all ingredients at bottom are stirred. Cover and cook on medium heat. When water has been absorbed, turn off heat. Add sake and serve.

FUNA MORI ZUSHI *vinegared rice in boat*

3 cups rice	8 medium prawns
3-1/4 cups water	2 cups water
3 tbsps mirin	3 tbsps vinegar
10 inch konbu	1-1/2 tsps salt
2 tbsps vinegar	3 tbsps sugar
1/2 tsp salt	3 eggs
1 tsp sugar	1/3 tsp salt
	1 tsp shoyu
Awase-Zu:	2 tsps sugar
6 oz white-meat fish, fresh	2 tbsps dashi
1-1/3 tsp salt	1 tbsp mirin
1-1/2 tsp sugar	2 oz pickled ginger
1/8 tsp red food coloring	4 cast-iron plant leaves or
8 oz fresh tuna	4 sheets 12-inch square silver foil

Special equipment: *square omelet pan*

Wash and rinse rice. Drain. In heavy metal pot, add water, mirin and konbu. When this comes to boil, remove konbu, add washed rice all at once. Stir. Cover, bring to boil, reducing to medium heat 5 minutes. Simmer 15 minutes. Turn cooked rice in wooden or enameled container. Combine vinegar, salt and sugar and pour over rice all at one. Mix rice with cutting motion while fanning.

continued on next page

Cut white-meat fish in 1-inch pieces. Boil in 1 cup water 4 minutes. Drain. Flake cooked fish meat. In saucepan, place flaked fish, 1/3 tsp salt, 1-1/2 tsp sugar and red coloring, holding 5-6 chopsticks in hand, stirring vigorously 3-4 minutes to make pink *soboro*. Slice tuna in 5/8-inch thick pieces, large bite-size. Devein prawns, insert skewer between shell and meat. Boil in 2 cups water with 1 tsp salt 4-5 minutes. Drain, remove skewer and shell. Marinate in 2 tbsp vinegar, 1/2 tsp salt, 1 tsp sugar. Set aside. Combine in bowl eggs, 1/3 tsp salt, shoyu, 2 tsp sugar, dashi, 1 tsp mirin and mix well. Using square omelet pan, make omelet 3-inch wide. Cut in 1/2-inch pieces. Make a boat with cast-iron plant leaves. Hold ends with toothpicks. If leaves are not available, fold aluminum foil in shape of boat for container. Spread 1 cup rice loosely in boat-shaped container. Divide flaked fish, tuna, prawns, sliced omelet and ginger in 4 parts. Arrange them decoratively over rice.

TEKKA DONBURI *vinegared rice topped with tunafish*

"Tekka" means 'iron in fire', symbolized by amber color of fresh tuna fish fillet.

3 cups rice	1-1/2 tbsps sugar
3-1/3 cups water	2 tsps salt
	1 lb tunafish fillet, fresh
Awase-Zu	2 sheets nori
4 tbsps vinegar	2 tbsps wasabi paste
	(horseradish)

Special equipment: *sushioke*

Wash 3 cups rice and measure 3-1/3 cups water, adding rice. Let stand for 30 minutes before starting to cook. Follow basic rice cooking method.

Awase-Zu: Combine vinegar, sugar and salt. When rice is done, turn into *sushioke*, wooden shallow bucket. Pour prepared awase zu all at once. Use paper or electric fan to cool while mixing the rice in cutting motion with spatula or rice paddle. Slice fish fillet in 1/4-inch thick bite-size pieces. Sprinkle hand-crushed nori on top of rice mound in donburi, topped with sliced fish fillet. Garnish with wasabi paste. Serve *shoyu* in another dish.

TEMAKI ZUSHI *help yourself sushi*

Let everyone get into creating his own sushi for a lazy Sunday brunch.

3 cups rice	1 sac codfish roe, broiled
3-1/3 cups water	5-6 chiso leaves
	4 oz takuwan (pickled daikon)
Awase-Zu:	2 tbsps white sesame seeds,
4 tbsp vinegar	roasted
2-1/2 tbsps sugar	4 eggs
1-1/2 tsp salt	2 tbsp sugar
8 sheets nori	1/4 tsp salt
1 cucumber, shredded	1/4 tsp shoyu
	1 tbsp sake

Wash rice and drain. Bring water to boil, add rice and bring to boil at once. Reduce heat to medium, cook 5 minutes then simmer 15 minutes.

Awase-Zu: Combine vinegar, sugar and salt. Pour over hot rice. Mix rice with cutting motion while fanning. Place seasoned rice in large serving bowl. Toast nori over burner, 4-5 inches away to crisp and then cut in 4 squares. Wash and shred cucumber. Broil codfish roe. Cut in 1/4-inch sliced rounds. Shred pickled daikon and mix with roasted sesame seeds. Combine eggs, sugar, salt, shoyu, sake and place in double boiler to make crumbly scrambled eggs. Arrange ingredients on platter and invite each person to create his own sushi. First take sheet of nori, then spread rice over. Whatever choice of ingredients choose 1, 2 or more, then close nori. Eat with shoyu. With miso or clear soup and vinegared salad, this makes a complete and no-fuss brunch.

Let everyone get into creating his own sushi for a lazy Sunday brunch.

TORI NANBAN *noodle and chicken in hot broth*

2-1/2 qts water	6 cups dashi
14 oz package udon,	1 tbsp sugar
wide noodles	1 tbsp shoyu
2-1/2 tsps salt	2 stalks green onion
1/2 lb chicken breast meat	

In 4 quart pot, bring water to boil. Drop in udon and return to boil. Stir occasionally. Cook uncovered 20 minutes or until noodles are soft. Stir in 1 tbsp salt. Cover pan tightly. Turn off flame and let noodles rest covered 5 minutes. Then drain in colander and run cold water over them 5 minutes. Drain again. Cut boned chicken breast horizontally in half, then into strips about 2-inches long by 1/4-inch wide. In 3 quart saucepan, combine dashi, sugar, 2-1/2 tbsps salt and shoyu. Stir and bring to boil. Add udon to dashi. Return to boil and remove from heat. Remove udon and place in 6 deep donburi bowls. Drop green onions, halved and sliced lengthwise, and chicken in dashi. Bring soup to boil over high flame 2 minutes, then pour over noodles equally and serve at once.

ODAMAKI MUSHI *egg custard with side noodles*

1 lb udon, wide noodles, uncooked	1 stalk green onion
2/3 lb chicken meat	4 cups dashi
1/2 tsp plus 1/2 tbsp shoyu	1-1/2 tsps salt
1/2 kamaboko, fish cake	2 eggs, lightly beaten

additional salt and shoyu are required for preparation

Boil wide noodles until tender. Rinse and drain. Divide in 5 equal portions and place in individual donburi bowls. Slice chicken meat in small pieces. Sprinkle 1/2 tsp shoyu over meat and let stand. Cut fish cake in half and then slice 1/6 inch in thickness. Slice green onion diagonally in 1-1/2-inch lengths. Mix dashi, 1/2 tbsp shoyu, salt. Beat eggs, add dashi and mix well. Arrange chicken meat, kamaboko, and green onions over cooked noodles. Pour beaten eggs over until everything is covered. Steam until eggs are set like thin egg custard. Serve while hot.

OKAME SOBA *fishcake and noodles in soup*

1 lb cooked soba	**Tare no moto:**
5 shiitake	2 tbsps mirin
1 medium carrot	6 tbsps shoyu
1 kamaboko	2 tbsps sugar
1 aburage	
7 cups dashi	

Boil soba according to basic recipe for soba. Soak shiitake in warm water to soften. Peel and cut carrots. 1-1/2-inches long, slice in half diagonally, cut deep notches to make fan-like shape. Cook in water until soft. Drain, set aside. Pour boiling water over aburage to remove excess oil. Squeeze, cut in 4-5 pieces. Combine dashi and tare no moto ingredients. Bring to boil, add shiitake and simmer 5 minutes to season. Add cooked carrots, kamaboko, aburage to warm. Place soba in donburi or any serving container. After rinsing other ingredients with hot water and draining well, arrange on top. Pour hot broth over and serve.

UDON SUKI *sukiyaki with thick noodles*

1-1/2 lbs Chinese cabbage	**Cooking Sauce:**
1 lb spinach	6 cups dashi
1 lb chicken meat	1-1/2 tsp salt
1 grilled tofu	1 tsp shoyu
8 oz kamaboko	2 tbsps sake
2 stalks green onion	1/2 cup lemon juice
6 oz carrots	
6 oz mushrooms	
1 lb udon, cooked	

Special equipment: *Sudare*

Wash and dip Chinese cabbage and spinach in boiling water. When wilted, remove. Spread cabbage on sudare. Lay spinach on top of cabbage. Roll like sushi-making and squeeze out water. Roll out from sudare and cut 3-inch long pieces. Cut chicken meat in large bite-size pieces. Grill tofu in half horizontally then cut in 1-inch cubes. Slice kamaboko in 1/2-inch pieces. Cut green onion diagonally 2 inches long. Cut carrots in 3/4-inch thick rounds. Boil in water until tender. Wash mushrooms and cut in half. Break enoki dake mushrooms in 4-5 bunches and discard orange-brown stem ends. Arrange ingredients on large plate at dining table. If dried udon are used, follow cooking instructions. In ceramic tabletop cooking pot, bring dashi, salt, shoyu and sake to boil. Then place desired ingredients in pot. Serve, placing lemon juice in small sauce dish.

YUZU GAMA *snapper steamed in grapefruit casing*

4 grapefruits	1 lb spinach, fresh
1/2 lb snapper	1 large carrot
1/2 tsp salt	2 tsp shoyu
4 os enoki dake mushrooms	

Special equipment: *flower cutter/ume gata*

Slice top 1/3 portion of grapefruit. Spoon out grapefruit meat from bottom part. Divide snapper in 4 parts. Sprinkle with salt. Wash and cut off orange part of enoki dake. Divide in 4 parts. Wash and dip spinach in boiling water until wilted. Dip in cold water. Drain. Cut in 1-1/2-inch lengths. Cut carrot using flower cutter to cut out 4 plum blossoms, 1/2-inch thick. Boil carrots until tender. Inside grapefruit, arrange snapper, 1/4 part of enoki dake, spinach and carrot. Pour 1/2 tsp shoyu into each casing. Steam 15 minutes. Replace grapefruit lids and serve while hot.

UDOFU *soybean curd pot*

6 cups water	4 squares tofu
7 inch square konbu	3 tbsps green onion, minced
6 tbsps shoyu	2 tbsps ginger, grated
3 tbsps bonito shavings	2 limes

Preferably in a ceramic tabletop cooking pot, place 6 cups water and konbu and let stand 30 minutes. Bring to boil slowly. Mix shoyu and bonito shavings in small cup. Place on top of konbu in ceramic cooking pot. When water starts to boil, cut tofu into bite-size cubes,   preferably using bamboo knife. A metal knife will harden cut sides of tofu. Spoon out warmed shoyu in individual saucers. Dip cooked tofu in warm shoyu mixture with minced onion, minced ginger and lime juice.

Udofu is eaten the year round. However, each household has a special dashi to cook tofu. In my parents' household in Tokyo when we were served udofu, it was only later in the fall and winter. I was told the reason was because the ayu fish when caught in mid-September has less oil in its flesh. Broiled and dried in the autumn sun, it is at its premium taste, when used for the dashi in which the tofu is cooked. More commonly, dashi is made of kelp. My grandmother, however, never made a compromise on ingredients.

KAKI NO CHAWAN MUSHI *egg custard soup with oyster*

2 eggs	**Kuzu An:**
2 cups dashi	1 cup dashi
1-1/3 tsps salt	1/4 tsp salt
12 medium oysters	1/2 tbsp cornstarch
12 oz spinach	

Beat eggs. Combine with cold dashi and salt. Wash oysters, drain well. Wash spinach. Dip in boiling water 2 minutes. Drain. Rinse in cold water, drain. Cut in 2-inch long pieces. Place shiitake in warm water to soften. Drain, slice in thin strips. Divide spinach, mushrooms evenly in 4 individual ceramic or oven-proof serving bowls. Strain egg mixture over and cover. With lid or foil cover, place in hot steamer. Cover steamer. Reduce heat to medium. Steam 15 minutes and remove.

Kuzu An: Combine cold dashi, salt, cornstarch in small saucepan, Cook and stir until slightly thickened. Pour over custard soup. Serve hot with spoon.

UCHI KOMI JIRU *clear soup with noodles*

4 oz udon	2 tsps sugar
8 fresh clams	2 tbsps mirin
1/2 square of aburage	2 stalks green onion
4 shiitake	4 cups dashi
1/2 oz bamboo shoots	1/2 tsp salt
3 tbsps shoyu	

Cook udon, rinse and drain. Cook clams until shells open, drain and set aside. Pour boiling water over aburage to remove excess oil. Cut in thin strips. Soak shiitake in warm water to soften, remove stems, squeeze out water and quarter. Slice bamboo shoots into this pieces. Combine 1 tbsp shoyu, sugar, 1 tbsp mirin. Cook aburage, shiitake and bamboo shoots over low flame until all seasoning is absorbed. Cut green onion into 2-inch long pieces, then slice lengthwise into thin strips. Combine dashi, 2 tbsps shoyu, salt, 1 tbsp mirin and bring to boil. Divide ingredients into four parts and arrange in serving bowls. Pour dashi over and serve immediately.

ISHIKARI NABE *one-pot simmer with salmon*

3/4 lb fresh salmon	8 oz carrots
1 cake grilled tofu	1 lb potatoes
1 cake konyaku, canned	6 oz watercress
2 lbs daikon	6 cups dashi
1-1/2 cups rice	2/3 cup miso paste
4 cups water	

Cut salmon in 1-1/2-inch pieces. Dip in boiling water for 1 minute, remove and drain. Cut grilled tofu in 1-1/2-inch cubes. Slice konyaku in 4-inch x 2-inch pieces and pour boiling water over pieces. Peel and cut daikon in 3/4-inch thick pieces, then cut in half-moon shapes. In large pot bring to boil daikon, rice and water. Cook until chopstick can pierce daikon easily. Drain and rinse with cold water. Cut carrots in 1/4-inch thick rounds and cook until tender. Peel and cut potatoes in large bite-size pieces. Soak in water 20 minutes to blanch. Drain and cook in 3 cups dashi until tender. Wash and cut watercress in 3-inch long pieces. Drain. In large ceramic tabletop cooking pot, add cooked potatoes and dashi. Add remaining 3 cups dashi. Stir in miso and bring to boil. Add ingredients. Simmer at table for pleasurable dining on cold winter night.

Ishikari is one of the ports of Hokkaido, for crab and salmon fishing. Hokkaido is the largest Japanese producer of Irish potatoes. During short evening breaks from exam cramming, I could hear the sound of **yomawari** *in the distance. The yomawari, a sign of winter, were making their nightly rounds. Literally translated night-going rounds,* **yomawari** *made their rounds from late in the evening until dawn carrying a lantern and sounding the warning signal by clapping two wooden sticks together. The sound carried in the still winter's night is very*

Continued on next page

evocative, and the practice arose to give warning of fires started by the open **hibachi** *or* **kotatsu,** *glowing with charcoal. Mingled with the sounds are memories of my mother staying up with each exam crisis and feeding me* **ishikari,** *hot from the pot, which she had prepared herself.*

TEPPAN YAKI *grilled on iron sheet*

1/2 lb pork fillet
1/2 lb beef fillet
1/2 lb chicken breast meat
4 oz squid, fillet fresh or frozen
4 oz scallops
4 oz shrimps
1/2 lb broccoli
4 oz mushrooms
1 round onion
1 green pepper
6 oz zucchini
1 medium eggplant

Dipping sauce A:
1/3 cup shoyu
1/3 cup dashi
1/3 cup lemon juice
1/4 cup salad oil

Dipping sauce B:
1 tbsp garlic, grated
1 tbsp ginger, grated
2 tbsps onion, grated
4 tbsps shoyu
1 tbsp sake
1 cup dashi
1/4 cup salad oil

Dipping sauce C:
3 tbsps shoyu
4 tbsps sugar
3 tbsps sake
6 tbsps apple, grated
1 tbsp ginger juice
1 tbsp lemon juice
1 tbsp sesame seeds, ground
6 tbsps miso paste
1 tbsp sesame oil

Slice pork fillet and beef fillet in 1/4-inch-thick slices. Cut chicken breast meat in large bite-size pieces. Remove outer skin of squid and score surface with criss-cross diamond-shaped cuts. Devein and shell shrimp. Slice broccoli in bite-size pieces. Dip in boiling water 2 minutes. Drain and rinse in cold water. Brush and wash mushrooms and cut in half. Slice onion in 1/2-inch thick rounds. Slice green pepper in 1/8-inch rounds. Slice zucchini horizontally in 1/4-inch thick slices. Slice eggplant 1/4-inch thick rounds. Arrange ingredients on platter on table. Prepare all dipping sauces by combining all ingredients listed under each heading. Heat grill and coat with 1 tbsp oil. Grill meat, fish and vegetables. Each person will have 2 small dishes for dipping sauces. One helps himself to the food desired to be grilled. Soup, pickled vegetables and rice with this dish make a very hearty meal. This is my stand-by when I have an unexpected guest or had a busy day and want to prepare something simple. It also is very popular with young people!

KAZE NABE *cold cure one-pot simmer*

1/2 lb pork fillet	8 oz shimeji mushrooms,
2 aburage	canned
8 oz rice cakes, 4 pieces	8 oz fresh enoki dake mushrooms
1 lb Chinese cabbage	4 cups water
8 oz spinach	1 cup daikon, grated
2 oz carrot	shoyu for serving
2 stalks green onion	
8 oz fresh shiitake,	
if dried, 6 medium	

Cut pork fillet in 1-1/2-inch bite-size pieces. Pour boiling water over aburage to remove excess oil. Cut in half and hit between hands to remove air, open gently. Stuff each pouch with rice cake. Rinse Chinese cabbage, cut in 2-inch long pieces. If too wide, cut in half. Wash spinach, cut off stems and use only leaves. Cut carrot diagonally in 1/2-inch thick pieces. Wash and slice green onion in 1-inch diagonal pieces. Clean and wash fresh shiitake, discarding stem. If dried ones are used, place in warm water to soften, but also discard stem. Remove stem ends from shimeji and enoki dake mushrooms. Break in 4-5 clusters. Wash under running water. Line bottom of large ceramic pot or electric skillet with Chinese cabbage, then carrot. Add remaining ingredients. Add 4 cups water and bring to boil. Simmer until carrot is cooked, 5 minutes. Serve with grated daikon and a little shoyu as desired.

When I lived at my parents' home in Japan, Suni sen was the cook and chief of household. If anyone was in bed with a cold, he or she was treated with this dish. Strangely enough, we always got better. I don't think there was any magical potion brewed into the pot. However, won't you try it?

YOSENABE *a pot with a little of everything*

2/3 lb medium prawns,	1 stalk green onion
uncooked	3 pz bamboo shoot
1/2 lb pork, sliced bacon-thin	3 oz carrot
5 scallops	15 shiitake
1/2 kamaboko	3 eggs
1 carton harusame noodles	5 cups chicken stock
1/2 lb Chinese cabbage	1 tbsps salt
5 oz spinach	

Shell prawns except for tail and adjoining section. Devein and slice underside to open shrimp flat. Slice scallops across the grain, very thin. Slice kamaboko thin. Fry harusame quickly and drain on absorbent paper. Wash and cut Chinese cabbage in 1-1/2-inch lengths. Wash and remove stems from spinach. Cut green onion in 1/8-inch thickness. Slice bamboo shoots 1/8-inch thick. Slice carrots 1/5-inch thick and boil until tender. Soften shiitake in enough cold water to cover.

Continued on next page

Squeeze out liquid when softened and cut off stems. Hard boil egg and peel. When egg is cool, slice. Arrange all of these on large plate to be placed on table. Bring 5 cups chicken stock with 1 tbsp salt to boil. Add one kind of vegetable at time, cook well and eat. Strong flavored foods usually are saved for last.

JOYA NABE *pork and spinach with ginger sauce*

2 lbs spinach	10 inch konbu
1-1/2 lbs pork fillets, sliced bacon-thin	1 cup daikon, grated
	1/4 cup carrots, grated
3 cups dashi	1 stalk green onion, minced
1 cup sake	2 tbsps ginger, grated
1 tsp salt	lemon wedges

Wash and drain spinach. Arrange on large platter with pork fillets. Combine dashi, sake, salt with konbu. Let stand 30 minutes for cooking broth. Combine grated daikon and carrots. This is called *momiji oroshi,* autumn maple leaves. Each person is served a small dipping bowl for grated daikon and carrots, minced onion, ginger and lemon juice as desired. On serving table, place electric cooker. Bring cooking broth to boil and remove konbu. Each person will dip spinach and pork in boiling broth. When cooked, remove and dip in sauce. Dipping in sauce cools some heat before placing in mouth. Try it. You'll want it every night!

Joya, *meaning 'every night,' is a simple one-part dish that is surprisingly hearty.*

KAKI NO DOTE NABE *oyster and vegetable cooked in ceramic pot*

1-1/2 large fresh oysters, shucked	1-1/2 lbs spinach or other leafy vegatable
1/2 cup daikon, grated	1 cake tofu
8 oz 1 can shirataki, white waterfall, gelatin-like noodles	1/2 cup miso
	3 tbsps mirin
3 stalks green onion	1 cup dashi
1 carrot	

Combine grated daikon, oysters. Toss lightly with hands. Rinse in cold water. Drain well and set aside. Rinse and cut shirataki into shorter lengths for easy serving. Slice green onion into 1/2-inch diagonal pieces. Cut carrots into 1/2-inch rounds, using a flower cutter to make *hane ninjin,* carrot flowers. Cook in water until tender, 8 minutes. Set aside. Remove stems from spinach. Wash in cold water. Cut tofu into 1-1/2-inch cubes. Make miso paste by mixing miso and mirin. Inside walls of ceramic pot, using entire mixture, apply miso paste, like making mud pie. On bottom of pot, arrange tofu, shirataki, oysters, carrot flowers, green onion. Pour dashi over. Place burner on dining or serving table. Heat ceramic pot with ingredients. When it starts to bubble, add spinach leaves a little at a time. Each person has little saucer dish to serve himself.

Imagine a cold winter night, everyone eating out of a communal earthenware ceramic pot. This simmering oyster dish is a true winter's delight, a get-closer-together dish.

HAKUSAI TO GAN MODOKI NO NIMONO *braised wonbok with*
fried tofu patties

cabbage
3 tbsps shoyu
3 tbsps sake
1/2 tsp salt
1-1/2 cups water

6 gan modoki (fried tofu
   patties, see index)
8 wonbok leaves
1 red pepper

Wash and cut cabbage widthwise in half. Bring to boil shoyu, sake, salt and water. Add gan modoki to this cooking sauce. Cook 3-4 minutes. Add bottom half of cabbage, then leaf ends and wonbok. Cover and cook 5 more minutes. Remove seeds from red pepper. Cut into needle-like *sengiri*. On serving dish, arrange cooked cabbage and *gan modoki*, garnish with shredded red. pepper.

GYUU KOMA TO SATOIMO TO DAINO NO MISONI
braised chopped beef, taro potatoes, radish with soybean paste sauce

2 lbs daikon
1-1/2 lbs satoimo
3 tbsps oil
1 lb beef, chopped
3 cups water

5 tbsps miso
1/2 tbsp shoyu
3 tbsps sake
1 tbsp sugar

Wash and scrub daikon without peeling skin. Cut into large bite-size pieces. Peel satoimo, cut in half. Heat oil in skillet. Saute chopped beef. When slightly browned, add radishes and satoimo. Add 3 cups water. When it boils, reduce to simmer 6-7 minutes. Skim off scum from time to time. Mix 3 tbsp miso with 1/4 cup cooking liquid from skillet. Pour into skillet, simmer until satoimo are tender. Mix remaining miso, shoyu, sake, sugar and add to skillet. Slowly bring to boil. Serve hot or cold.

TORI SOBORO DENGAKU *braised crumbly chicken with tofu*
and vegetables

3/4 lb chicken meat, ground
2 tbsps shoyu
3 tbsps mirin
2 tbsps sake
2 tsps plus 2 tbsps sugar
1 tsp cornstarch
1-1/4 lb daikon
8 inch konbu

5 cups water
8 oz konyaku, devil's tongue
   tuber vegetable cake, canned
1 cake tofu
1/2 cup miso
1/4 cup dashi
1 tbsp grated lemon peel

In small saucepan, place chicken meat, shoyu, 2 tbsps mirin, sake, 2 tsps sugar and cornstarch. Using 4 chopsticks to make *tori soboro* stir ingredients until crumbly in texture. Cut daikon in 1/4-inch thick rounds. Peel, score one side of daikon with criss-cross. Place in boiling water for 2-3 minutes. Drain. Bring to boil 5 cups water and konbu. When it boils, remove konbu. Add blanched daikon. Simmer 30 minutes. Cut konyaku into bite-size pieces. Dip in and out of separate boiling water. Cut tofu in 8 squares. Combine miso, 2 tbsps sugar, 1 tbsp mirin, dashi. Place on burner. Remove at boiling point and set aside. When daikon becomes tender, add konyaku and tofu and simmer 5-6 minutes. Turn into serving bowl. Pour miso sauce over, then sprinkle seasoned crumbly chicken on top. Garnish with lemon peel.

MISO DENGAKU *simmered meat and vegetables with miso dipping sauce*

3/4 lb pork fillet	12 large scallops
1-1/2 lbs daikon	1 tsp salt
8 medium satoimo	1 7-inch square sheet konbu
7-8 cups rice water, sufficient to prepare gohan	
3 cups water	**Dipping Sauce:**
1 tsp vinegar	1/2 cup miso
8 oz konyaku, devil's tongue	1/2 cup sugar
1 square tofu	2 tbsps sake
	2/3 cup dashi
	1 tbsp grated lime peel

Cut pork fillet in large bite-size pieces. Dip in and out of boiling water. Set aside. Peel and cut daikon 3/4-inch thick round. Boil in rice water saved from night before or morning when cooking rice. Boil until daikon is soft. Save rinsing water used for this daikon cooking. It gives an extra rich flavor. Peel satoimo. Wipe off sticky substance with a paper towel. Boil with 3 cups water and vinegar until tender, 8-10 minutes. Set aside. Cut konyaku in triangular large bite-size pieces. Dip in and out of boiling water. Cut tofu in 8 rectangular pieces. Dip in and out of boiling water. Sprinkle salt on scallops then rinse under running water. Skewer each ingredient onto bamboo skewers. In small saucepan, combine miso, sugar, sake, dashi. Stir constantly until slightly thickened. Add lime peel. Line large earthenware pot or electric cooker with konbu sheet. Fill with 4-5 cups of water. Bring to boil, add skewer ingredients and reduce to simmer. Serve dipping sauce in individual small bowls. Each person helps himself to the simmering skewered morsels and dips them in the sauce.

Dengaku is definitely a wintertime favorite. Here is a one-pot dinner prepared and cooked at the table in happy laughter, gathered around a **kotatsu,** *foot warmer. We would be a cozy group of people. Ingredients on bamboo skewers simmered away in large earthenware pot releasing an irresistible aroma. We would quickly forget the chilly, snowy outside. Because this is a help-yourself-with whatever pleases you type of dish, the hostess is able to engage in the conversation. If one does not like one thing, pick something else that pleases the palate.*

Fuke wa Uchi

Fuku wa Uchi! Fuka wa Uchi! Oni wa Soto!
Fortune in, Fortune in, Devil Out!

This is a chant heard from every traditional Japanese home the evening of *Setsubun,* literally meaning season-change. Closing the year's coldest season which ends usually the second or third of February, it is marked by the ceremony of *Mame maki,* bean-throwing or *Tsunan,* devil-driving.

A small branch of *hi iragi,* or holly, and the head of a dried sardine was placed as *mayoke,* at the entrance of each house to keep the devils out. The ceremony of *mame maki,* held in the evening, was always done by my father or my brothers.

A handful of parched soy beans was thrown in each room, taken from the *masu* or dry measurement box. A handful was thrown twice in the lucky direction of the year and once in the direction opposite, inviting good fortune to enter and to drive the devil out. This was repeated in every room and closed before we hurried to close every door and window to keep good fortune inside.

I picked up as many parched beans as my years of age, eating them to ensure health and good luck. Meanwhile, I could sense that *dengaku* was being prepared.

ORANGE ZUKURI *raw fish on orange slices*

1/4 lb fresh raw fish fillet	cellophane wrap
1 orange	ice
1 tbsp wasabi	1/2 tsp sesame seed
1 bunch alfalfa sprouts	1 tbsp shoyu
lettuce	

Slice orange crosswise 1/4-inch thickness. Cut fish in thin slices, arrange on orange like flower petals. Fill center with alfalfa sprouts and top with wasabi. Make ice mold size of plate and wrap with cellophane. Arrange orange topped sashimi on ice. Place chopped ice around this arrangement. Garnish with lettuce, serve with shoyu, and sesame seeds.

JOYO MANJU *steamed cake*

6 oz joshinko	15 oz koshian
6 oz sugar	1 tbsp grated lemon peel
4 oz yamato imo	1/4 cup cornstarch
1 tbsp water	waxed paper

Sift rice flour and sugar together in bowl. Peel and grate yamato imo. Combine with water. Mix well with dried ingredients until they have softness of earlobes. Divide dough in 15 parts. Also divide koshian in 15 parts. Shape in balls, dust fingertips with cornstarch. Wrap koshian with divided dough. Cut waxed paper in 1-1/2-inch squares. Place bottom of cake onto waxed paper. Steam over high flame 10 minutes. When cake is cooled, garnish center with lemon peel.

Spring

Hina Matsuri

As a young girl growing up in Japan, I would become aware one day that spring was coming. I had not seen the first crocus nor heard the first robin sing. A Japanese girl has a special sign.

Toward the end of February, I would come home from school, and, as I passed the hallway of the main room, my nostrils would be tickled by the odor of camphor. That instant my face would break into a very broad smile, and I would be guilty of a great rudeness. Without greeting any family members, I would slip into the main room. As I expected, the dolls and their things would be there in the wooden storage boxes where they had been placed a year ago.

As I did the previous year and the year before that, I would carefully unwrap and dust them.

This day of the women of Japan is called *Hina Matsuri,* or Festival of Dolls. It is the day most eagerly awaited by all girls in Japan and hardly less by mothers and grandmothers. The Doll Festival was designed to make girls emulate the highest household in the country with all its stately decorum. Even the lowliest Japanese woman is supposed to behave in a dignified and courteous manner. This decorum and protocol is demonstrated not only by the little ceremonial meals offered to visitors, but chiefly by the array of furniture exhibited with the *Hina.*

Hina Matsuri began to be observed around 1640, but its beginnings go back to the old, old celebrations of fertility and the reawakening of nature. It also is called *Momo-no-Sakku,* or the Peach Blossom Festival. The peach is the fruit of life. My grandmother always told me on that day, "You have to become a bride and that's where you find happiness. Little girls", She said, "should be gentle, sweet and peaceful as a peach flower."

We have a number of Hina sets in my family. Some belonged to my grandmother, some to my mother, some to me. My Hina set started to be built when I was first born. The first March 3, the third day of the third month, family members and relatives, as well as friends of my parents, all wished happiness to me. Later, my grandmother told me which Hina was given by which person. It took me a number of years to remember which Hina came from whom!

Each year I unmasked the faces of my dolls, talking to them as if they understood me. I took them to the Hina den, tiers of shelf-like steps built up against the main room wall and covered with a scarlet cloth called *himosen,* or fire blanket. I remember there were seven steps.

The doll order is very important. The Emperor and Empress always sit on the very top step, in a spendid palace called *Dai-Ri-Bina,* meaning "Lady on the Left." The Empress wears a costume called *jyu-ni-hito,* a twelve-layered, unlined silk kimono of different colors. Her hair falls down in a long cascade and in one hand she holds a fan. The Emperor usually wears a robe of purple and holds a flat scepter.

Three ladies-in-waiting, called *kan-jo,* sit on the second shelf in long-sleeved white kimono with wide trailing, crimson-colored trousers. Representing youth, middle and old age, they serve the festival sake and the food.

On the third shelf sit the court musicians, five in number called *goninbayashi*, or five-man orchestra. Reputed to be young men selected for their beauty, they usually are represented as young boys playing large and small hand drums, *tsuzumi*, flat drums on stands and the flute or *shakuhachi*. The one holding a closed fan is a singer.

Ministers of the Left and the Right fill the fourth row. carrying bows and arrows, they are the highest dignataries of the ancient imperial government. They are separated by three footmen who represent three human moods. One laughs, one weeps and one wears an angry face.

The Hina look as though a court scene had emerged from a magician's hand, each Hina with his worldly symbols or possessions. Hina have writing boxes, letter or document boxes of gold lacquer, equipment for the Japanese tea ceremony or *chan-no-yu*, musical instruments, furniture with drawers and shelves, chests, travelling trunks; colored boxes with bowls, trays and tall, screen-like racks. There even are tiny picnic boxes, complete with lacquer plates, sake bottles, cups and also the *norikago* or palanquin, and *goshoguruma* the imperial traveling cart. The Emperor and Empress come as visitors this day to be royally entertained by their little hostess. Trays of food are offered to the Emperor and Empress, and, indirectly, to the spirits of the ancestors, which was the original custom. Black and gold lacquer trays bear little bowls for soup and more solid food, correct to the smallest detail.

When the dolls and the miniature furniture have all been set in place, and the peach blossoms and paper lanterns, the excitement begins. The entire household has been busy getting ready for the festival. The evening before the festival, March 2, the family has a feast. On March 3, along with every other little girl in Japan, I would be allowed to invite friends for a party. Three colored rice cakes — pink, green, white — would be served with rice wine. Our festival food was clam broth and sushi. Girls would be the main guess and we would say to each other, "Aren't we lucky we were born as girls?" Our appetites were enormous.

After we had eaten, we would play games like *kai awase*, or matching clam shells. The clam shells look alike, but no clam is really shaped like another and only the two halves which grew together can ever match. The shells were lined with gold leaf. Inside each half was painted the identical portrait of an elegant court lady. When I helped unpack the shells from their silk wrappings, the gold leaf lining of the shell's inside darted out into my eyes as I separated them, the light reflecting shining like a treasure box. I often held my breath in excitement at this moment. My grandmother said, "Each of you will find another proper half when you grow up to stay with happily ever after."

"The game *Kai-ooi* or *Kai-Awasi* has 180 pairs of shells. One side of the shell is called *Ji-gai*, the other *Ide-gai*. The 'caller' will have all the *Ide-gai* and the *Ji-gai* are spread out on a crimson blanket which has been laid out on the *tatami*. The caller presents an *Ide-gai* and the players try to locate the matching half. Anyone can pick up a *Ji-gai*, but only one is a perfect match. Each match scores a point and the winner, of course, is she who amasses the greatest number of points."

We passed a happy time looking for matching halves, reading poems, and exclaiming over lovely ladies. We were surprised when, looking outside, night had fallen.

Some of my fondest memories are of having my friends around me on Hina Matsuri. Later, when we had grown out of little girl games, we sat in the warm reflection of the scarlet cover of the *hina den,* or doll steps, watching shadows of the peach blossoms cast by the *bon bori* or lanterns, on the steps, sipping our little cups of sweet rice wine or *shirozake.* We talked endless young girl dreams, giggled about nothing and wrote poetry. When I was 17, I wrote the following poem on Hina Matsuri.

> *Toatsyuo no*
> *Rotakeki mayu*
> *Utsukishiki egakana*
> *Kimi wa*
> *Anatsu otome go.*

> *You lived in long ago yesteryear. I do not know you, but I feel your presence and spirit of noble beauty. In spite of your elegantly-arched eyebrow, Yamato lady, I sense the sorrow hidden in your heart.*

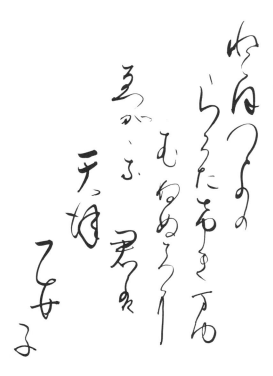

SHIROZAKE *sweet white rice wine*

2-1/2 cups sweet rice or mochi
3-1/2 cups water
2-1/2 cups rice malt
1/2 tsp ginger juice

Wash rice and drain. Add water and let stand 1 hour, then bring to boil on medium heat. Reduce to simmer when water starts to recede. Rice will be soft and sticky. Crumble rice malt with finger itps. Mix into warm, soft rice. Wrap and cover with newspaper or heavy towel to maintain temperature between 70 to 80 degrees. To stop germinating, after 24 hours bring to boil and allow to cool. Pour into bottle and store in refrigerator. It will keep one month. To serve, heat 2-1/2 cups shirozake with 1/2 cup sake in pot. Do not boil! Add ginger juice to mixture and stir. This beverage is a must to celebrate Hina Matsuri!

HAMAGURI NO KAIMORI *shellfish arrangement*

10 medium size, hard	3 tbsp white miso
shelled clams	3 tbsp sugar
salt water solution	1 tbsp sake
1/4 tsp salt to each cup water	2 tbsp rice vinegar
1 tbsp sake	1/4 tsp mild mustard
1/4 cup fresh or	
frozen green peas	

Scrub clam shells with a stiff brush. Rinse, then soak in salt water solution for 30 minutes. Heat steamer. Place clams on a large plate and sprinkle with 1 tbsp sake. Place plate in steamer and steam clams 5 to 8 minutes with high steam. Remove clams from steamer and when cool, remove clam meat from shells, saving shells. Cut clam meat into bite-size pieces and set aside. Throw green peas into pot of boiling water. Let cook for 30 seconds only! Drain, dip in cold water, and set aside. Combine miso paste, sugar, and sake in a small sauce pan. Cook on low heat, stirring frequently, until mixture bubbles. Remove from heat and let cool. Add vinegar and mustard and mix well. Add clam meat and peas and stir gently. Spoon mixture into clam shells and serve.

OKUCHI-TORI *sweet things*

MOMOZONO KAN *peach blossom garden gelatin*

    1 stick red kanten
    1-1/4 cup water
    1/2 cup sugar
    1 14 oz can minced peaches

Break kanten into bowl of water, soaking 30 minutes to soften. Squeeze out water and shred into a cooking pot with 1/2 cup water. Heat until kanten dissolves. Add sugar and stir. Strain into another pot, cooking another 3 to 4 minutes. Add liquid from canned peaches to cooked kanten. Let stand until warm before adding minced peaches. Pour into nagashi bako. When firm, cut into 2-inch diamond shapes and serve.

ZENSAI *sweet red beans*

    2-1/2 cups azuki beans
    7-1/2 plus 3 cups water
    3 cups sugar
    8 pieces mochi

Wash azuki beans. In large pot, cook beans in 7-1/2 cups water on high heat. Bring to a boil and when beans begin to surface, add one cup cold water. Repeat this three times, cooking until soft. While cooking use a wooden spoon to mash about 1/3 of beans. Add 1-1/2 cups sugar. Simmer 20 minutes then add another 1-1/2 cups sugar. Simmer 15 minutes. Place rice cakes under broiler. The rice cakes will be puffy after about 2 minutes. Turn over and continue to broil for another minute until soft. Remove from broiler and place 2 rice cakes in each small serving bowl. *Spoon warm, azuki mixture over rice cakes and serve.*

HACHIZAKANA *broiled things*

SAZAE NO TSUBO YAKI *turbo shellfish broiled in shell*

4 turbo	2 tsps shoyu
2 shiitake	2/3 tsp salt
6 sprigs coriander	1 tsp sugar

    1-1/2 cups dashi

Pry open shells. Take out body of shellfish and cut out dark intestines. Dice fishmeat into 1/4-inch thick pieces and set aside. Wash inside of shells well. Drain. Cut coriander into 1-inch long pieces. Soften shiitake in water and cut into 1-inch strips. Combine dashi, shoyu, salt, and sugar in saucepan and bring to boil. Divide ingredients into 4 parts and stuff into shells. Pour equal amounts of dashi into each shell. Broil until mixture bubbles then remove from oven. Set each shell in a bed of polished pebbles for balance.

CHIRASHI ZUSHI *decorated vinegared rice*

4 cups rice	3 oz carrots
15 shiitake	3 oz bamboo shoots
1-1/2 tbsp mirin	1/2 lb lotus roots
1-1/2 tbsp sake or dry sherry	8-1/2 tbsp vinegar
4 tbsp shoyu	5 uncooked prawns
3-1/6 tbsp sugar	1 egg
1 oz dried gourd	1/4 tsp cornstarch
9 tbsp dashi	5 tbsp green peas
salt	2/3 oz pickled ginger

Prepare rice for sushi rice. Soften shiitake in cold water (enough to cover). Remove stems. Bring to boil mirin, sake, 3 tbsp shoyu, and sugar. Add shiitake and cook over low flame until well flavored. Remove from sauce and drain. In salted water, soften dried gourd, then cook in plain water until soft. Add 5 tbsp dashi and 1 tsp salt to sauce in which shiitake cooked. Add gourd, cooking until well seasoned. Remove from sauce and gently sqeeze sauce out of gourd. Mince, peel and cut into thin slices 3/4-inch long. Add 4 tbsp dashi, 1 tbsp shoyu, 1 tsp salt and 2 tsps sugar to sauce in which gourd cooked. Add carrots and cook until well flavored. Remove carrots from sauce and drain. Slice bamboo shoots and cook in carrot sauce until sauce is nearly gone. Peel lotus roots, cut into quarters, slice thinly and add 4 cups water, 1-1/2 tbsp vinegar to lotus to prevent discoloration. Throw away water, then boil lotus roots in new solution using same proportions of vinegar and water. Drain. Mix well 3-1/2 tbsp vinegar, 1-1/2 tbps salt, 1-1/2 tbsp sugar. Marinate lotus roots at least 1 hour. Devein prawns by inserting skewer into back of prawns. Place prawns in salted boiling water, cook until tender. Shell except for tail and adjoining section. Slit and open underside flat. Mix 2 tbsp vinegar, 2/3 tsp salt, 1 tsp sugar. Marinate for 1 hour. Beat egg with 1/6 tsp salt, 1/2 tsp sugar, 1/4 tsp cornstarch dissolved in 1 tsp water. Fry, making sheets as thin as possible. When cool, cut into strips. Cook green peas, being careful not to overcook in order to retain the color. Cut kamaboko in half lengthwise and then into 1/8-inch thin slices. Cut red pickled ginger into fine strips. Mix carrots and gourd with rice and divide into 5 individual rice bowls. Arrange the other prepared ingredients in an attractive manner on top of rice. Serve warm or cold.

OHANAMI *Cherry Blossom Festival*

Around April 10 the typical cherry blossom in Tokyo becomes soft cotton candy-like pink. Grandmother began listening for the forecast of the cherry blossom blooming and we knew that Grandmother's cherry blossom viewing party soon would be in the making.

As soon as the blossoming was forecast, Grandmother instructed the cooks to order bamboo shoots from the South. They would be ordered at least ten days ahead of time so that shoots could arrive and be prepared the day before the party. It was the 'big deal' in the party preparation. What with house cleaning and arranging things in a spotless manner, the whole household spent a busy few days preparing to entertain grandmother's guests. I recall my grandmother instructing our cook to make many tid-bits to place in the half-moon boxes, or *obento,* so that her guests would find many surprises. This was grandmother's way of bringing joy to her friends.

A few days later in the main room, where all was in readiness, grandmother first served tea to her guests, then lunch with soup, prepared in lacquer boxes of half-moon shape.There usually were six to eight beautiful elderly ladies in kimono, looking very elegant, all of them behaving as though they were high-school-age girls, joking and poking fun at each other. I often was amazed at their behavior.

At the elegant, leisurely lunch they recited poetry and practiced their calligraphy. Such very lazy, gentle spring afternoon memories go through my mind like a magic, revolving lantern.

Obento has taken on another significance for me more recently. And those are the lunches for Robert Joffrey, artistic director of the Joffrey ballet, a member of the Council for the Arts of the National Endowment for the Arts, and the American chairman for the judges for the International Ballet Competition, Jackson, Mississippi.

I first met Mr. Joffrey with the Joffrey Ballet's principal choreographer, Gerald Arpino, when they came through Hawaii in 1963. They were returning to New York via Japan after the company's State Department-sponsored tour of the Middle East and India. Since I was teaching ballet in Hawaii at the time, the introduction was quite logical.

Soon after, when I moved to the Mainland from Hawaii, I naturally gravitated toward the ballet life in my new area. I eventually started to teach ballet again when I moved to Portola Valley.

The Joffrey Ballet had reformed at this time and had started to spend part of its summer touring schedule in residence at Stanford and Berkeley. My daughters and I regularly attended their seasons. At the end of their local engagments, we gave company and crew members leis of tiny orchids flown in from Hawaii for closing night. This was our way of showing appreciation for the company's dancing artistry.

In conversation, I found out that Mr. Joffrey liked Japanese food, so that when the Joffrey Ballet started appearing at the San Francicso Opera House, I brought Mr. Joffrey and Mr. Arpino obento as a gesture of appreciation. So that is how Obento Joffrey began, wrapped in a *furushki* and, in the beginning packed in a

continued on page 107

Capezio toe-shoe slipper box! I used some of the recipes which follow of grand-mother's *Ohanami Bento* and still others you will see later under summertime obento. It is a helpful snack to someone who works in the theatre from late morning to equally late at night.

OHANAMI BENTO *Menu*

Habutae Mushi *steamed custard soup*
Takenoko Gohan Nagamusubi Kinome *young bamboo shoots, cooked with rice, made into small, oblong rice balls*
Shigure Mushi *steamed tofu and pork*
Shingiku no goma Bitashi *Shungiku with sesame soy marinade, encased in a lemon shell.*
Gyuuniku no goma age *Beef slices with sesame seeds*
Shinoda oni *Stuffed fried soybean curd*
Shiro Ingen Mame no Amani *sweet kidney beans*
Sakura Mochi *cherry leaf-wrapped sheets*

OHANAMI BENTO
HABUTAE MUSHI *flower lunchbox*

3 cups dashi
3/4 tsp salt
1 tsp shoyu
3 eggs
6 salted cherry blossoms,
   canned or bottled

Sauce:
1 cup dashi
1/2 tsp salt
1/2 tsp shoyu
1/2 tsp cornstarch
1 tbsp water

Season dashi with salt and shoyu. Beat eggs and pour through sieve into individual porcelain, chawan mushi containers or teacups. Using medium heat for steaming, steam 20 minutes. When done, place rinsed, salted cherry blossoms on top and steam another 2 minutes, then remove from steamer.

Sauce: In small pot, place dashi, salt, shoyu and bring to boil. Add cornstarch, water, and mix together. When it thickens pour over cherry blossoms and serve.

TAKENOKO GOHAN NAGAMUSUBI KINOME
young bamboo shoots cooked with rice made into small, oblong riceballs

3 cups rice
1 fresh bamboo shoot or
    12 oz can bamboo shoots
3/4 cup dashi
1-1/2 tbsp sake
2-1/2 tsp shoyu

1-1/2 tsp sugar

Additional seasoning:
1 tbsp shoyu
2-1/2 tbsp sake

One hour before cooking time, wash 3 cups rice and drain. Shred bamboo shoots in 1-inch length pieces. In pot, place dashi, sake, shoyu and sugar. Bring to boil and add shredded bamboo shoots. Simmer until bamboo shoots are well seasoned. Drain and save liquid to cook rice. Using seasoned liquid, add enough water to measure 3-1/3 cups, combine with washed rice and place in rice cooker. Follow basic rice cooking instruction. When rice is cooked, mix together seasoned bamboo shoots and rice. Shape into oblong riceballs.

It is a springtime delight. Springtime is when young, tender bamboo shoots are plentiful. We always make an occasion to serve them for springtime festivals.

SHIGURE MUSHI *steamed tofu and pork*

1 square tofu
1 lb ground pork
2 tbsp sake
1 tsp ginger, grated
3 tsp sugar
2-1/2 tbsp shoyu

2 eggs (one separated)
1/4 tsp salt
1 tsp cornstarch
parsley
pickled ginger,
    canned or packaged

Cut tofu into fourths. Place in pot, add enough water to cover and bring to boil.

Drain and squeeze water out of boiled tofu through cheesecloth. In pan, use half ground pork, 1 tbsp sake, ginger and tofu. Mix together, cook like scrambled eggs and cool. Add remaining ground pork, 1 tsp sugar, shoyu and egg whites. Mix well, then spread mixture onto large plate forming flat square shape. Using steamer, steam 7 to 10 minutes and remove from steamer. Combine egg, egg yolks, remaining sugar, sake, salt and scramble. When done, mix in cornstarch. Spread this yellow mixture evenly over steamed ground pork mixture. Place in steamer an additional 3 minutes. When done, cut into small squares. Garnish with sprigs of parsley and serve with pickled ginger.

SHINGIKU NO GOMA BITASHI *shungiku with sesame soy marinade encased in a lemon shell*

1 bunch shungiku or 1 bunch spinach as substitute
boiling water
1 tsp salt
3 tbsp white sesame seeds, toasted
2 tbsp shoyu
3 lemons cut in half lengthwise, insides removed

Snip off stems of shungiku or spinach, using only leaves. Wash and drop leaves into boiling water and salt. Stir and when color of leaves become bright green, place in colander, rinse with cold water to stop cooking and to set color. Squeeze water out and cut into bite-size pieces. Grind toasted sesame seeds and mix with shoyu. Marinate cooked shungiku or spinach. Use the lemon shells as casing and serve.

GYUUNIKU NO GOMA AGE *beef slices with sesame seeds*

3/4 lb beef, sliced into bite-sized pieces
1-1/2 tsp salt
2 tsp shoyu
2 tsp sake
4 tbsp cornstarch
1 cup white sesame seeds
oil for deep frying

Combine beef, salt, shoyu and sake. Add cornstarch and mix well. Roll seasoned beef slices into sesame seeds. Heat cooking oil to 360 degrees and fry beef slices until sesame seeds turn lightly golden brown. Serve hot or cold.

SHINODA NI *stuffed fried soybean curd*

6 fried tofu
1 cup bean threads
1/2 cup green peas
4 shiitake
1/2 lb chicken, minced
2 tbsp sake
1 tsp salt
1 tbsp shoyu
1/2 cup bamboo shoots, cut into 1-inch strips
1/2 cup carrots, cut into 1-inch strips
1/2 cup tofu, drained
1-1/2 cups dashi
2 tbsp sake
3 tbsp sugar
1 tsp salt
2 tbsp shoyu

Pour hot water over fried tofu to remove excess oil. Cut in half crosswise and carefully separate sides to form pocket, being sure not to break outer skin. Soften bean threads in warm water and cook in hot water 1 minute. Drain and cool, cut into 1/2-inch pieces. Pour boiling water over peas and set aside. Soften shiitake in water, then cut into thin strips. Place chicken meat in large bowl. Add 2 tbsp sake, 2 tsp sugar, 1 tsp salt, 1 tbsp shoyu. Add bean threads, peas, shiitake, bamboo shoots, carrots and drained tofu. Stuff fried tofu with chicken mixture. Secure opening with toothpicks. In skillet bring to boil dashi, sake, sugar, salt and shoyu. Place stuffed fried tofu in skillet. Simmer 25 minutes. Do not stack them! Serve 2 stuffed, fried tofu per person.

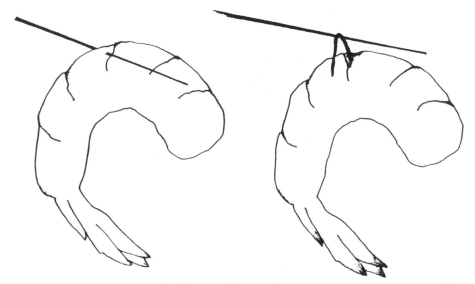

How to devein shrimp

How to keep shrimp straight

SHIRO INGEN MAME NO AMANI *sweet kidney beans*

    15 oz can kidney beans
    2/3 cup water
    2/3 cup sugar
    1/4 tsp salt

Drain and rinse kidney beans. In small saucepan place water, sugar and salt and bring to boil. Add cooked beans and simmer 10 minutes. Remove when cool. Cook remaining liquid until half original amount remains. Return cooled beans to saucepan. Simmer for few minutes. Allow beans to cool in liquid. Serve cold.

SAKURA MOCHI *cherry leaf wrapped sweets*

    1-1/2 cups do myo ji ko
    1 cup sugar
    1/3 cup hot water
    1-1/4 lb koshi an
    1/4 tsp red food coloring
    16 salted cherry leaves

Wash do myo ji ko and drain. Place wet dishcloth in steamer rack. Arrange do myo ji ko evenly and steam over high heat for 30 to 35 minutes. Combine hot water, sugar and heat until sugar is dissolved. Turn do myo ji ko in bowl and pour sugar water over and mix. Cover with wet towel and steam for 15 minutes. Add red food coloring. Using 2 tbsp koshi an, shape into 16 balls, wrap with steamed do myo ji ko. Wrap pastry with salted cherry leaf.

When cherry trees are in blossom, sweet mochi is wrapped in cherry tree leaves. The leaves are removed before eating but the delicate fragrance permeates the sweet mochi and lingers in the mouth.

EBI NO AMAZU *sweet pickled prawns*

12 uncooked prawns	1 tbsp sugar
1/2 tsp salt	1/2 tsp salt
3 cups water	1-1/2 oz ginger
2 tbsp vinegar	2 tbsp shoyu
1-1/2 tsp shoyu	2 tsp sesame seeds, roasted

Devein prawn, inserting skewer or toothpick in back. Also insert short skewer between shell and meat of prawn before boiling to maintain a straight shape, rather then curled or hunched look. Boil in salted water until tender, 5 minutes. Cool. Shell prawns and remove skewer. Mix vinegar, salt and sugar. Marinate cooked prawns in this sauce. Peel and mince ginger. Add shoyu and cook together over low flame, stirring constantly until minced ginger has absorbed the shoyu. Cut marinated prawns into 3/4-inch lengths, place on serving plate with ginger, sprinkled with roasted sesame seeds.

ASPARAGUS NO GOMA KARASHI AE *asparagus with mustard and sesame sauce*

1-1/2 lb asparagus
2 tsp roasted black sesame seeds
1 egg yolk
1 tsp shoyu
2 tsp mustard

Snap off hard, lower part of asparagus stalks. Wash, remove scales and cook in boiling water until done. Rinse under cold water and slice into thin, diagonal pieces. Grind sesame seeds a little, mix with egg yolk, mustard and shoyu. Toss sliced asparagus with sauce.

BUTANIKU NO SUMISO AE *pork and beansprouts with mustard miso sauce salad*

1/4 lb pork fillet	2 tbsp water
3 stalks green onion	2 tbsp sake
1/4 lb beansprouts	2 tbsp sugar
	1/2 tbsp mustard paste
Sauce:	3 tbsp vinegar
1/4 cup miso	

Slice and cut pork fillet into thin bite-size pieces. Cook in boiling water 3 minutes or until done. Trim tails off beansprouts and wash. Parboil and rinse in cold water. Cut green onion into same length as beansprouts. Slice in half lengthwise and cook in boiling water until wilted. Rinse in cold water. Using small pot, combine miso, water, sake and sugar, stirring constantly over medium heat. When mixture becomes smooth, thick and creamy, remove from heat adding vinegar and mustard paste. Squeeze water out of cooked beansprouts and green onion. Add cooked pork mix gently with mustard-miso sauce and serve immediately.

IKA TO TAKENOKO NO LEMON ZUKAKE
cuttlefish or squid and bamboo shoots with lemon sauce

1/2 lb bamboo shoots, canned or fresh
1 lb cuttlefish or squid
2 tbsp vinegar
1 tbsp uni fresh or preserved
1 egg yolk
1 lemon, cut in wedges
1/4 tsp salt

Cut bamboo shoots in 1/4-inch strips. Remove legs from squid and peel off skin. Dip quickly in and out of boiling water. Place in colander and pour cold water over to cool. Cut squid in same manner as bamboo shoots. Mix squid and bamboo shoots well with 1-1/2 tbsp vinegar. This technique is called "vinegar wash".

Squeeze out excess liquid. Mix uni with 1/2 tbsp vinegar, egg yolk and salt. Dress squid and bamboo shoots with uni mixture. Serve with lemon wedge.

IKANO KIMI ZU KAKE *squid with egg yolk dressing*

1 lb squid	**Sauce:**
1 tsp salt	5 tbsp vinegar
2 medium cucumbers	2 tbsp sugar
2 tsp salt	1 tsp salt
	2 egg yolks

Remove outer skin of squid and split open to make a flat piece. Score surface of squid without cutting through and cut into thin strips. Bring water to boil and add 1 tsp salt. Dip squid pieces in boiling water, turn into colander and pour cold water over squid to cool. Sprinkle 2 tsp salt, on cutting board, roll cucumber under palms of hands, slice very thin without cutting through, then divide into 1/2-inch pieces, cutting all way through every 1/2 inch. In double boiler, place sauce ingredients, vinegar, sugar, salt and egg yolks and cook until thickened. Arrange cucumber and cooked squid in individual dishes. Pour egg yolk sauce over. Serve immediately.

MIYAKO AE *Capital-style salad*

1/4 lb white meat fish fillet	**Amazu sauce:** —bring to boil—
1/2 tsp salt	1/2 cup dashi
1/2 carrot	1/2 cup vinegar
1 daikon	1/2 cup shoyu
1 cucumber	1 cup sugar
1/2 tsp salt	1/2 tsp salt
6 kikurage	
2 eggs	
2 tsp black sesame seeds	

Salt fish and leave 2 hours. Rinse with water and cut in thin strips. Cut carrot, daikon and cucumber in slivers and salt. Let stand 10 minutes and squeeze out water. Soak kikurage in water. When soft, drain and slice thin. Scramble eggs in ungreased frying pan. Sieve through mesh. Marinate all ingredients with Amazu sauce. Garnish with chopped roasted black sesame seeds.

AJI NO SALAD *vinegared horse mackerel salad*

2 tbsp lemon juice	1 green pepper
3 tsp white wine	1-1/2 tsp mustard paste
6 vinegared horse mackerel	2 tsp salt
1 onion	1-1/2 tbsp vinegar
1/2 tsp salt	3 tbsp oil

Sprinkle 1 tbsp lemon juice and white wine over prepared vinegared mackerel and let stand 3 minutes. Peel skin and slice diagonally into thin pieces. Peel onion and cut in 1/4-inch slices and separate into rings. Parboil and drain. When onion is cooled, sprinkle with remaining lemon juice and salt. Cut green pepper in 1/4-inch slices. Parboil, drain, cool. Combine mackerel, onion and green pepper. Serve with mixture of mustard paste, salt, vinegar and oil.

BUTA TO MOYASHI NO KARASHI AE *pork and bean sprout salad*

1/2 lb pork	**Sauce for Karashi:**
1 tsp salt	1-1/4 tbsp powdered mustard
1 tbsp sake or sherry	1 tbsp hot water
1 stalk green onion	3 tbsp vinegar
1 small finger fresh ginger root	3 tbsp shoyu
3/4 lb beansprouts	2 tsp sugar
2 tbsp vinegar	

Cut pork in two parts and rub with salt. Place pieces on fireproof plate, sprinkle with sake, topping with green onion and slices of ginger. Using steam basket, steam salted pork 40 minutes. When done, allow to cool before cutting into 2-inch strips. Clean and pinch off hair-like roots of bean sprouts, rinse with boiling salted water and place on colander to drain. Squeeze water out gently and place in bowl. Sprinkle with vinegar and mix thoroughly. Squeeze liquid out gently once more. Quickly mix powdered mustard and hot water. Add vinegar, shoyu and sugar for mustard sauce and mix well. Place pork and bean sprouts in large bowl. Pour mustard sauce over to marinate and serve.

YASAI NO SHIRA AE *vegetables marinated with tofu, bean curd and goma dressing*

1 tofu	**Tofu and Goma dressing:**
2/3 lb radishes	3 tbsp goma
1 small carrot	2 tbsp sugar
1 cucumber	1 tsp salt
1 tbsp salt	2 tsp shoyu
5 medium shiitake	1/4 cup dashi
2 pieces canned konnyaku	

Wrap tofu in kitchen towel or cloth napkin and squeeze water out, placing between two cutting boards with an added weight on top. Shred radishes, carrot, cucumber, and sprinkle with salt. Allow to stand 30 minutes and then squeeze water out. Soften mushrooms in enough cold water to cover and squeeze water out. Cut into strips.

Goma Dressing: Grind goma until it becomes paste, add sugar, salt, shoyu, dashi and mix well. Combine all ingredients and fold in tofu dressing.

IKEBANA *Flower Arrangement*

Every Japanese woman, no matter what her social status, studies *Ikebana*. I am no exception. However, the history of women and Japanese flower arrangement is a comparatively recent development.

As with so many other important arts in Japan, *Ikebana* has both early and religious beginnings. In the sixth century, when Buddhism and Chinese culture and writing were first being introduced to Japan, the Buddhist priest, Ono-no-Imako was dissatisfied with the idea of placing flowers carelessly around the Buddha's altar.

Pondering deeply, Ono-no-Imako came to realize that the arrangements symbolized the whole universe and man's relationship to it. From this, *Ikebana* as an art form evolved. For many centuries only priests made flower arrangements and those in the temples. Sketches of a style known as *rikka* depict some arrangements towering fifteen or twenty feet high! This might be considered a real emphasis in the heaven part of the earth-man-heaven principle, which must be present in all proper Japanese flower arrangements.

Eventually flower arranging caught the interest of the court nobility and many of them took it up as a pasttime. Women were not engaged in its practice until about 1860.

When I lived in Japan with my parents, my teacher, Madame Ikeda, would arrive at our home each Wednesday evening about six. After the greetings the main room with hot tea, grandmother, mother and I took seats for the lesson in the style of *senke-kogi*.

Sometimes we would arrange three different vases during a lesson. I can never remember Madame Ikeda explaining anything about arranging. The lesson was conducted in a graceful silence. Madame would make a sample arrangement which I disassembled and rearranged. With very few words, Madame Ikeda would make remarks on my arrangement. Then grandmother and mother would follow me. This teaching and relationship in silence continued for over a decade, until I moved with my children to Hawaii.

Madame Ikeda's way of *O-Hana* is unlike most Western floral arrangements, since it is based on the concept of "less is more." Full bloom flowers would be used only for a specific reason. An ideal arrangement might employ a bud, a half-open bud and perhaps a fully-bloomed flower, representing future, present and past.

With this foundation of understanding, I practice *Ikebana* almost every week for purely personal enjoyment, bringing nature and the seasons from outdoors indoors for my contemplation.

CHAWAN-MUSHI *egg custard soup*

3-1/2 cups dashi	a few shiitake
1 tsp salt	10 small prawns
1/2 tsp shoyu	1 lime
2 large eggs	1 small bamboo tip
1/2 lb chicken breast meat	15 ginkyo nuts
1/2 tbsp shoyu	salt
1/2 kamaboko	shoyu
15 sprigs fresh coriander	

After heating and seasoning dashi with salt and shoyu, allow to cool. Beat eggs, add cooled soup stock and strain. Allow chicken to stand in shoyu 20 minutes. Cut kamaboko lengthwise and then slice into fan-shapes. Trim ends of coriander. Soften shiitake in enough cold water to cover. Cut off stems. Shell and devein prawns by using a skewer. Salt slightly. Divide ingredients equally into 5 chawan mushi bowls or custard cups, placing coriander leaves on top. Add small piece of lemon peel. Fill cups with egg mixture. Chawan mushi cups usually have lids and are made of porcelain. Place covers on cups and set in steamer making certain water in steamer does not boil but only makes steam. Boiling water makes the chawan mushi "hole-y." Steam 20 minutes or until set. Test with silver knife. Serve cups with lids.

ATSUYAKI TAMAGO *thick Omelet*

4 eggs	1/4 tsp salt
4 tbsp warm dashi	1/2 tsp shoyu
5 tbsp sugar	1 tbsp vegetable oil
1 tsp mirin	1/2 cup grated daikon
1 tsp sake	1 tsp shoyu

In mixing bowl beat eggs well. In small sauce pan combine warm dashi, sugar, mirin, sake, salt and shoyu, stirring well until sugar and salt have dissolved. Add mixture to beaten eggs and blend. Pour oil into pan, heating pan to medium heat. When pan is warm and well coated with oil, pour out excess oil and pour in 1/4 of egg mixture, cooking it with medium heat until eggs start to set. Fold egg in half. Oil pan lightly, pour another 1/4 of egg mixture in oiled part of pan. When it starts to set, lift it and turn it over first 1/4-portion, laying it on top. Oil pan again before pouring another 1/4 of egg mixture. Pour in third 1/4-egg mixture. Lifting cooking omelet, allowing some mixture to run under it. Cook for few moments and when it begins to set fold over again. Repeat operation four times. The omelets will have undetermined number of layers. Cook and slice into 1-1/2" x 2" x 1" pieces. Serve with grated radish, barely colored with drops of shoyu.

This recipe is followed in Nigiri sushi. Atsyuyaki Tamage was my favorite lunch box surprise in my youth and it was sushi topping in picnic lunches. It traditionally is cooked in a rectangular or square copper pan called "Tamage yakinabe". It is also possible to make thick omelet with methods used for square pans when cooking with a round pan.

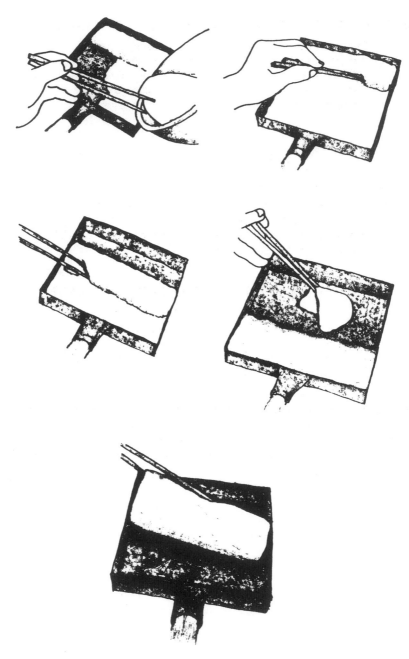

How to make a Japanese omelet

HIJIKI NO SHIRO AE *black sea vegetable with tofu dressing*

3/4 cup hijiki	**Dressing**
3 cups water	1 square tofu
2 tbsp sake	2 tbsp roasted sesame seeds,
1 tbsp sugar	ground
1 tbsp shoyu	1-1/2 tbsp sugar
	1 tsp shoyu
	1/3 tsp salt

Wash hijiki in cold water and soak in 3 cups cold water 1/2 hour. Drain and cook in warm water until tender, about 10 minutes. Drain. Add sake, sugar and shoyu and simmer 5 minutes. Set aside.

Dressing: Boil tofu 3 minutes and drain. Wrap in cheesecloth to squeeze moisture out. Using blender, blend 2 minutes until tofu texture becomes very smooth. Add sesame seeds, sugar, shoyu, salt and work another minute. Drain liquid from sea vegetable and toss lightly with tofu dressing.

KANU TO SAKURA NO HANA TO KONBU NO AMAZU ZUKE
pickled turnips, cherry blossoms and seaweed

4 medium sized turnips	**Sauce for pickling:**
1 tbsp salt	4 tbsp vinegar
4-inch square seaweed	3 tbsp sugar
2 tbsp salted cherry blossoms	

Pare, slice turnips into paper-thin sheets and sprinkle with salt. Place weight over sliced turnips until they become wilted. Using pair of scissors, cut seaweed into matchstick pieces. Rinse both seaweed and salted cherry blossoms with cold water. Combine vinegar and sugar, adding turnips, seaweed and cherry blossoms after having squeezed out any excess liquid. Pickle ingredients at least 30 minutes before serving.

TEMPURA

Made in the following way, Tempura should melt in your mouth. The coating of batter should appear as delicate as a bridal veil.

Tempura batter mix:
1-1/4 cup soft wheat flour, cake or non-glutenous, sifted
4 tbsp rice flour
4 tbsp cornstarch
1-1/3 cup water
1 egg yolk
3 cups vegetable oil

Mix egg yolk and 1/2 cup water. Add sifted wheat flour, rice flour and cornstarch, mixing very quickly. Add remaining water and stir. Do not let batter set more than five minutes before using. To add sesame flavoring for tempura, substitute 1/2 cup sesame oil to cooking oil. Deep frying tempura at 365 degrees will turn out lovely, tantalizing tempura.

Tentsuyu dipping sauce:
1 cup dashi
1/3 cup sweet wine, or mirin
1/3 cup shoyu
2 fingers fresh ginger root, grated
1 daikon or radish, grated
Bring liquid to boil. Serve with fried tempura.

Tempura frying: Gather ingredients and wipe dry. Oil should be placed in large, deep skillet or deep fryer. One at a time, dip ingredients into batter, then into oil. Cook a few at a time to prevent lowering temperature of oil. When temperature is low, food absorbs oil and becomes soggy. Remove when evenly browned, drying excess oil on wire rack or on paper towel. If latter, change towels frequently to avoid too much grease. Serve immediately with tentsuyu, grated ginger and daikon. Watch the happy faces.

Materials for Tempura Frying:
12 fresh prawns
12 fresh scallops
1/4 lb sea bass, fillet of sole and any white fish meat in season
1 small egg plant, 1/8 lb
1 green pepper
12 asparagus spears when in season
8 okra pods
1/4 lb broccoli
1/8 lb green beans
slices of yam or squashes

With a creative mind and imagination, many other ingredients can be utilized in tempura.

Various ingredients suitable for tempura

Preparation:

Prawns: Devein, using toothpick inserted or skewer as illustrated. Shell except for tail and adjoining segment. Remove water from tail to prevent oil spattering in deep frying. Cut tail tip end off, pressing water out with knife or fingertips. Then bend peeled prawns backwards until they lie straight when placed on flat surface. Wipe dry.

Scallops: Clean and wipe dry.

Sea Bass,   *or white-meat fish:* Cut in small, thin pieces and wipe dry.

Egg plant: Slice into thin pieces.

Green pepper: Cut into long strips.

Asparagus: Clean and cut off tough bottom end. Wipe dry.

Broccoli: Wash and cut tip portions into thin slices. Wipe dry - wet broccoli is the oil-spattering champion!

Green beans: Use whole or sliced. Wipe dry.

Yam or squash: Slice in thin rounds and wipe dry.

Tempura provides many varieties of delicacies with the seasonal changes, and, as you can see by the list of suggested ingredients, is not limited to shrimp or fish, but includes vegetgables. Fruit fried the tempura way makes an excellent dessert, one of the most enjoyable I serve to my family and guests.

Tempura most often is eaten as it is cooked. Of course, you may create an arrangement of assorted tempura in a dish. It usually is served individually and has tentsuyu as the dipping sauce, which is the 'heavenly dew' in literal translation! The sauce has ginger and grated daikon to distinguish it.

Tempura never was intended for the Japanese, surprisingly enough. In the mid-1600's, the Kamakura period, the Dutch first arrived in Japan. They could not accustom themselves to eating raw fish, or sashimi. Some very clever Japanese chef created fish, French-fried! Though served with a Japanese-style sauce, many claim tempura is due to the Western influence on our culture!

Oil for Tempura:

The tempura I sampled as a child somehow tasted lighter and better in my taste bud memories. When my brother Take-chan visited me, I mentioned this to him, while we were doing a *pas de deux* cooking tempura in my kitchen. We both decided that the secret was the oil.

Our late mother gave instructions to the family cook to use mostly olive oil and a small portion of camellia oil, normally only used as hair oil in Japan and extracted from the deep red single petal camellia seeds grown in southern Japan. Our mother was an eternal romantic and loved the aroma of the Mediterranean, and waxed poetic about the olive trees.

Continued on next page

In my memory I don't remember using soy oil or cottenseed oil. Mustard seed oil, or *natane abura,* was common for tempura cooking. When olive oil was not available to us during the second world war sesame oil was used mixed with *Kaya-na-abura,* an oil from a pampas-grass-like plant, harvested in late September.

Now to my students I recommend the following for tempura oil: 2 parts olive oil and 1 part sesame oil; or, 2 parts vegetable oil and 1 part sesame oil. The end result will be very tasty and fragrant.

Prawns for Tempura:

Prawns for tempura must not be too large, but a maximum of 3-1/2 inches long. There is an old saying "One does not use teeth to eat Prawn Tempura. "That sounds illogical and unthinkable to eat anything without chewing! However, when prawns are too large, the batter, or *Koromo* necessarily becomes overcooking in order to ensure a cooked prawn. The prawn meat will then be hard and chewy.

ASPARAGUS TO TORI NO KAORI AGE *asparagus and chicken in spiced batter*

1/2 lb chicken meat	1/2 cup flour
18 pieces asparagus	
1 egg	**Sauce:**
4 tbsp water	5 tbsp dashi
1/2 tsp salt	2 tbsp mirin
1/2 tsp red pepper, finely minced	2 tbsp shoyu
3 sprigs parsley, finely minced	oil for deep-frying

Snap off hard, lower part of asparagus stalk. Wash and remove scales. Slice chicken meat into bite-size pieces. Combine egg and water, mix well. Add salt, red pepper, parsley and flour to make batter. Combine dashi, mirin and shoyu in sauce pan, bring to boil and set aside. Heat cooking oil to 370 degrees. Coat chicken meat slices in batter and deep-fry until crisp. Coat asparagus in same manner as chicken meat and deep-fry until crisp. Serve with sauce.

EBI DANGO *tofu balls with shrimp*

1-1/2 cubes tofu	dash of pepper
2-1/2 tsp salt	2 tbsp cornstarch
400 gms or 1/2 lb shrimp	2 tbsp minced onion
1 egg yolk	oil

Break tofu in 3 or 4 pieces. Boil 3 cups water, add tofu and 1/2 tsp salt. Cook 3 minutes. Drain. Cool with cold water. Squeeze water out of tofu. Knead well or use blender. Shell shrimp, wash with salted water and chop fine. Mix tofu, shrimp, egg yolk, remaining salt, pepper, cornstarch and minced onion. Shape into balls 1-1/2-inch in diameter and deep fry until golden brown. Serve with shoyu seasoned with mustard.

TAKENOKO MAKI AGE *bamboo shoots wrapped in pork*

1-1/2 lb pork fillets

Sauce A:
1 tbsp shoyu
1 tbsp mirin
1 tbsp ginger juice
8 oz can bamboo shoots

Sauce B:
1 tbsp shoyu
1 tbsp mirin
1/2 cup cornstarch
oil for deep frying
parsley
prepared mustard

Cut pork fillets into very thin slices. Sprinkle mixture of Sauce A over meat and stand for 15 minutes. Cut bamboo shoots into matchstick-size pieces. In small saucepan combine Sauce B and bamboo shoots and cook over low flame until all liquid is gone. Cool. Place seasoned pork fillets on sudare in the exact manner as making wrapped sushi. Arrange one-fifth of bamboo shoots horizontally across 1 inch from edge nearest you. Lift edge closest to you and with a slight pressure, roll cylinder away from you. Use toothpicks to prevent from unrolling. Dust pork with cornstarch, making sure ends are well-dusted. Heat oil to 350 degrees, then deep fry dusted pork rolls until surfaces become crispy. Drain. Remove toothpicks and cut into 1-1/2-inch pieces. Serve with prepared mustard and shoyu garnished with parsley.

KAORI AGE *fragranted pork*

1-1/2 lb pork fillets
1 tbsp ginger, minced
1 stalk green onion, minced
2 tbsp shoyu
1 tsp sugar
1/2 tbsp sake

2 tbsp sesame seeds
1 celery
1 cucumber
1/2 cup flour
oil for deep frying

Cut pork fillet into 3/4-inch cubes. Marinate in ginger, green onion, shoyu, sugar, sake, and sesame seeds 30 minutes. Clean and wash celery and cut into thin diagonal pieces. Split cucumber in half lengthwise and remove seeds. Slice into thin diagonal pieces and soak in water to crisp. Mix flour in pork marinade. Each piece should be well-coated with flour. Heat oil to 360 degrees and deep fry pork cubes, five or six pieces at a time. Fry until meat surfaces to top, then cook another two minutes. When all are fried, remove. Bring cooking oil to 370 degrees two minutes. Return fried pork cubes to oil again. Remove when all are crispy. Drain. Serve with crispy celery and cucumber.

AGE TOFU NO ANKAKE *deep-fried tofu in sauce*

1 square tofu	1 egg
2 cups dashi	1 cup breadcrumbs
3 tbsp shoyu	1/4 cup sesame seeds
1 tbsp mirin	1 finger ginger, grated
2 tbsp cornstarch	1/4 lb broccoli
2 tbsp water	2 carrots
oil for deep frying	1/2 cup water
1/2 cup flour	

Cut tofu in half lengthwise, then crosswise into 1/2-inch thick pieces. Pat each piece dry with cloth or paper towel. Bring dashi, shoyu and mirin to a boil. Stir together with cornstarch, water and keep warm. Heat cooking oil to 360 degrees in deep skillet or fryer. Dust each piece of tofu with flour. Dip into beaten egg, then roll in breadcrumbs and sesame seeds mixed *together* . Deep fry until golden brown. In serving bowl, top tofu with grated ginger accompanied by cooked broccoli, cut into bite-size, dipped in boiling water 2 minutes. Drain, rinse in cold water. Drain carrots, cut into 1/2-inch length, cut out with any cutter. Cook in water until tender and drain. Pour warm sauce over and serve warm.

AGE NIKU DANGO *fried meatballs*

1/2 lb ground pork	2 eggs
2 tbsp onion, grated	3 tbsp cornstarch
1 tsp garlic, grated	4 tbsp flour
2 tsp sugar	oil for deep frying
2 tbsp sake	parsley
2 tbsp shoyu	mustard
1 tsp salt	vinegar
2 tsp sesame oil	shoyu

Combine ground pork, onion, ginger juice, garlic, sugar, sake, shoyu, salt and sesame oil in large bowl. Mix well with wooden spoon. Add eggs, cornstarch, flour and mix until smooth in texture. Coat palms of hands with oil. Divide mixture an make 30 individual balls. Heat cooking oil to 360 degrees and deep fry balls 5 minutes. When meatballs are cooked, increase the oil temperature to 375 degrees and cook an additional minute. Serve deep-fried balls with parsley, mustard, vinegar and shoyu.

TORI NIKU NO DANGO *chicken and tofu balls*

1 square tofu	3 tbsp cornstarch
2 stalks green onion	oil for deep frying
3 shiitake	parsley sprigs
1 egg	
1 lb chicken meat minced	**Dipping sauce:**
1 tsp salt	2 tbsp shoyu
	2 tbsp vinegar

Break tofu into fourths. Cook in large pot with enough water to cover tofu. When it reaches boiling point, remove from heat. Drain and squeeze out water. When cooled, knead cooked tofu with hands. Wash and mince green onion. Soak shiitake in warm water to soften. Remove stems and mince fine. Beat egg and combine with chicken meat, tofu, green onion, shiitake, salt and cornstarch. Mix well. Shape into large bite-size balls. Heat cooking oil to 360 degrees and deep-fry meatballs, frying until inside is well-cooked, 7 to 10 minutes. Garnish with parsley on top. Serve with sauce made by combining shoyu and vinegar.

SHINJAGAIMO TO TORI NIKU NO UMANI *new potatoes and chicken*

1/2 lb chicken meat	2 tbsp mirin
1 lb new potatoes	3 tbsp sugar
2 tbsp salad oil	4 tbsp shoyu
2-1/2 cups dashi	1/2 cup green peas, fresh or frozen

Cut chicken meat into bite-size pieces. Peel potatoes and cut into squares. Heat oil in pot and saute potatoes and chicken until chicken is golden. Add dashi. Spoon out residue. Add seasoning and simmer until liquid is almost gone. Add green peas just before removing pot from heat. Serve individually or in large serving bowl.

SAKANA NO NITSUKE *fish cooked in seasoned liquid*

SHIROMI ZAKANA *white meat fish*

1 lb fish cut into 2-1/2-inch long pieces
4 tbsp sake or sherry
4 tbsp shoyu
3 tbsp mirin

Combine in saucepan sake, shoyu and mirin and bring to boil. Add fish and cover with small-sized lid which fits inside pan, touching fish. Then cover with saucepan lid to prevent evaporation. Cook over high heat until well flavored. (Sauce will boil up and over small-sized lid.) Remove from heat and serve on individual plates, pouring sauce over fish.

AKAMI SAKANA *red meat fish*

> 1-1/3 lb fish (such as mackerel) cut into 2-1/2 inch long pieces
> 6 tbsp shoyu
> 4 tbsp mirin
> 4 tbsp sake or dry sherry
> 1-1/2 tbsp sugar

Cook like white fish recipe, except when fish sauce boils, turn flame to low and continue cooking 5 to 6 minutes. Remove inner lid, cooking another 20 minutes before serving.

GOMOKU NI *soybeans cooked with pork*

1 cup dried soybeans	4 cups dashi, soup stock
3/4 lb pork fillets	3 tbsp sake
1 carrot	2 tbsp sugar
1 piece ginger, size of little finger	3 tbsp shoyu
1 tbsp oil	

Wash dried soybeans. Soak overnight in 4 cups water. Drain. Cut pork fillets into 1-inch length strips. Peel and cut carrots size of soaked soybeans. Cook until almost done. Peel and cut ginger into sengiri. In large heavy pot, heat oil, add ginger and stir until wilted. Add pork strips and saute until slightly browned. Add to soaked soybeans 3 cups dashi and sake. Boil until bubbles form on top, then reduce to low flame. From time to time skim off any scum which rises to top. (Soybeans are tender and done when easily crushed between fingers.) Add carrots, 1 cup dashi, sugar and shoyu. This also can be served as a snack.

MAME TO KOEBI NO ITAME NI *peas and shrimp or small prawn dish*

2 cups fresh or frozen peas	1/4 tsp ginger juice
2 tsp salt	1 egg white
3 cups plus 2 tsp water	4 tsp cornstarch
1 stalk green onion	1/2 cup plus 2 tbsp cooking oil
1/2 lb small, uncooked prawns	1/2 cup dashi
2 tsp sake or dry sherry	1 tsp shoyu

Sprinkle salt onto fresh peas and allow to stand 10 minutes. Bring 3 cups water to boil and add salted peas. Bring to boil again and cook 5 minutes. Let peas cool in cooking water to keep pea skins smooth. When cooled, drain in colander. Cut green onion size of peas. Clean, devein and shell small prawns in bowl. Mix prawns with sake, ginger juice and egg white. Sprinkle with cornstarch. In deep frying pan heat 1/2 cup oil. When oil reaches 350 degrees F, divide prawns into two parts. Deep fry each separately until prawns turn to pink color. (Caution: cook prawns in two parts since cooking all at one time lowers heat and causes prawns to clump together. Prawn meat would also become hard.) Remove and drain. Heat 2 tbsp oil in skillet. Saute chopped onions, peas and fried prawns. Add seasoning mixture of sake, dashi, shoyu and 1 tsp salt. Stir, then pour in 1 tsp cornstarch and 2 tsp water which have been mixed together.

DENGAKU TOFU *grilled soybean curd with miso dressing*

The appearance of this dish may remind Americans of a popsicle.

> 2 tofu
> 2 cups water
> 1/4 lb fresh spinach leaves
> 1/2 cup miso
> kona sansho

Cut tofu into 8 pieces, each 3/4-inch wide by 3-inches long. Preheat broiler. Making only one layer, place pieces of tofu in flameproof baking dish. Add enough cold water to come halfway up sides of tofu, then place dish as close to broiler as possible. Sear tofu on one side, then other for few seconds. Tofu will be speckled but not evenly browned. Remove dish from broiler and set aside. Bring water to boil in 1-1/2 or 2 qt saucepan. Trim stems from spinach leaves and cook about 2 minutes. Quickly remove and place into colander, immediately running cold water over spinach to stop cooking and to maintain green color. Squeeze liquid out and chop fine. In suribachi (serrated mortar bowl) pound or mash spinach to paste. With back of large spoon, rub spinach through sieve into bowl. Stir half the miso and a few sprinkles of kona sansho with spinach until miso has turned green. Place remaining miso in small bowl and mix until smooth. Over moderate heat, bring pan of seared tofu, water remaining, almost to boil. Remove from heat and spoon green miso dressing into pastry bag equipped with a No. 47 ribbon tip.

Squeeze miso along top of 4 pieces of tofu, covering each top. Spread a thin film of miso on each piece of tofu, running prong of fork down miso to create serrated line. Cover remaining tofu with plain miso. Insert two 4 to 6-inch bamboo skewers or small lobster forks halfway through length of each piece of tofu. Place tofu back into baking dish and broil few seconds. Serve at room temperature.

TORINIKU NO TSUKE YAKI *pan-fried*

> 1-1/2 lb chicken leg meat, deboned
>
> **Tare sauce:**
> 3-1/3 tbsp shoyu
> 3-1/3 tbsp mirin
> 2 tbsp sake
> 2 tbsp oil
> 1 tbsp prepared mustard

Use fork or skewer to pierce hole through chicken skin. Combine sauce mixture and marinate chicken 40 minutes, turning meat while marinating. Heat heavy skillet with oil, saute chicken meat with skin side down. Cook over medium flame from 10 to 15 seconds, reduce flame, cover and simmer 5 to 6 minutes. Turn chicken meat over, bring flame up to medium and repeat cooking method. Check doneness after ten minutes cooking time. Thick part of meat should bounce back when pressed. Remove from skillet and set aside. Place marinade sauce in skillet and simmer until half original amount remains. Brush with tare sauce. Serve chicken skin side up, sliced diagonally. Serve with prepared mustard.

TORI NO GINGAMI YAKI *foiled wrapped chicken*

3/4 lb chicken breast meat	**Sauce:**
1/2 tsp salt	4 tbsp dashi
1 tbsp sake or sherry	1 tsp salt
4 wakame, dried	5 tbsp sake
6 shiitake or 2 fresh button	aluminum foil cut into 12-inch
mushrooms per serving	squares
3 stalks green onion	
1 lemon	

Cut chicken meat into bite-size pieces. Sprinkle with salt and sake and set aside. Soak wakame in water and when soft, remove hard vein. Soften shiitake in warm water. Cut off stem and cut into strips. If fresh mushrooms are used, wash and cut into thin slices. Shred green onion, cut lemon into slices. On each piece of aluminum foil, place chicken meat, vegetables, lemon slice. Sprinkle sauce over, wrap and place under broiler for ten minutes. Serve on plate with foil.

WAKADORI NO YUAN YAKI *pan-fried chicken*

3/4 lb chicken breast meat	1 tbsp mirin
2-1/2 tbsp shoyu	1 tbsp salad oil
1-1/2 tbsp sake	mustard

Pierce skin of chicken breasts using tip of a skewer. Marinate in mixture of shoyu, sake and mirin for 3 hours. Heat skillet with oil. Remove chicken from marinade and wipe off excess moisture. With skin side down, saute until brown. Turn and finish cooking. To check doneness, when pressed down, chicken meat springs back. Remove chicken from skillet. Place remaining marinade in skillet, cook and stir until slightly thickened. Slice chicken into 1/8-inch diagonal pieces, brush over with thickened sauce and serve with mustard.

BUTANIKU NO MISO YAKI *To-Kiku   Ka-Kabu broiled pork with miso marinade pickled turnips*

1/2 cup miso paste	**Pickle recipe:**
1 stalk green onion, minced	6 small turnips
1 tbsp ginger, grated	6 tbsp vinegar
3 tbsp sugar	4 tbsp sugar
3 tbsp sake	3 tbsp water
1-1/2 tbsp mirin	1/2 tsp salt
1-1/2 lb pork fillet	3 inch ita konbu
	red pepper

Combine miso paste, minced green onion, grated ginger, sugar, sake and mirin and mix well for marinade. Slice pork fillet in 6 thin pieces. On bottom of baking dish, spread miso marinade. Add pork fillets and spread remaining half of marinade evenly over pork. Cover and refrigerate 1 to 2 days. Broil evenly on

Continued on next page

both sides. Serve with pickled turnips. Peel skins off turnips. Place between two chopsticks, cut in 1/8-inch slices and make half turn, repeat cutting. Chopsticks help prevent from cutting through. Combine vinegar, sugar, water and salt. Bring to boil and let cool. Place seaweed in vinegar mixture and flower-cut pickled turnips. Store overnight in refrigerator. Squeeze out vinegar. Serve garnished with red pepper.

DAIZU IRI HAMBURG *soybean added hamburger*

3 cups cooked soybeans	dash of pepper
1 onion, minced fine	1 egg
1 tbsp butter	1 cup breadcrumbs
1/3 lb ground beef	1/4 cup flour
1 tsp salt	2 tbsp oil

Drain cooked soybeans well. Using food processor or blender, crush soybeans. Mince onion fine. Saute with butter, add ground beef, season with salt, dash of pepper and let cool. Combine with crushed soybeans, egg, breadcrumbs and mix well. Make 10 even-sized patties and dust with flour. Heat skillet with oil. Saute patties, browning both sides well. Serve with tomato ketchup or shoyu.

CALIFORNIA FU *apricots California*

1/4 lb dried apricots	**Seasonings:**
1/2 cup warm water	3 tbsp sugar
1 round onion	1 tsp salt
1 green pepper	2 tbsp shoyu
3/4 lb beef, sliced thin	2 tbsp catsup
1 egg yolk	
2 tbsp sake	1 tbsp cornstarch
1 tbsp cornstarch	2 tbsp water
1 tbsp flour	
1 tbsp shoyu	1/2 cup almonds, blanched
1 tbsp minced ginger	
2 tbsp oil	

Soften apricots in water. Cut onion and green pepper into apricot-sized pieces. Saute beef in oil and set aside. Saute onion and green pepper until cooked, but still crisp, before adding beef, apricots and seasoning mixture which has been combined in a small bowl. While stirring add cornstarch and water which has been previously mixed in a small bowl. Top with almonds and serve with rice.

KATSUO NO YAKI TATAKI *partially broiled bonito sashimi —*
Variation #1

1/2 fresh bonito fish fillet,
   approx 1-1/2 lb
1 tsp salt
1-1/2 tbsp vinegar

Sauce:
1/4 cup fresh grapefruit juice
1 stalk green onion, minced

1 clove garlic, grated
beefsteak plant leaves, cut sengiri
1 cucumber
1 carrot
1 bunch beansprouts
1 cup daikon, grated
mustard paste, as desired

Split fish to make two narrow fillets. Slice and remove dark portion of fillet. Using four metal skewers, securely skewer through fillets in shape of fan. Sprinkle 1/4 tsp salt over the fish. Broil skinside first until slightly browned, then turn. Broil another minute. Remove skewers with twirling motion. Immediately sprinkle vinegar and pat with hands to tighten the meat. Combine grapefruit juice, shoyu, minced green onion, grated garlic, and beefsteak plant leaves. Slice broiled bonito straight down into 1/4-inch slices. Place sliced bonito into shallow pan, sprinkle 1/3 of grapefruit sauce over bonito and let stand 10 minutes. Repeat, using another 1/3 portion of sauce, store remainder in refrigerator. Slice cucumbers widthwise into very thin slices. Sprinkle with 1/4 tsp salt. Let stand 10 minutes. When wilted, rinse with water, drain and squeeze with hands. Cut carrot sengiri style. Keep in water until crisp. On serving platter, place seasoned bonito. Sprinkle remaining 1/3 portion sauce over fish. Arrange cucumber, carrot, beansprouts and serve with mustard paste.

KATSUO NO YAKI TATAKI *partially broiled bonito sashimi —*
Variation #2

1/2 bonito fresh fish fillet,
   1-1/2 lbs
1 tsp salt
2 tbsp lemon juice
2 cups grated daikon
1 stalk green onion, minced
2 tbsp ginger, grated

Sauce:
2 stalks green onion, minced
1 tbsp ginger, grated
1/2 cup daikon, grated
2 cloves garlic, grated
lemon wedges

Split fish to make two narrow fillets. Slice and remove dark portion of fillet. Using four metal skewers, securely skewer through the fillets in fan shape. Broil skinside first until slightly browned, then turn and cook another minute. As soon as fillet is broiled, sprinkle with salt. Remove skewers with twirling motion. place salted fillet in shallow pan. Pat fish with mixture of grated daikon, lemon juice, green onion and ginger. Store in refrigerator until serving time. Cut into 1/2-inch slices straight through as in Variation #1. Combine ingredients for sauce. Garnish with lemon wedges.

May has been boys' month in Japan for many years. This particular fish 'katsuo' is translated as "winner" or "survived through obstacles." On the day of May 5, the dinner table is on parade with this fish. I can appreciate how much spiritual investment parents in Japan had in their young sons to carry on the family name and traditions.

端午の節句

TANGO NO SEKKU *Boys' Festival*

For centuries the Boy's Festival has been celebrated yearly on May 5, or fifth day of the fifth month.

One interpretation of *Tango* is "first day of the horse." Displayed in the festival, the horse implies the attributes of manliness, bravery and strength desirable in boys. The festival also is known as *Shobu-no-Sekku*, a variety of iris whose long, narrow leaves resemble a sword's blade. The festival calls for many leaves of *shobu*. On this day the boys bathe in *shobu-yu*, an iris-leaf hot bath, to instill the warrior spirit in them.

The flag of warrior ancestors, the armor, helmets, leg guards and so forth are brought out and placed in the main room *tokonoma* on a tier of shelves very much like that used March 3 for Hina Matsuri or Girls' Festival Day. Small figurines of famous feudal generals and warriors with miniature swords, armor, helmets, banners, drums, spears and pictures, depicting scenes and characters of well-known feudal stories, also are placed on the tiers.

Koi-no-bori, large balloon carp, are hoisted in the garden on a long pole. Wind fills them out, making them swim in the air like real fish. The carp is known for fighting its way up swift streams and its determination to overcome obstacles. It therefore is held to be a fitting example for growing boys, typifying ambition, strength and will to overcome difficulties. Usually a carp is flown for each son, 15 feet long or more for the eldest, diminishing in size to a small one if there is a baby boy in the family.

The absolutely indispensable dish at Boys' Day is *Chimaki*, glutinous rice soaked in water. Placed in small three-cornered cases made of the bamboo leaves, the rice is steamed until very soft and is eaten with soy-bean flour, mixed with sugar and a bit of salt. Etiquette requires that *Chimaki* be sent to all those from whom gifts are received on the first celebration of Boys' Day.

Another food, *Kashiwa-mochi*, oak-rice cake, is rice flour mixed with hot water and steamed with sweet beans wrapped with it. It is very much like camellia cake, *Tsubaki-mochi* or Cherry-leaf wrapped cake, *Sakura-mochi*, but wrapped in fresh oak leaves and steamed again. The fragrance of mountain oak leaves makes an interesting contrast with cherry or camellia leaves.

SABA ZUSHI *vinegared rice with marinated mackerel*

4 cups rice	1 tbsp sugar
4 cups water	1 tbsp wasabi paste
1/2 cup mirin	
1/2 oz konbu	**Awase-zu:**
1 medium to large mackerel	1/2 cup vinegar
4 tsp salt	3 tbsp sugar
1 cup vinegar	1 tsp salt

Cook rice with water, mirin and konbu, and when cooked, use awase-zu ingredients as sushi recipe. Prepare mackerel into 3 piece fillet manner. Sprinkle with 3 tsp salt and let stand for half hour. Rinse and pat dry. Combine 1 tsp salt, vinegar and sugar and marinate fish fillets for 2 hours. Debone. A pair of tweezers may be necessary. Peel off skin. With wet towel on sudare, place fish with skin side down. Spread wasabi paste evenly on fish. Shape rice length and width of fish fillet and press together. Bring both ends of bamboo mat together and turn. Give good squeeze to form rectangular shape. Also press from both open ends. Let stand unwrapped 10 minutes. Cut 1-inch in width with wet knife. Serve with small dish of shoyu.

Sushi is for the Japanese what the hamburger is for Americans, our national fast food. While it has begaun to capture the imagination and the taste of many Americans, let me say that this method of preserving rice with fish originally was imported to Japan as it now is becoming one of America's favorite imports. During that remarkable flowering of Japanese culture under Hideyoshi, just before the start of the Tokugawa Shogunate, we acquired the beginnings of our Sushi habit from Southeast Asia and particularly from the area which is now Vietnam. While we have refined and added to our original lessons, Sushi owes its origins to cuisines to the south of Japan.

AJI-ZUSHI *vinegared horse mackerel sushi*

6 vinegared horse mackerel	2 tbsp sugar
4 cups rice	6 tbsp vinegar
4 cups plus 2 tbsp water	1 finger ginger
2-1/2 tsp salt	2 leaves beefsteak plant

Wash and drain rice. Bring rice to boil over medium flame. When it reaches boiling point, reduce flame to very low. Allow to stand a few minutes and then turn flame up as water diminishes. Lower flame to simmer. When cooked, turn rice into large shallow pan. Pour over it prepared mixture of salt, sugar and vinegar. Mix with wooden rice paddle using cutting motion. Cut ginger into sengiri. Shred beefsteak plant leaves in same manner. Remove skin from vinegared mackerel. Slice into bite-size pieces. Shape rice into oblong balls, and place mackerel on top. Garnish with ginger and beefsteak plant leaves.

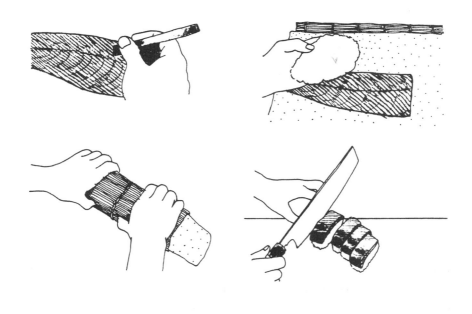

Sushi

NAGINATA *Halberd, Japanese-style*

Naginata, the only martial art exclusively for women, was taught as part of the athletic program in the all-girls high school I attended during World War II. We were told to use *naginata* in combat with enemy soldiers. Thinking back, I find the admonition interesting, since it would have been not only inefficient, but fatal versus guns!

We were all outfitted in white kimono and navy-blue *hakama*, the divided shirt once used by the samurai. Our heads were tied with white *hachimaki*, or head band, and we wore a criss-cross *tasuki*, a tie for the kimono sleeves.

The history of *Naginata* goes back to the thirteenth century, when it first was used by fighting monks to defend the wealth and property of large Buddhist temples. A sword with an extremely long handle, *naginata* became the favorite self-defense weapon for women during the Edo period, 1603-1867. Naturally, the blade was shortened. The handle frequently provided an opportunity for beautifully decorated lacquer work in gold or silver.

Naginata also was used by horseless samurai during the Japanese medieval period.

SUJIME AJI *vinegared horse mackerel*

8 horse mackerel	3 tsp salt
2 cups water	2 tbsp vinegar

Remove heads and tails from mackerel and split in half lengthwise. Bone, soak in mixture of water and add salt and store overnight in refrigerator. After taking fish out of refrigerator, before serving, remove small bones and sprinkle with vinegar. This is the basic preparation to use horse mackerel in early summertime. Increase ingredients for larger servings. Aji, or horse mackerel are plentiful during early summertime. Although horse mackerel is named in the following recipe, mackerel may be substituted.

SHIMESABA *vinegared mackerel sashimi*

1 fresh mackerel	1/4 lb red radish
1 tbsp salt	1 tbsp wasabi powder
1/2 cup vinegar	shoyu

Remove bones. On plate sprinkle 1/3 tbsp salt. Place mackerel fillet skin side down and sprinkle with remaining salt. Allow to stand to 10 minutes. Wrap fillets with plastic wrap and refrigerate 5 to 10 hours. When fillet is well salted and becomes firm, using a tweezer, pick out small bones. Wipe fish using half vinegar. Refrigerate for 20 minutes, then turn skin side up. Peel off thin skin from head side. Using very sharp knife slice into 1/2-inch thick oblong shapes. Garnish with red radish, cut into matchstick size. Serve with wasabi and shoyu.

NORIMAKE ZUSHI *vinegared rice wrapped with nori*

4 cups rice	1-1/2 tbsp mirin
2 eggs	1 oz kanpyo
9-1/2 tbsp dashi	10 shiitake
3-1/3 tbsp shoyu	7 sheets of nori
3/4 tsp salt	1 lb spinach
2-1/2 tsp sugar	1 kamaboko
2 tbsp sake or dry sherry	1 oz red pickled ginger

Cook and season rice as for sushi rice. Beat eggs and add 1-1/2 tbsp dashi, 1 tsp shoyu, 1/4 tsp salt and 1-1/2 tsp sugar. Fry in square skillet making omelette 1/3-inch thick. Cut into pieces a little smaller than little finger. Soften shiitake in enough water to cover, season by boiling in 3 tbsp dashi, 2 tbsp shoyu, 2 tbsp sake or dry sherry, 1-1/2 tbsp mirin and 1 tsp sugar. Season well, drain and cut into thin strips. Save sauce. Soften kanpyo in salt water 30 to 40 minutes and bring to boil in same water. Add 5 tbsp dashi, 1/2 tsp salt and kanpyo to sauce used for shiitake. Cook until flavored, drain and cut into lengths measuring width of nori. Cook spinach in boiling, salted water until tender. Rinse in cold water and gently squeeze out water. Sprinkle with 1 tbsp shoyu and mix well, gently squeeze again. Slice fish into rolls 1/2-inch in diameter and lengths that measure width of seaweed. Cut red pickled ginger into extremely tiny strips. Hold nori over burner and remove when crisp. Place sheet of nori on sudare. Place rice on nori, leaving 2-inch gap. Center ingredients, include fish cake, spinach, shiitake, kanpyo and egg. Using little of each ingredient, roll seaweed as illustrated. Make sure grip is firm in step shown in illustration. When finished rolling, give gentle squeeze, then unroll mat. Slice in inch-wide rounds. Serve with cut side up.

SUSHI SANDWICHES

3 cups rice	4 tbsp dashi
1 small cucumber	1 tbsp plus 1 tsp shoyu
2 tbsp vinegar	3 eggs
1 tsp salt	2 slices boneless ham
6 tsp sugar	on oshiwaku* (molding box)
1/3 oz dried kanpyo	1 oz red pickled ginger
1/3 oz shiitake	6 sheets nori
	sake or dry sherry

Cook rice for sushi. Slice cucumber crosswise 1/8-inch thick. Salt and allow to stand until soft. Gently squeeze out liquid and place cucumber in mixture of vinegar, 2/3 tsp salt, 2 tsp sugar, marinate until ready to use. Boil dried kanpyo until cooked. Soften shiitake in enough cold water to cover. Mix 1-1/2 tbsp dashi, 1 tbsp shoyu, 2 tsp sugar and bring to boil. Add shiitake continuing to cook until well flavored. Mince shiitake after removing from sauce. Mix with shiitake and gently squeeze liquid out. Beat eggs, add remaining dashi, 1/3 tsp

*Available in Japanese hardware store. *Continued on next page*

salt, 2 tsp sugar, 1 tsp shoyu and mix well. Fry in square skillet making an omelette 1/3-inch thick. Slice across width of square 1/4-inch thick and diagonally from top to bottom. Slice red pickled ginger in fine strips. Divide cooked rice in 6 portions. Mold and press half of portion of rice in box. On rice, place slice of ham, spread thinly with mustard, place layer of cucumber on mustard and place other half of rice on top. Press and mold. Remove and wrap in sheet of nori crisped (by holding over a burner for a minute). Make another ham sandwich. In this manner, make 2 shiitake and kanpyo sandwiches by placing between rice and minced shiitake and kanpyo and 2 of egg and ginger sandwiches. Cut them into 5 or 6 pieces per sandwich. Serve them on a large plate.

NIGIRI ZUSHI

4 cups rice	1/2 cup water
3 eggs	10 medium prawns
1 tbsp sugar	1 cuttlefish
1 tsp shoyu	1/4 cup snapper fillet
1/3 tsp salt	1/4 cup tuna fillet
1-1/2 tbsp mirin	1/4 cup flounder or sea bass fillet
2 tbsp dashi	1/4 cup salmon fillet
1/2 tsp oil	1/8 cup abalone meat
2 tbsp wasabi	1 sheet asakusa nori, cut into
1/2 cup amazu shoga	1/4-inch ribbons
2 tbsp vinegar	Shoyu for dipping

Prepare rice for sushi following master sushi meshi recipe. Do not refrigerate. Cover container with damp cloth to prevent drying and hardening. In small bowl, beat eggs well, adding sugar, shoyu, salt, mirin, dashi and mixing well. Make Atsuyaki Tamago like recipe on page 117. Cool before slicing 2-1/3 x 1-1/2 x 1/4 inch pieces. These slices will drape over rice ovals. The sea food must be absolutely fresh. Boil prawns according to ebi no amazu method. Chill. Remove skewer and shell prawns. Then slit underside, open flat and set aside. Remove legs from cuttlefish and remove 2 layers of thin skin of body and cut into side of Atsuyaki Tamago. Cut snapper, tuna, flounder, sea bass, salmon fillet and abalone meat in the same manner. To make nigiri-zushi, follow illustration. Size of rice oval measures 1-1/2 inches long. Give good squeeze to the rice when in the palm of your hand. Use wasabe only with fish. Spread small amount on the underside of each fish fillet, drape over rice oval, press together. Use asakasa-nori strips to give 'tied' look to Atsuyaki Tamago and cuttlefish. Arrange Nigiri zushi on wooden tray or large plate, garnished with amazu-shoga. Serve shoyu in small dish for dipping. *When serving guests, atsuyaki tamago-zushi always is served first.*

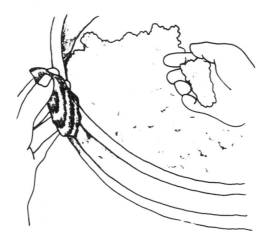

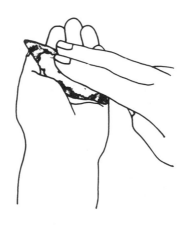

Nigiri sushi

SUKIYAKI

Soup stock:

2 cups water	2/3 lb Chinese cabbage
10 inch konbu (for seasoning	2 bunches shirataki, available
soup stock only)	also in cans
1/4 cup soybeans	2 squares tofu
2/3 cup shoyu	1/3 lb celery
1/2 cup sugar	2/3 lb bamboo shoots
10 stalks green onion	2 lb beef, sliced bacon-thin

Mix water, soybeans and konbu to make soup stock and allow to stand 10 hours. Add shoyu and sugar, bring to boil. Remove from fire and strain. Cut green onions at slanted angle 1/4-inch lengths. Wash Chinese cabbage and drain. Wash and cut shirataki into 3-inch lengths. Cut tofu into 12 squares. Slice celery into thin strips. Cut bamboo shoots into thin slices by cutting crosswise. Arrange vegetables colorfully on large plate. Put pieces of suet into skillet. When melted add some of each vegetable starting with those taking longest to cook. Brown them. Add some meat on top of vegetables and add soup stock. Last of all, add shirataki and tofu. Do not put in all the foods at once. Adjust seasoning to taste by adding more shoyu or sugar. This is to be eaten as it is cooked. More food is added when there is room in skillet. Allow 1 egg per person when serving. Individuals break and mix egg at the table. Dip sukiyaki in egg and eat with rice.

In Japanese history, meat-eating has existed ever since the very first inhabitants in Yamato, an early name for Japan. After the 7th Century and the adaptation of Buddhist teachings, however, the Emperor Teumu, the ruler or Yamato, forbade anyone from consuming meat of ox, horse, dog, monkey and chicken. However, animals not on the list were hunted by many tribesmen and farmer. In the mid-13 century there were many "momonuji-ya" or animal meat restaurants in Edo.

Sukiyaki is enjoyed world over by people as representative of Japanese cuisine. It is, however, recent in Japaneses history because the Meiji Restoration way of adapting Western culture was by eating from the very same pot without strict Japanese or newly-learned Western table manners. Sukiyaki was designed to kindle friendships and conversation. In the Meiji period the sukiyaki house was called *"Gyu Nabe Ya"* or "Beef Pot Restaurant". Gyu Nabe restaurants became as popular as cafes in France as gathering places for the young and seekers of new ideas.

As a general rule, Western meat cooking hardly requires any sugar. When I demonstrated sukiyaki to some Westerners, one of my guests asked with a bewildered look in her eyes whether I was making some kind of desert dish or cake. I am sure she was quite puzzled the way I was putting sugar onto thin slices of beef. When I finally added some shoyu she looked somewhat relieved. I will never forget the expression on her face.

TENDON *tempura on rice*

    4 tbsp mirin
    4 tbsp sake (rice wine) or dry sherry
    2 tbsp shoyu
    2 tbsp sugar
    4 cups cooked rice

Bring to boil mirin and sake until it becomes thick. Add shoyu and sugar, bring to second boil and remove from burner. Into deep bowl with cover, place individual servings of rice. Dip fried foods quickly in and out of hot sauce and place on top of rice. Pour 1 tbsp sauce over fried foods. Cover and serve.

I serve tendon for lunch whenever I cook tempura the evening before. The literal translation of "ten" is an abbreviation of tempura and "don" is the short form of donburi (large container).

ABU DAMA DONBURI *fried soybean curd and onion with egg over rice*

    4 cups cooked rice
    4 squares aburage
    1 medium onion
    1/8 lb green beans
    3/4 cup dashi

    1/4 cup shoyu
    1/4 cup mirin
    1 tsp sugar
    5 eggs

Cut aburage into 4 triangles. Cut onion in half, then slice very thin. Clean. Cut green beans julienne style. Parboil and set aside. In small pot, combine dashi, shoyu, mirin and sugar. Bring to boil to make cooking sauce. Divide all ingredients into 5 equal parts. In small skillet or oyako-nabe (mother and child pan), put 1/5 of cooking sauce and 1/5 of ingredients. Bring to boil before turning flame low. Cook until onion is wilted. Add 1 beaten egg. Be careful not to stir like scrambled eggs since a velvety texture is desired. When egg is almost cooked, remove and slide onto bowl of rice. Repeat 5 times. Cover and serve.

FUKAGAWA-DONBURI *clam and carrots with egg over rice*

    1/2 lb clam meat
    1-1/2 tsp sake
    1-1/2 tsp shoyu
    1 medium carrot
    1 medium green pepper

Sauce:
    3/4 cup dashi

    1/4 cup shoyu
    1/4 cup mirin
    1 tsp sugar

    5 eggs
    4 cups cooked rice
    4 tbsp green seaweed

Marinate clam meat with sake and shoyu and set aside. Cut carrots and green pepper into sengiri. **Sauce:** Combine dashi, shoyu, mirin and sugar and bring to a

Continued on next page

boil to make cooking sauce. Divide all ingredients into 5 equal parts. In small skillet or oyako-nabe put 1/5 cooking sauce and 1/5 of ingredients. Bring to boil, then turn flame down to low. Cook 2 minutes until all vegetables are cooked. Add 1 beaten egg. Be careful not to stir like scrambled eggs since velvety texture is desired. When the egg is almost cooked, remove from fire, slide on top of bowl of rice and sprinkle with aonori-nori, green seaweed. Cover and serve.

MUSHI-URI

Another cue of summer was the visible signs of construction for *Ennichi-yo-mise* or vendor festival stalls, as one passed by *Kishibojin* Temple.

I made certain that particular vendors were there, and I had already made my selections returning home from school in the afternoon. Of particular importance was the mushi-uri or cricket seller. On the prescribed festival day I begged older family members to accompany me to the temple to purchase the merchandise. I ran ahead to the *mushi-uri* stall, waiting for whomever accompanied me. They always knew where to find me!

The miniature bamboo cage for the cricket came in every imaginable size and shape, constructed of very fine split bamboo, match-stick size. I must have accumulated ten or more such cages from each summer.

I made my selection with the recommendation of the *mushi-uri*. Some were champions of sound, and some, alas, became deaf-mutes when we got them home and hung the cages under the eaves. But most of them sang with the sweetest of melody. My memories of the past are saying it might have been my imagination, but my favorites were always *suzu-mushi,* or bell cricket and lin-lin-ling.

The cricket chorus seemed to stir gentle breezes on hot summer nights. I don't recall much singing in the daylight, so I guess they partied only at night, happy with each day's diet of cucumber and egg plant slices.

Just as summer vacation was nearing its end at the end of August, we held a ceremony in the crickets' honor in the garden to thank them for the pleasure of keeping us cool. That night we opened the small cage door to allow them to return to nature, being careful not to step on the cricket, now free. With a paper lantern in our hands and with a good-bye song, we guided them into a soft grassy area. The crickets treated us continually with symphonic sound from the garden into October. I recognized each key they sang, and it mingles with my memories of summers of yesteryear. The smell of the carbide lamps on the *mushi-uri* stalls still seems to tickle my nostrils as my mind hears the special notes of the *mushi.*

HIRAME NO HAKATA OSHI KIMIZU KAKE *flounder, pressed, with egg yolk dressing*

3/4 lb fresh flounder	2 egg yolks
1 tsp salt	1 tbsp sugar
1 tbsp sake	1/3 tsp salt
1 cucumber	2 tsp mirin
1 tsp salt	3 tbsp vinegar
1 oz fresh ginger	1 tsp shoyu
2 oz beansprouts	2 tbsp dashi

Cut flounder fillet into 1/8-inch slices, arrange on plate and sprinkle with salt and sake. Slice cucumber into very thin pieces. Sprinkle with salt and when salt is wet, squeeze out water. Cut ginger, hari-shoga style, and soak in cup of water to bleach. Drain and dry of moisture. Using Oshiwaku, lined with waxpaper, cover bottom with flounder fillet. Then later with cucumber, ginger and beansprouts. Repeat layers 3 times before covering with wax paper. Press with oshiwaku cover. Ingredients are enough to make two sandwiches, 5-1/2 by 2-1/2 inches. In top of double broiler beat egg yolks. Combine with yolks, the sugar, salt, mirin, vinegar, shoyu and dashi. Blend well and place pan on double boiler. Using weed spoon, stir continuously until slightly thickened. Remove from heat and allow to cool. Slice pressed flounder in 5 or 6 pieces. Serve with egg yolk sauce over.

OHAGI *sweet rice wrapped in auki beans, soybean flour and sesame seeds*

1-1/2 lb mochi rice	1-1/2 cup sugar
1-1/4 tsp salt	1/2 cup kinako, roasted
cups + extra cold water	soybean flour
1 tsp + 1/5 tsp + 1/8 tsp salt	
1-1/3 cups azuki beans	1/2 cup black sesame seeds, roasted and coarsely ground

Wash sweet rice and soak in 5 cups water at least 5 hours. Drain. Place dishcloth on steamer rack. Spread rice evenly. Steam for 1/2 hour over high flame. Turn into bowl and pour boiling water over rice combined with 1 tsp salt. Cover tight. Steam inside bowl 20 minutes. Wash azuki beans and place in large pot with 5 cups water. Bring to boil. Add 1/2 cup cold water each time it reaches boiling point, repeating 3 or 4 times, until all beans are at bottom of pot. Pour out bean-cooking water except for 1-1/2 inches water to cover beans. Cook with medium heat 1 hour. Turn beans and water into blender. Grind 2 to 3 minutes. Use large mesh strainer to catch skins from beans. Discard skins and strain through cloth to drain water from bean paste. Combine bean paste with sugar and 1/5 tsp salt. Simmer and stir constantly with wooden spoon until thick and of even consistency. Place well-wrung-out wet dishcloth on palm of hand. Spread 3 tbsp sweet beanpaste. Place in center 2-1/2 tbsp

Continued on next page

rice. Wrap rice with sweet bean paste into an oblong shape by closing palm of hand. Make 5. Then reverse procedure by wrapping rice around bean paste. On well-wrung-out wet dishcloth in palm of hand, place 3 tbsp rice and 2-1/2 tbsp sweet bean paste. Shape as others and make 10. Mix kinako with 1 tsp salt. Pat 5 with kinako mixture, remaining five with coarsely-ground black sesame seeds. Arrange 3 different colored pastries on laquered tray with serving dish with nanden sprigs.

The ladies in Japan have great love affairs with ohagi. It is a party time must for ladies' gatherings. As I recall, it is served on ancestor days, birthdays, the first day of spring and tea ceremonies. Made of steamed glutinous rice coated with various sweet stuff, it is a good contrast to green tea.

AWAYUKI *powdered snow jello*

1 stick kanten (agar-agar)   1/2 tsp lemon extract
2 cups water   1/4 tsp salt
1-1/4 cups sugar   few mint leaves
2 egg whites

Soak kanten in water for half hour. Then cook until kanten melts. Add sugar and cook on slow flame 15 minutes. Beat egg white until 1/4 tea salt stiff. Fold into warm syrup of Kanten. Add lemon extract. Pour into 10 small molds or square nagashi-bako. Garnish with mint leaves.

Summer

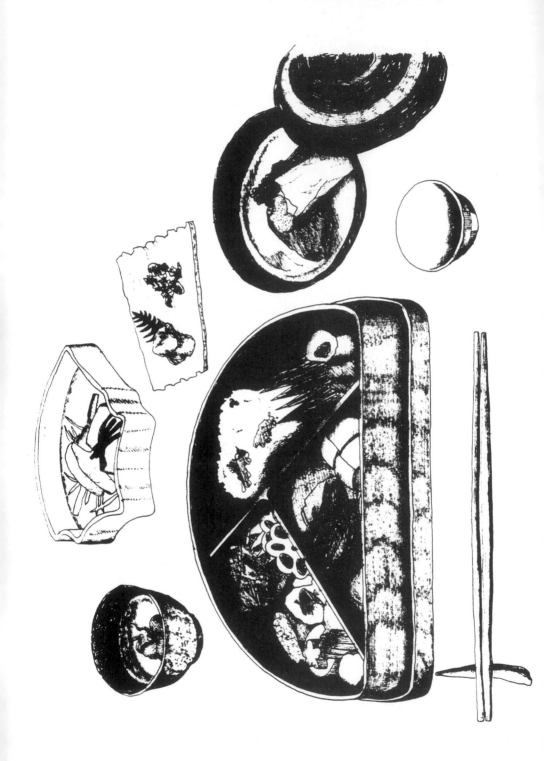

A smile comes to my face as I remember a visit to my aunt one early summer's evening.

My mother, in her cheery, light-hearted voice, directed my attention to a small, flowered cucumber at the dinner table, the size of one's large finger with tiny, yellow flowers on the tips, placed on an almost white, blue Seiji porcelain dish. The cucumber glistened like an ornament carved of deep green jade. The contrast of the colors were in such harmony I felt this epitomized the art, or, shall I say, the heart of Japanese cooking.

This arrangement possessed all the ingredients of entertaining. With this gentle suggestion, our hostess brought us news of the season. I felt, somehow, a gentle summer evening breeze brush my hair although we were behind a shoji screen, seated inside.

This image of the tiny flowered cucumber made a very vivid impression on my heart. It is, to this day, one of my most cherished memories of childhood in Japan.

NATSU NO MAKU NO UCHI BENTO *summertime lunchbox for entertaining guests*

MENU:

Maguro no sashimi to hakuhatsu daikon *tuna fish sashimi with white-haired daikon*

Kyuri to kurag e no sunomono *cucumber and jellyfish vinegared salad*

Shiromi zakama no teriyaki *glazed whitemeat fish, using any fish glaze cooking method (see index)*

Toriniku no tatsutaage to peaman no suage *deep-fried chicken and pepper*

Sayaingen iri dashi tamago maki *wrapped omelet with green beans*

Nasu no dengaku *eggplant with miso sauce*

Ingen mame no amani *honeyed kidney beans (in Japan, this is often store-bought)*

Kyuri no nukazuke *pickled cucumber in rice bran (see index)*

Nameko to tofu no akadashi *nameko mushroom and tofu miso soup*

Maku no uchi gohan *pressed rice ball with black sesame seeds*

Most foodstuffs are served chilled or cold in summertime entertaining. This lunchbox is prepared ahead so the hostess will be able to engage her guests. Preparation starts with the sashimi, followed by miso dashi. Marinate chicken for tatsutaage and fish for teriyaki. The eggplant should be sliced next and sauce made for this dish. Vegetables should then be cut for salad. Cook the omelet and shape rice balls. Have pickled cucumber and honeyed kidney beans ready.

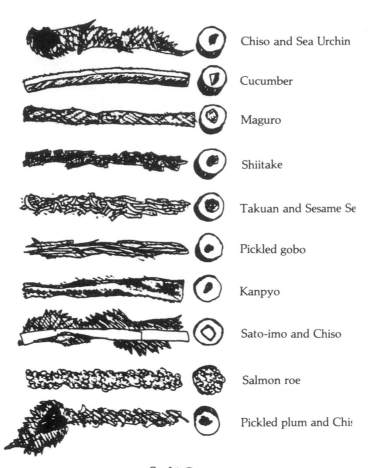

Chiso and Sea Urchin

Cucumber

Maguro

Shiitake

Takuan and Sesame Se

Pickled gobo

Kanpyo

Sato-imo and Chiso

Salmon roe

Pickled plum and Chi

Sushi Centers

Haran or Sasa-no-ha

MAGURO NO SASHIMI TO HAKUKATSU DAIKON

  3/4 lb fresh tuna fish
  4 inches daikon
  6 chiso leaves
  1 tbsp wasabi powder
  3/4 tbsp water

Cut tuna fish in 2-inch wide slices, 3/8 inches thick. Cut daikon in very thin sengiri and soak in iced water until serving. It should resemble white hair, thus *hakukatsu,* or white-haired. Make paste from wasabi powder and water. Using chiso leaves, arrange tuna fish, daikon and wasabi paste on top.

TORINIKU TATSUTA NAGE TO PEAMAN NO SUAGE
deep-fried chicken with green pepper

  3/4 lb chicken thigh fillets   1 green pepper
  1-1/2 tsp salt   1 egg white
  2 tbsp shoyu   1/4 cup cornstarch
  1 tbsp sake   oil for deep frying

For directions on cutting chicken fillets, see index. Marinate chicken thigh fillets with 1/2 tsp salt, shoyu, sake. Set aside 15 minutes. Cut green pepper into 8 pieces. Beat egg white until foamy. Dip seasoned chicken thigh fillets in egg white, dust with cornstarch. Heat oil to 360 degrees F. Deep-fry green pepper until bright green in color, Drain. Sprinkle with 1 tsp salt. Bring oil temperature to 370 degrees F. Deep-fry dusted chicken pieces until golden brown. High temperature for deep-frying is necessary to retain crispness of egg white and cornstarch coating.

KYURI TO KURAGE NO SUNOMONO *cucumber and jellyfish vinegared salad*

  1 cucumber
  1-1/5 tsp salt
  1 cup water
  4 oz jellyfish, dried
  1/2 tsp vinegar
  1 tsp sugar

Cut cucumber in half lengthwise. Then cut in small sangiri style. Soak in water with 1 tsp salt. When slightly wilted, remove, squeeze out excess water, and set aside. Wash dried jellyfish. Soak in water 15 minutes until salty taste is removed. Place jellyfish in colander and pour boiling water over. Cut in 1-inch thick strips. Combine vinegar, sugar, 1/5 tsp salt and mix well. Toss cucumber and jellyfish with sauce. Chill until serving time.

SAYAINGEN IRI DASHI MAKI TAMAGO *wrapped omelet with green beans*

1/4 cup dashi	1/2 tbsp cornstarch
1/2 tsp shoyu	3 eggs, beaten
1/4 tsp salt	2 medium green beans
1 tsp sugar	1 tbsp oil
1 tsp mirin	cotton pad
Special equipment: *sudare*	

In bowl, combine dashi, shoyu, salt, sugar, mirin and cornstarch. Mix well, adding beaten egg a little at a time. Wash green beans, remove strings and ends and boil until tender but crisp. Heat omelet pan and oil well with cotton pad. Pour 1/3 egg mixture into pan. When surface begins to harden, place cooked beans horizontally across middle. Lift up, roll away edge of the omelet nearest you. Wipe skillet with oiled cotton pad, pour another 1/3 egg mixture into pan. When almost half cooked, roll wrapped omelet toward you. Wipe skillet with oiled cotton pad again. Cook remaining egg mixture and repeat rolling away. After removing omelet from pan, roll in sudare to shape the omelet. When cool, cut in 3/3-inch pieces.

NASU NO DENGAKU *eggplant with soybean paste sauce*

3 Japanese eggplants	1 tsp mirin
1 tsp salt	2 tsp sugar
2 tbsp oil	1 tbsp chiso leaves, minced
2 tbsp white miso	

Cut eggplant across in 1-inch thick slices. Place in water with salt to bleach. Drain and pat dry. Heat skillet with oil. Saute both sides of eggplant until soft enough for skewer to pierce it. Do not stir. Remove from skillet. Cool. In small saucepan combine miso, mirin and sugar. Simmer until shiny. Coat one side of eggplant with miso sauce. Garnish with minced chiso leaves.

INGEN MAME NO AMANI *honeyed kidney beans*

15 oz can cooked kidney beans
1 cup brown sugar
2 tbsp honey
dash of salt

Bring kidney beans to boil with liquid from can. Add half the brown sugar and simmer 10 minutes. Add remaining brown sugar, honey and dash of salt. Simmer until sugar is dissolved. Cool beans in cooking liquid.

NAMEKO TO TOFU AKADASHI *nameko mushroom and tofu miso soup*

> 1/2 can nameko mushrooms
> 1 tofu
> 4 cups dashi
> 1/2 cup red miso
> parsley sprigs
> Special equipment: *misokoshi*

Bring dashi to boil. Use small meshed misokoshi to strain miso into pot. Add mushrooms and 1/2-inch cubes of tofu. Bring to boil immediately. Serve garnished with parsley sprigs.

TANABATA or HOSHI MATSURI

Star or Weaving Loom Festival

I can almost recapture the summer evenings of those special stars. July 7 is the night the Weaver, princess star, *Shukujo*, is supposed to meet the herd boy star, *Kengyu*, with the help of the bridge of magpies, *Kasasagi-no-Hashi*. The galaxy of the Milky Way is naturally thought of as a heavenly river and the magpies form the bridge with their spread wings. On this night the two brilliant stars on opposite sides of the river of heaven meet in happy reunion. In the fairy tale the stars represent Man and Woman. For the festival, a freshly-cut bamboo tree from a nearby garden is placed on the veranda in a tub of sand. It is there as part of the Milky Way gazing and the bamboo is part of the legend.

The evening of July 6, with the help of grandmother, I would hang on the bamboo tree limbs the fair weather wish paper dolls, or *Teru-Teru-buzu*. These dolls ensure a fair weather blessing for the once-a-year rendezvous for the princess and prince.

While the festival really began well after sundown July 7, in my little childhood world the festival began early in the morning, especially when I knew the stars would not be washed away by teardrops of rain. Hearing grandmother's voice beckoning me toward the garden, I slipped into my wooden geta and skipped through the lawn grass, wet with morning dew, feeling its tickling sensation on my bare feet. As I approached the morning glories, their trumpet-like bases holding the morning dew were just beginning to open. As I tilted the flowers.

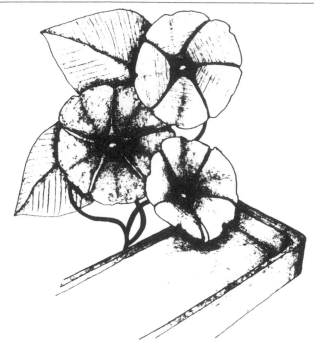

to gather enough dew for the ink stones to make ink for the calligraphy, the dew was transformed by the sun's rays into little pearls as the drops rolled out of the morning glories and into my container. We composed the finest possible poems for *Tanabata*, reverently brushed in our best calligraphy onto the gaily-colored paper strips, the *tanzaku*.

Since the weaver princess is an accomplished artist, anyone wishing to emulate her in the gentle arts needs to make an offering to celebrate this day. Fruits of many kinds and threads of five colors—green, red, yellow, white, purple—are among the offerings on the tray. These colors are like the traditional five spiritual root organs of Buddhism which are faith, energy, memory, meditation and wisdom. As a result, the Japanese commonly use five for everything.

The house is readied with festival lanterns. The harp and flute, *koto* and *shakuhachi*, are laid out to suggest the harmony of music, the *koto*, the feminine, the *shakuhachi*, the masculine. Together they are a melodic duet as they are often played together.

The first dish of the season for this evening meal was a small, sweet, fresh water fish called *ayu*, something like a brook trout. It was prepared with salt and broiled on a stick, *shio yaki* style. Next, tofu was served, floating in a bowl of iced water. Each piece of tofu was dipped in a mixture of shoyu, roasted and ground sesame seeds, green onion and minced ginger.

The last to come was buckwheat noodles, *zarusoba*, piled high in their bamboo basket container. *Zarusoba* was accompanied by a sauce made of dashi, shoyu, sake and mirin. The entire meal was accompanied by plenty of tea made from roasted barley grain, called *mugi-cha*.

The morning after the star gazing, the bamboo tree was taken to a stream to float away on the current. The magpies have separated their wings and flown away.

O BON

O *bon* literally translates as honorable server or tray, but also refers to the Bon Festival or "Feast of Lanterns." Buddhists call it "Soul's Day," and it occurs annually three days in July on the 13th, 14th and 15th.

My childhood memories of Obon were filled with painted and decorated paper lanterns hung across the family altar. In our home, we had a separate room for this, but in most homes it is simply a special place in the family living room. Obon was the time when the family priest from the temple visited our home to chant the sutras in the altar room.

An additional wooden table was set on the altar for Obon with all sorts of offerings — vegetables, fruits, melons, etc. Fish, fowl and meat, however, were not part of the offerings. Special vegetarian dishes were cooked and served on lotus leaves.

My grandmother told me Obon is the time of year to honor the ancestors' spirits when they pay a three-day visit to their former terrestrial home. To help welcome the ancestral spirits, I helped prepare *O-mukae-bi*, or welcome fire. This blaze was made on a clay dish in front of the main entrance to light the way of the ancestral spirits to our home.

An essential part of Obon was a bull and a horse created from eggplant and white melon. I helped grandmother to create them, so that when the spiritual visitors ended their three-days' visit, they rode the eggplant bull and the white melon horse back to their celestial abode.

The evening of the third day of Obon, the eggplant bull and the white melon horse, together with other offerings, were gathered and placed on a small wooden boat illuminated with a paper lantern on the bow. These were taken to the ocean. It was my task to remove my geta and wade into the water with the boat, its offerings and spiritual passengers. With the lantern lit, I placed the boat afloat in the waves of the sea, darkened by the night. There our boat joined many others set afloat by other families, the waves gently pushing the ancestral spirits toward *Meido*, the Celestial World of Darkness. We stood on the seashore watching the boats drift seaward, lights bobbing with the crests and cradles of the waves, the darkness of sea and sky blending, broken only by lantern and star light.

MAKU NO UCHI GOHAN *pressed rice ball with black sesame seeds*

> 4 cups cooked rice
> 1/4 cup roasted black sesame seeds
> salt
> Special equipment: *maku-no-uchi*

Use maku no uchi to form rice balls, sprinkle with dash of salt. Garnish with roasted black sesame seeds.

KOGORI DORI *amber chicken*

1-1/2 to 2 cups dashi of	2/3 lb cubed chicken
chicken bone and pork bone	1/2 cup water chestnut, cubed
green onion	1 tbsp shoyu
crushed ginger	1 tsp salt
2 tbsp sake	2 tsp sugar
1 kanten	

Make dashi of chicken and pork bone, green onion and crushed ginger. Add sake while still boiling. Strain dashi. Soak kanten in water, squeeze, tear in small pieces, add to dashi and bring to boil. When kanten is dissolved, add chicken and water chestnut with seasonings. Skim. Place chicken and dashi in a mold or deep dish. Refrigerate and serve shilled.

HAKATA TOMATO *tomato and egg sandwich*

6 slices day-old, thinly sliced bread
1 4 oz tomato (large)
2 eggs
1/3 tsp salt
1/2 tsp sugar
1 tbsp cooked green peas

Peel tomato and slice 1/4-inch thick. Beat 2 eggs, add salt, sugar and mix well. Saute, stirring constantly, to paste-like consistency. Remove from fire and add green peas. Divide egg and tomato to make 2 triple-deck sandwiches. Place tomato on top of egg between 2 slices of bread, add more egg and tomato and additional slice of bread. Wrap in damp cloth and place under heavy object — between cutting boards weighted with tea kettle filled with water — 15 minutes. Cut off edges and slice into small sandwiches.

TOMATO ZUME *stuffed cherry tomato*

1/2 cup cooked crab meat, fresh or canned
2 tbsp vinegar
1 finger grated ginger
1 tbsp sugar
2/3 tsp salt
1-1/2 tsp shoyu
cherry tomatoes

Mix together crab meat, vinegar, ginger, sugar, salt and shoyu. Scoop out seeds from cherry tomatoes. Stuff cavity with crab meat mixture and serve chilled.

GYUUNIKU NEGIMAKI *steak and scallion rolls*

1/4 lb sirloin steak, sliced 1/4-inch thick
2 scallions, including green stem

Teriyaki sauce:
1-1/2 tbsp mirin or substitute 1-1/4 tbsp dry
sherry and 1-1/2 tsp sugar
1-1/2 tbsp shoyu
1 tbsp dashi

Place steak between sheets of waxed paper. With meat pounder, pound to 1/8-inch thickness. Cut steak in half crosswise. Arrange strip of scallion down length of each piece of meat. Starting with wide side of meat, roll pieces in tight cylinders. Secure end with toothpicks. Preheat broiler or hibachi. With chopsticks or tongs, dip rolls in teriyaki sauce, broil 3 inches from heat 3 minutes. Dip again in sauce and broil other side one minute. Remove toothpicks, trim ends of rolls with sharp knife, and cut rolls in 1-inch pieces. Stand each piece on end to expose scallions and serve.

TORINIKU NO ZERII YOSE *chicken aspic mold*

2 tbsp gelatin	15 cups water
1 tsp salt	4 tbsp water
2 tbsp sake	1 cucumber
1 stalk green onion	salad oil
2 pieces thin ginger slices	1 lemon wedge
1/2 lb chicken meat	5 lettuce leaves

Combine water, salt, sake, green onion, ginger slices and bring to boil. Add chicken meat. Turn flame to low and cook 15 minutes. Remove chicken meat from cooking broth and slice in very thin pieces. Soak gelatin in water. Strain cooking broth, then add gelatin mixture. Slice cucumber in very thin pieces. Coat a deep bowl or mold with salad oil. Pour 2 cups of cooking broth in the bowl. When jellied slightly, place lemon wedge in the center and fill sides with cucumber slices. Line cucumber slices alternately with chicken meat slices. Gently pour over remaining cooking broth. Repeat until all ingredients are used. Refrigerate 4 to 5 hours. To serve, turn the mold over. Serve on lettuce leaf bed.

GYUUNIKU NO KAORI MAKI *beef-wrapped celery*

1 lb beef sirloin	2 tbsp cooking oil
1 tbsp ± 2 tsp shoyu	
1 tbsp mirin	**Sauce:**
3 stalks celery	3 tbsp sugar
1 lemon	2 tbsp shoyu
3 tbsp sugar	2 tbsp sake

Slice beef in thin slices. Marinate in 1 tbsp shoyu and mirin. Wash celery and parboil 5 minutes. Cut in 1/2-inch wide sticks. Sprinkle with 2 tsp shoyu. Spread marinated beef on cutting board and place 2 pieces of celery in center of beef. Roll up, using toothpick to secure. Slice lemon in thin wedges. Dust with sugar. Heat skillet with oil. Brown beef rolls. When cooked, remove. In same skillet, add sauce ingredients. Simmer. When thickened, return cooked beef rolls. Stir, cut in 1-1/2 inch pieces. Serve with sugared lemon wedges.

MUSHI DORI NO SUNOMONO *steamed chicken salad*

1/4 lb chicken breast meat	1 tbsp vinegar
2 tsp sake or dry sherry	6 red radishes
1-1/4 tsp salt	
1 medium size cucumber	**Sanbaizu (seasoning):**
1 stalk celery	6 tbsp rice vinegar
1/8 lb lotus root	3 tbsp sugar
2 cups water	2 tsp shoyu

Place chicken breast meat in soup dish. Sprinkle with sake and 1/4 tsp salt. Let stand 10 minutes. Place in steamer and cook with high steam 8 minutes. Remove and shred. Keep in cooked juices. Wash and peel cucumber, leaving some green skin on to give color to finished dish. Slice in very thin round pieces. Sprinkle with 1 tsp salt. Cut celery in 1-inch pieces first, then slice legnthwise 1/4-inch wide. Skin and clean lotus root. Cut to same size as cucumber. Cook in water and vinegar 5 minutes. Drain. Wash and clean radishes. Cut to matchstick size. Combine in bowl: cucumber, celery, lotus root and half of red radish with 1/4 portion of sanbaizu. Squeeze out liquid gently. Add steamed chicken meat. Mix well with another 1/4 portion of sanbaizu. Garnish with remaining matchstick-cut radishes and pour remaining sanbaizu over ingredients. For Western style meal, serve in large bowl, or in small individual dishes for first course of Japanese meal.

EBI TO KYURI NO SUNOMONO *cucumber and prawn, or crab meat, vinegared salad*

1 lb cucumber	**Sauce:**
1 tsp salt	3 tbsp vinegar
1/4 lb prawns or crab meat, cooked	1 tsp salt
4 tbsp vinegar	1 tbsp sugar
1 tbsp sugar	
1 finger fresh ginger	

Slice cucumber lengthwise in quarters. Scoop out seeds with little spoon. Slice crosswise in 1/4-inch pieces. Salt and mix, let stand 20 minutes or until soft. Mix again and squeeze out water gently. Stir in 1 tbsp vinegar and mix well (this is called "vinegar wash"). Drain and squeeze liquid out gently. Slice prawns to size of cucumbers or shredded crabmeat. Mix 3 tbsp vinegar, 1 tsp salt, 1 tbsp sugar. Add prawns or crab. Slice ginger root paper-thin lengthwise, then cut in *hari shoga* style. Leave in water until bleached, drain. Arrange cucumbers and meat in individual small bowls, garnish with ginger. Combine sauce ingredients and pour over salad.

TORI TO KYURI NO PEANUTS SHOYU AE *peanut sauce over chicken and cucumber*

1/2 lb chicken meat	2 cucumbers
4 cups water	4 tbsp peanut butter
1 tsp salt	4 tbsp shoyu
1 tsp sake	2 tbsp vinegar
2 stalks green onion, 1 minced	1 tsp new pepper oil
2 ginger slices	

Bring to boil water with salt, sake, 1 green onion and ginger slices. Cook chicken meat over medium flame 10 minutes. Remove and cool. Slice into small bite-size pieces. Save water for dashi later. Cut cucumber in half lengthwise, then into thin slices. Make cucumber bed on serving platter, arrange chicken meat on top. Refrigerate. Combine peanut butter, shoyu, vinegar, sugar, hot oil and 1 minced green onion. Stir until very creamy. Serve cold cucumber and chicken with this sauce.

MOYASHI TO NINJIN NO NANBAN *Nanban style beansprouts and carrot salad*

1 lb moyashi
2 medium carrots

Sauce:
2-1/2 tbsp shoyu
1/2 tsp sugar

1 tbsp sake
2 tsp sesame oil
1/2 tsp green onion, minced
1 tbsp white sesame seeds,
    roasted and chopped
1/4 tsp red pepper, minced

Wash and clean moyashi. Remove tail-like roots and cook in boiling water 1 minute. Rinse in cold water, drain and set aside. Cut carrots in half, then slice into thin pieces lengthwise. Cook 2 to 3 minutes, until soft, drain. Combine shoyu, sugar, sake, sesame oil, minced green onion, sesame seeds and red pepper. Mix well.

Unlike other Japanese dressings, this sauce has sesame oil, and therefore is called "nanban," or foreign.

INGEN NO GOMA MISO AE *string beans with seame-miso sauce*

1/2 lb green beans
1 tsp salt
3 tsp white sesame seeds
1/2 cup white miso
3 tbsp mirin

Remove ends and strings, if any, from beans. Wash and cook in boiling water with salt. When tender, place in colander, rinse with cold water and drain. Cut in 2-inch long pieces and set aside. Roast and grind sesame seeds. In small pan, combine miso and mirin. Stir vigorously and add ground sesame seeds. Mix well, add cooked green beans to sauce and toss gently. Serve in small individual bowls.

KYABETSU TO HAM NO SUNOMONO *cabbage and ham salad*

1 lb cabbage
1-1/2 cups water
1/4 lb boneless ham
3 tbsp white sesame seeds

4 tbsp vinegar
1 tsp shoyu
1 tsp salt
1-1/2 tbsp sugar

Finely shred cabbage. Place in covered saucepan and cook with water until tender. Drain and cool. Shred ham. Roast and grind sesame seeds to a paste. Add vinegar, shoyu, salt, sugar and mix well. Add cabbage and ham, toss and serve.

RENKON NO KURUMI AE *lotus root with walnut sauce*

1/2 lb lotus root	1/4 oz beansprouts
1 tbsp vinegar	1½ oz green beans
3/4 cup dashi	1/2 cup walnut meats
3-1/2 tbsp sugar	1 tbsp mirin
2 tsp salt	1 tsp shoyu
1 medium carrot	

Peel and cut lotus root in half lengthwise. Slice horizontally in very thin pieces. Rinse in cold water and cook 20 seconds in boiling vinegared water. Rinse again in cold water. Cook in mixture of 1/4 dashi, 1/2 tbsp sugar and 1/3 tsp salt. Cut carrots in strips. Cook in 1/2 cup dashi until tender. Clean beansprouts. Dip quickly in and out of boiling water. Rinse in cold water. Clean green beans. Cook in salted water until tender. Rinse in cold water and cut in julienne strips. Sprinkle 1/3 tsp salt over cooked carrots, beansprouts, green beans. Crush walnuts in a mortar or use blender to make a paste. Add 3 tbsp sugar, mirin, 1 tsp salt, shoyu and mix well. Combine cooked ingredients and sauce just before serving. Can be served as an individual or a communal dish.

TORI NIKU NO TOMATO ZUME SUMISO *stuffed tomato with miso dressing*

3 lb chicken breast meat	1/2 oz ginger
1/5 tsp salt	1/2 cup white miso
3-1/2 tbsp sake	1-1/2 tbsp sugar
4 small tomatoes	2 tbsp dashi
1 cucumber	1 egg yolk
2 chiso leaves	1/2 tbsp vinegar

Arrange chicken breast meat in skillet. Sprinkle with salt and 1-1/2 tbsp sake. Cover and cook over low flame 5 minutes. While meat is still warm, shred in thin pieces and set aside. Wash and slice off 1/3 top end of tomatoes. Scoop out pulp and seeds. Shred cucumber and chiso leaves. Soak in water to crisp. Drain. Cut ginger hari shoga style. Soak in water 10 minutes and drain. Combine miso, sugar, dashi, 2 tbsp sake in small saucepan. Cook over low flame, stirring constantly and when thick, remove from heat. Add egg yolk and stir. Then add vinegar. Mix miso sauce, chicken and ginger and stuff tomatoes with mixture. Garnish with chiso leaves and serve on cucumber bed.

SUDORI SHOGA *vinegared new ginger shoots*

> 8 new ginger roots
> 1/3 + 1/5 tsp salt
> 3 tbsp vinegar
> 1 tbsp sugar

Cut off tops of ginger roots, leaving 6 inches of root. Peel skin off new ginger roots, boil 30 seconds. Marinate root in mixture of vinegar, sugar, and 1/5 tsp salt 30 minutes before serving.

This makes a lovely garnish and condiment for broiled fish, fried chicken or beefsteak as well as a delight to the eye.

SUNO MONO WITH MISO DARE *vinegared salad*

> 1/4 cup miso   1 tbsp grated ginger
> 2 tbsp sake   lettuce
> 1/4 cup dashi   cucumbers
> 2-1/2 tbsp sugar   avocado
> 6 tbsp vinegar   carrots
> 1/2 tsp sesame seed oil   red radishes
> 1/3 cup vegetable oil   celery
> 1/4 cup mayonnaise   mandarin oranges
> 1/4 cup ground almonds

Cook and simmer together miso, sake, dashi and sugar. Let cool. Add vinegar, sesame oil, vegetable oil,mayonnaise,almonds and ginger. Mix well. Cut the rest of the ingredients in bite-size pieces. Toss, serve with miso dressing.

BUTA TO MAME NO SHIRA AE *pork and green beans with soybean curd dressing*

> 2 cups water   2tbsp sugar
> 1 square tofu   4 tsp shoyu
> 2 tbsp sesame seeds   1/2 lb boneless pork
> 2 tbsp dashi   2/3 lb green beans
> 1-1/2 tsp salt

Bring water to boil. Cut tofu in 4 pieces. Drop in water and simmer 5 minutes, drain and cool. Wrap tofu in cheesecloth and place a heavy weight — 4 to 6 lbs — on top to press out water. Roast and grind sesame seeds in mortar or blender to make a paste and mix with dashi, 1/2 tsp salt, sugar, 1 tsp shoyu. Stir in tofu and set aside. Cut pork in 2-inch strips and sprinkle with 1 tsp salt. Drop in boiling water and boil until tender. Drain and chill. Drop green beans in boiling salted water. When tender, rinse in cold water and drain. Cut in julienne strips like the pork. Sprinkle with 3 tsp shoyu and squeeze. Mix pork and beans. Stir in sesame-tofu mixture. Serve as small individual dish or as a communal dish.

EEL

Each summer when the weather was extremely hot and the humidity high, one's appetite dropped and stamina vanished. The Japanese call this condition *nat-suyase*, summer time weight loss.

Sometime in mid-July we had an eel-eating day to consume protein-laden eel to prevent the summer lassitude from weakening the body condition. This is called *doyo-no-ushi-ho hi*. The succulent, delicious Unagi no Kabayaki is most surely a summertime favorite of mine. The aroma rising from broiling and glazing the eel does make one realize suddenly that one is hungry!

Formerly, whenever Japanese ships were on a long voyage, Unagi no Kabayaki faithfully appeared on the weekly menus.

I was told eels caught in the mouth of the river where it joins the sea are the best tasting and most tender in texture. Each eel fillet with skin should weigh 1/2 pound. Methods of cooking eel vary in the Knate and Kansai regions.

UNAGI NO KABAYAKI *glazed and broiled eel*

> 3 eels, filleted with skin, 1-1/2 lb
>
> **Tare sauce:**
>
> | | |
> |---|---|
> | mirin | 3 tbsp sugar |
> | 4 tbsp sake | 1 tbsp mizuame |
> | 6 tbsp shoyu | 1/2 tsp sansho |
>
> Special equipment: *bamboo skewers*

Cut eel fillets into 5-inch pieces and insert 3 to 4 skewers in each piece. Broil skewered eels several inches from heat a few minutes each side, then place inside steamer. Steam 5 minutes with high heat. In saucepan cook broiled eel head and bones with mirin, sake, shoyu, sugar and mizuame until liquid is reduced one third. Using pastry brush, brush this tare on steamed eels. Broil 4 to 5 minutes. Repeat procedure 3 times. Remove skewers before serving. Sprinkle with sansho and serve as main dish. When served over white rice, eel becomes *unagi donburi*.

Unagi-no-Kabayaki is more likely found at restaurants in Japan these days than on the family table! Regarding the tare, my mother stored tare year after year in beer bottles. She felt it gave a richer flavor.

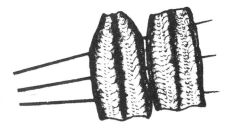

MAGURO NO MISOZUKE YAKI *miso-marinated tuna fish*

1-1/2 lb tuna fillet, fresh or frozen
1/2 cup miso
2 tbsp sugar
2 tbsp mirin
1/2 cup daikon, grated

Spread mixture of miso, sugar, and mirin on bottom of baking dish to marinate tuna fish fillet slices. Spread tuna fillets in mixture. Cover and refrigerate 2 days. Gently wipe the mixture off the surface of the tuna fillets. Broil without burning until golden brown. Serve with a mound of grated daikon beside each fillet.

BUTANIKU TO YASAI NO OIL YAKI *pork and vegetables cooked on grill or skillet with oil*

1-1/2 lb pork fillets	**Tsuke Jiru:**
1 eggplant	1/2 cup shoyu
6 shiitake, or 1/4 lb fresh mushrooms	1/2 cup mirin
	1 tsp vinegar
1-1/2 onion, medium	1 tbsp garlic, grated
2 green peppers	1 tbsp ginger, grated
3 tbsp oil	1 tbsp sesame seeds, roasted and coarsely ground

Slice pork fillets in thin bite-size pieces. Split eggplant in half lengthwise and then cut into 1/2-inch slices. To soften, place shiitake in warm water. Remove stems and cut in half. If fresh mushrooms are used, wash, clean and cut in half lengthwise. Slice onions in 1/2-inch rings. Split green peppers lengthwise into eight pieces. Combine shoyu, mirin, vinegar, garlic, ginger and sesame seed. Mix well and set aside until serving time. Heat skillet, coat with oil.

Hostess can cook and serve, but in our household each person cooks his own portion. When cooked this way, serve Tsuke Jiru in individual bowls. It's delicious!

IKA NO TATAKI AGE *deep-fried minced squid with chiso leaves*

1 lb squid	1/4 pumpkin
1 tsp salt	1 egg
1 tbsp sake	2 tbsp flour
20 chiso leaves	3 cups oil for deep-frying
1/2 cup cornstarch	lemon wedges

Remove intestines and cartilage   of squid. Peel off skin. Chop legs and fillets fine. Add salt and sake. Mix well and divide in 10 equal parts. Wash chiso leaves and pat dry. Using 2 leaves as a set, dust one side with cornstarch. Spread one portion of minced squid on cornstarch-dusted leaf. Place another leaf on squid. Dust with cornstarch again and set aside. Slice pumpkin in 1/4-inch thick wedges. Beat egg and mix with flour. Coat pumpkin wedges with egg and flour mixture. Heat cooking oil to 365 degrees F. Deep-fry pumpkin wedges and squid sandwiches.

WAKADORI NO SHICHIMI AJI chicken cooked with seven spices

2-1/2 lb whole chicken	6 tbsp shoyu
4 tbsp onion, minced	3 tbsp sesame oil
4 tbsp parched white sesame	1 carrot
seeds	8 oz bamboo shoots, canned
4 tbsp garlic, minced	6 shiitake
3 tbsp sugar	1 green pepper
1/2 tsp black pepper	1/2 cup dashi
1/2 tsp red pepper, minced	

Cut chicken in small chunks leaving bone in. In bowl combine chicken with onion, sesame seeds, garlic and mix well. Add sugar, black pepper, red pepper and mix again. Then add shoyu and sesame oil. Mix ingredients and marinate 30 minutes. Peel and cut carrot to size of chicken pieces. Cut bamboo to a similar size. Soak shiitake in enough warm water to soften, remove stems as necessary, and cut in half. Cut green pepper to conform to vegetable sizes. Parboil 3 minutes, rinse with cold water and set aside. Bring dashi to boil and add chicken with marinade. Cook over high flame 5 minutes. Stir quickly, cover, and simmer 20 minutes. Add carrots, bamboo shoots, shiitake, stir and cook 15 additional minutes. Add green pepper when carrots are done. Simmer until liquid is absorbed. Serve warm or cold.

TORI NO UMANI *chicken boiled with vegetables*

1 lb chicken, cut with bones	15 small shiitake
8 cups water	a few string beans
2 tsp salt	2 tsp cornstarch
1 tsp shoyu	sugar
1-1/2 lb bamboo shoots	1-1/2 cups dashi
1/3 lb carrots	

Cut chicken in bite-size chunks. Bring water to boil and cook chicken 40 minutes over low flame. Skim several times while cooking. After 40 minutes, add salt and shoyu, continue to simmer 10 minutes. Cut pointed end of bamboo shoots crosswise 1-1/4-inch thick,then quarter. Because of tough, thick ends, cut cross-sections into 2/3-inch thick rounds, using it as is. Cut carrots in rounds, and flute edges in flower shapes using flower-shaped cutter. Soak shiitake in enough water to cover until soft. Squeeze out water and cut off stems. String green beans and cut off ends so that all are the same length. Drop beans in salted, boiling water and parboil. Rinse in cold water immediately to keep green color, drain. Place dashi in large pot, add shiitake, carrots and bamboo shoots, cooking long enough to flavor. Drop in string beans just before removing from burner. Thicken remaining dashi with cornstarch. Arrange vegetables and chicken on serving dish. Pour over thickened dashi and serve.

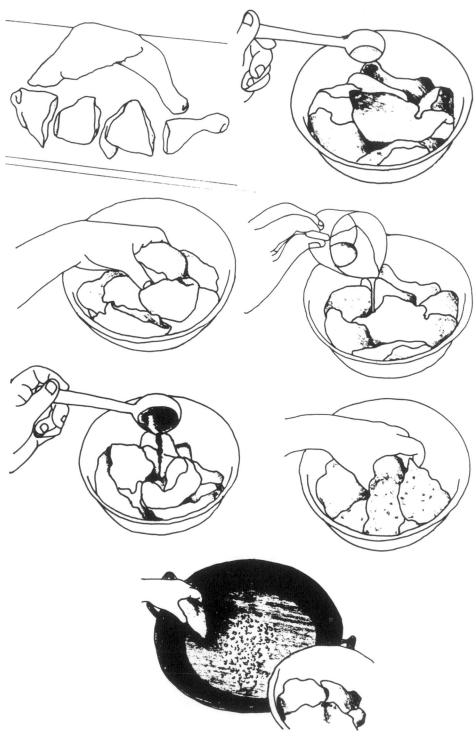

Tori no kara age

TORI NO KARA AGE *fried chicken*

2 lb chicken breasts, thighs, legs	2 tbsp sake or sherry
2 eggs	4 tbsp sugar
3 tbsp flour	2 tsp salt
4 tbsp cornstarch	2 tsp minced white part of
5 tbsp rice flour	green onions
2 tbsp shoyu	1 finger ginger, crushed
	oil for deep-frying

Prepare chicken parts by cutting in finger-food size pieces. Place in bowl and break both eggs over the chicken. Add remaining ingredients and mix well. Marinate 30 minutes for best taste. Heat oil to 340 degrees F. Fry each piece of chicken until nicely browned, then drain excess oil. Just before serving, heat oil to 370 degrees F, fry all the chicken pieces together then drain on rack. This means that you can prepare this in stages, particularly if you want to double or triple the recipe. You can refrigerate or freeze the chicken before final frying, leaving second frying until just before serving.

American fried chicken is noted the world around as Southern Fried Chicken. Very much influenced by Chinese cooking, this is Japanese fried chicken, and can be enjoyed as part of a family dinner, a party dish, or the center of a picnic menu. The delicious juices of fried chicken Japanese style spill all over your mouth when you take a bite. This is also one of the favorite ingredients in the Obento Joffrey menus when the company visits San Francisco each summer. One Christmas Robert Joffrey and Gerald Arpino had me serve it for their annual Christmas Eve party in Greenwich Village, New York City.

TONKATSU *pork cutlets*

6 boneless pork chops, 1/3-inch thick	1 cup breadcrumbs
	oil for deep-frying
1/2 cup flour	6 lettuce leaves
1/2 tsp salt	half head cabbage, finely
dash of pepper	shredded
1 egg, beaten	1 carrot, finely shredded
1 tbsp water	tonkatsu sauce, as desired

Pound pork chops with meat mallet or bottle. Cut edges to prevent curling. Dust chops with flour seasoned with salt and pepper. Combine beaten egg with water and dip each chop in the mixture. Coat with breadcrumbs, patting each piece with fingers to cover well. Heat cooking oil to 370 degrees F. Fry maximum of 2 chops at a time to maintain even frying temperature. Fry 4 minutes then turn. When both sides are golden brown and cooked through, remove and drain. Lean chops against a mound of shredded cabbage and carrot and serve hot with tonkatsu sauce. This often will be accompanied by boiled potatoes or a bowl of rice. Many times a knife will be inserted in the cutlet for those eating with chopsticks.

(Continued on next page)

Tonkatsu is an interesting example of the combined cultures of the West and Japan. Tonkatsu is an adaptation of the European breaded deep-frying method having become thoroughly Japanese. It is served at home as well as in restaurants in Japan. There are tonkatsu restaurants specializing in serving tonkatsu dishes. In translating the word "tonkatsu," "ton" means pork, "katsu" is the Japanese way of saying "cutlet."

BUTA NIKI NO TATSUTA AGE

1 lb pork fillets
1 tbsp shoyu
1 tbsp mirin
1 tsp ginger juice
4 tbsp cornstarch
oil for deep-frying
mustard sauce

Cut pork fillets in bite-size pieces. Marinate 10 minutes in shoyu, mirin and ginger juice. Dust pork with 2 tbsp cornstarch. Heat cooking oil to 360 degrees F, Dust pork again with remaining cornstarch, but shake off any excess when ready to fry. Deep-fry pork pieces 3 minutes, a few at a time. When all are fried, bring oil to 375 degrees F, frying pieces a second time until golden brown. Remove, drain and serve hot or cold with mustard sauce.

This makes a fine addition to a picnic, obento or lunch.

TORINIKU NO YANAGAWA *mock Yanagawa chicken*

1/4 lb chicken meat	1 tsp mirin
2 tsp shoyu	4 oz bamboo shoots, sliced
1 tsp sake	5 eggs
4 oz gobo	1 tbsp sugar
1-1/4 cup dashi	1 bunch Chinese parsley

Slice chicken in bite-size pieces. Sprinkle with 1 tsp each shoyu and sake. Scrape off gobo skin with wrong side of knife. Shred gobo into small bamboo leaf shapes. Soak in water to bleach. In a shallow pan, combine dashi, 1 tsp shoyu, 1 tsp mirin and bring to boil. Cook chicken pieces in the broth. When almost done, about 3 minutes, remove from pan and set aside. In same broth, cook gobo 10 minutes. Add bamboo shoots. Place chicken back in pan and stir gently. Beat eggs well and pour over bubbling ingredients. When egg is partially cooked, add chopped Chinese parsley.

A summertime favorite of the Japanese.

TOFU TO HIKINIKU NO KASANE YAKI *bean curd and open-face ground pork sandwich*

2 tofu
1 lb ground pork
1 tsp fresh ginger juice
1 tsp salt
1 tsp sugar
1 tsp sake or dry sherry
1/2 cup cornstarch
3 tbsp water

3 tbsp cooking oil

Sauce:
3/4 cup dashi
2 tbsp shoyu
2 tsp sugar
2 tsp cornstarch
1 tbsp water

Drain liquid from tofu by placing it on slanted board in bowl. Combine pork, ginger juice, salt, sugar, sake, sherry, 1 tsp cornstarch and water. Mix well until very smooth in texture. Slice drained tofu in half lengthwise then crosswise — there will be 8 pieces. Pat each piece dry with cloth and sprinkle with cornstarch. Scrape excess cornstarch off gently. Spread pork mixture on top of cornstarch tofu. Heat large skillet with cooking oil. Place tofu and pork sandwich face down in pan and shake pan gently. Cook 3 minutes or until pork is done. Turn and cook until tofu side is slightly browned.

Sauce: In small saucepan combine dashi, shoyu, sugar and bring to boil. Add mixture of cornstarch and water. Stir and remove from heat. Sauce will be slightly thick. Serve each cooked open-faced sandwich topped with sauce.

SHIROMI ZAKANA TO TOFU NO ANKAKE *codfish and tofu with soy sauce*

3/4 lb codfish fillet, fresh
  or frozen
1/2 ginger juice
1-1/2 tbsp shoyu
2 tbsp sake
1 egg white
2 tbsp cornstarch
oil for deep frying
1 tofu
1 large tomato

4-inch green onion
2 tbsp oil
2 slices ginger
1 cup dashi
1-1/4 tsp salt
2 tsp cornstarch mixed with
  1-1/3 tbsp water
1/2 cup green peas
1 tsp sesame oil

Cut codfish fillets in bite-size pieces. Marinate in ginger juice, 1/2 tbsp shoyu, sake. Beat egg white until slightly foamy, sift in cornstarch to make batter. Heat deep-frying oil to 360 degrees F. Before frying, pat excess moisture from marinated fish and dip in batter. Fry until light brown. Cook tofu in boiling water 3 minutes. Drain and pat off excess water with cloth. Cut in half lengthwise, then in 1/2-inch thicknesses. Dip tomato in boiling water. Peel, cut in 8 wedges. Cut green onion in 4 or 5 pieces. Heat skillet with oil. Saute tomato wedges and ginger slices. Add dashi, 1 tbsp shoyu, salt and half the cornstarch and water mixture. Add sliced tofu and deep-fried fish and stir gently, adding remaining water and cornstarch mixture, green peas, sesame oil stirring gently. Serve warm.

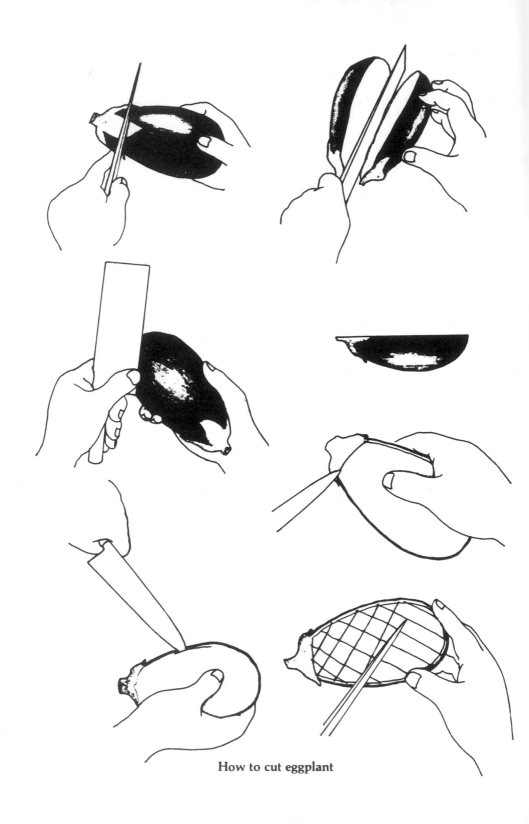

How to cut eggplant

NASU NO HASAMI AGE *Japanese eggplant, fried and stuffed*

1 lb pork fillets	**Batter:**
1 tbsp shoyu	1 egg
1 tbsp sake	3 tbsp water
1 tsp ginger juice	1/2 cup flour
6 Japanese eggplants	1/2 cup flour (for dusting)
6 ginger roots	
	oil for deep frying
	1/2 cup daikon, grated
	shoyu

Cut pork fillets in 6 thin pieces. Marinate in shoyu, sake, ginger juice 20 minutes. Trim tip of eggplant stem and score both sides of the newly cut face. To bleach, soak 10 minutes in water. Clean and wash ginger root. Cut in 6-inch lengths. Wipe eggplant dry. Dust each pork fillet with flour.

To make batter, mix egg, water and flour. Coat scored eggplant slits with batter. Fold pork fillet in half and sandwich between eggplant halves. Dip ginger root in batter. Heat oil to 350 degress F. Deep-fry ginger root and drain. Deep-fry eggplant/pork sandwiches. Arrange sandwiches and ginger roots on individual serving dishes and serve with grated daikon and shoyu.

If you are puzzled by the descritpion of eggplant, please remember that Japanese eggplant is long and slender, like the shape of zucchini or the yellow-necked summer squash, and not like the large ovular Western eggplant. The shape makes it possible to treat the Japanese eggplant as if it were a sandwich.

HIYASHI MUSHIDORI KYURI NO MIZORE GAKE *cold chicken with cucumber sauce*

2 pieces chicken breast meat	2 tbsp dashi
1 tsp salt	2 tbsp vinegar
1 bunch parsley	1 tbsp sugar
2 tbsp sake	1 tsp shoyu
1 cucumber	1 carrot

Salt breast meat slightly and line steaming plate with half the parsley. Place salted chicken meat on parsley and sprinkle with sake. Cover meat with remaining parsley and place inside steamer. Cook over high steam for 20 minutes or until done. Cool when it is cooked. Grate cucumber, squeezing out excess water. Add dashi, vinegar, sugar, shoyu and blend well, with cucumber. Cut and slice carrot, sengiri style. Slice cold chicken into bite-sized pieces. Use individual dish to arrange chicken. Top with cucumber sauce and garnish with sengiri-style cut carrot.

AGE TOFU NO CURRY SAUCE *fried tofu with curry sauce*

3 squares tofu	1/2 cup dashi
2 tbsp oil	1 tbsp curry powder
1 medium onion, minced	1 tbsp shoyu
1 tbsp garlic, minced	1 tbsp miso
1 tbsp ginger, minced	oil for deep-frying
1/4 lb ground pork	1/2 cup cornstarch
1 tbsp flour	1/4 cup green onion, minced

Place tofu on cutting board placed on slant so that liquid will drain, then cut each tofu in 12 even square cubes. Set aside. Heat skillet with oil. Saute onion, garlic and ginger. Add ground pork, sprinkle with flour to thicken and stir until brown. When cooked, add mixture of dashi, curry powder, shoyu and miso. Simmer 10 minutes and set aside. Heat cooking oil to 360 degrees F. Dust tofu with cornstarch, deep-fry until golden brown. Serve fried tofu topped with curried meat mixture garnished with minced green onion.

BUTANIKU MAKI *rolled pork with cheese*

Cheese is not used often in Japanese cooking but this is an exception.

3/4 lb pork fillets	1/4 tsp salt
1/4 lb cheese (mozzarella	dash of pepper
preferred)	2 tbsp flour
1 green pepper	2 tbsp cooking oil
1 onion	1-1/2 tbsp shoyu
1/4 lb cabbage	

Slice pork fillets into ten very thin sheets. Cut cheese into ten equal portions resembling carrot or celery sticks. Cut green pepper in thin strips lengthwise. Divide in ten equal portions. Cut onion into thin rings. Shred cabbage sengiri style. Place cheese stick and green pepper on sliced pork fillet. Wrap rolling away from you. When all are rolled, sprinkle with salt and dash of pepper. Let stand 10 minutes, then dust with flour. Heat skillet with oil. Saute onion and remove when wilted. Set aside. In same skillet, place pork rolls with seam side down. Turn gently until all sides of pork are cooked, sprinkling with shoyu while turning. Return onions to skillet and stir. Serve pork rolls on shredded cabbage bed.

MISODARE TSUKE YAKI *pork fillet with miso sauce*

1-1/2 lb pork fillets	1 tbsp ginger juice
3 tbsp miso	1 tbsp sesame seeds, roasted
1 tbsp sugar	lettuce leaves
2 tbsp sake	

Slice pork fillets into thin pieces. Using mixer at medium speed, combine miso, sugar, sake and ginger juice. Add roasted sesame seeds, when ingredients are well-mixed. Marinate sliced pork in sauce 15 minutes. Broil until meat is done and serve on lettuce bed.

LEMON YAKI *lemon beef*

1/2 lb sirloin tips, rump short cut	1 tbsp ketchup
2 cloves garlic	1 tbsp salad oil
1 lemon, cut in wedges	1 lb green beans
1 tsp salt	3 tbsp butter
1 tsp curry powder	salt and pepper
1 tsp Worcestershire sauce	

Slice beef chunk in 8 thin pieces. Combine garlic, lemon wedges, salt, curry powder, Worcestershire sauce, ketchup, oil and marinate beef in mixture 30 minutes. Remove ends and any strings from string beans, wash and parboil. When tender, drain and saute in 1 tbsp butter, season with salt and pepper to taste. Heat skillet, melt 2 tbsp butter and saute marinated meat. When brown, remove from skillet. Pour remaining marinade sauce with lemon wedges into skillet and bring to boil. Return browned beef to skillet, heat, and serve with green beans. *This makes a delightful summer dish.*

ABURA YAKI TOFU NO ANKAKE *tofu with shrimp sauce*

2 squares tofu	2 tbsp green onion, minced
2 tbsp dried shrimp	2 tbsp shoyu
1 cup water	1 tbsp sake
1 egg	1/2 tsp salt
4 tbsp oil	2 tsp cornstarch

Place tofu on bamboo basket to drain water. Wash dried shrimp and soak in water to soften. When soft, remove, rinse and mince, saving soaking water for dashi. If necessary, add water to make 1 cup dashi. Beat egg. Cut tofu in half lengthwise then slice in 1/2-inch pieces. Heat skillet using 3 tbsp oil. Dip sliced tofu into beaten egg, then fry until both sides are golden brown. In large skillet or wok, heat 1 tbsp oil. Stir minced shrimp, add minced green onion, then 1 cup dashi from soaking shrimp, shoyu, sake, salt, cornstarch and bring to boil. When slightly thickened, add fried tofu gently. Serve warm.

NASU NO SHIGI YAKI *stir-fried eggplant with miso sauce*

1 lb eggplant	4 tbsp sake
1/2 lb green pepper	2 tbsp niboshi ko
2/3 cup miso	4-1/2 tbsp oil
3 tbsp sugar	

Cut eggplant in large bite-size pieces and soak in water 10 minutes to blanch. Drain and pat dry with paper towel. Cut green pepper in bite-size pieces. Combine miso, sugar, sake niboshiko powder and mix well. In large skillet, heat oil and add eggplant, stir mix quickly. When eggplant white becomes slightly brown, add green pepper, stirring again. Add miso sauce mixture. When shiny in texture, remove from heat. Serve immediately hot. Can be served cold.

NASU TO HIKINIKU NO ITAME MONO *eggplant with meat sauce*

1-1/2 tbsp shoyu
3 tbsp oil + 1 tsp hot oil
1 tbsp green onion, minced
1 tbsp garlic, minced
1/2 lb ground beef

1 eggplant
2 tsp sugar
4 tbsp water
1 tsp cornstarch

Wash and cut eggplant in quarters lengthwise, then slice in thin pieces. Soak in water 10 minutes to bleach, then dry. Using a skillet or wok, heat 3 tbsp oil and saute minced onion, garlic and ground beef. Add eggplant continuing to saute. Stir seasonings, hot oil, shoyu, sugar and 2 tbsp water. Simmer until eggplant is cooked. Combine cornstarch and remaining water, adding to eggplant and ground beef to thicken.

YAKITORI *broiled chicken, scallions and chicken livers*

1 inch piece peeled fresh ginger
3 tbsp sake or dry sherry
1 tbsp shoyu
2 tsp sugar
8 chicken livers, trimmed of
    all fat

2 whole chicken breats or
    4 legs, boned
8 scallions, including 3-inch
    green stems
1-1/2 cup teriyaki sauce
kona sansho

Cut fresh ginger root in paper-thin slices. Combine sake, shoyu, sugar and sliced ginger in mixing bowl and add chicken livers. Turn over to moisten. Marinate 6 hours or overnight in refrigerator. Remove from marinade and cut each liver in half. Reserve marinade. Cut boned chicken in 1-inch pieces. Cut scallions in 1- to 1-1/2-inch long pieces. On each of 4 small skewers, string 4 halved chicken livers. On each of 8 additional skewers, alternate 4 chunks of chicken with 3 strips of scallion. Preheat broiler, or light hibachi or charcoal broiler. Broil skewered livers 3 inches from heat 4 minutes. Then dip in teriyaki sauce and broil 4 to 5 minutes on other side and set aside on plate. Quickly dip chicken and scalliion skewers in teriyaki sauce and broil on one side 2 to 3 minutes. Dip again in sauce, grill 2 minutes; dip once more and broil other side 2 minutes. The entire grilling should take 6 to 7 minutes. On each plate, place one skewer of chicken livers and 2 skewers of chicken and scallions. Sprinkle with kona sansho, and moisten each skewer with a little   marinade.

GYUUNIKU TERIYAKI *broiled sliced beef with a shoyu-seasoned glaze*

1-1/2 lb lean boneless beef,
preferably tenderloin or
boneless sirloin

Teriyaki sauce:
1 cup mirin or sherry
1 cup shoyu
1 cup dashi

Teriyaki glaze:
1/4 cup teriyaki sauce
1 tbsp sugar
1 tsp cornstarch mixed with
1 tbsp cold water

Garnish:
4 tsp powdered mustard
12 sprigs fresh parsley

Teriyaki sauce: To make sauce, warm mirin or sherry in 1-1/2 quart enameled or stainless steel saucepan over moderate heat. Take pan off burner, igniting mirin with match. Shake pan back and forth until flame dies out. Stir in shoyu and chicken stock and bring to boil. Pour sauce in bowl and cool to room terperature. **Teriyaki glaze:** To make glaze, combine teriyaki sauce and sugar in enamel or stainless steel saucepan. Bring almost to boil over moderate heat, then reduce heat to low. Stir combined cornstarch and water in sauce, stirring constantly, until sauce thickens into clear, syrupy glaze. Pour immediately in dish and set aside. Preheat broiler, light hibachi or charcoal broiler. Dip meat in teriyaki sauce one at a time. Broil 2 inches from heat 1 minute on each side, or until lightly browned. Broil additional minute for well-done. Slice meat into 1-inch strips and place on individual serving plates. Spoon a little glaze over each serving. Combine powdered mustard with just enough hot water to make thick paste, set aside 15 minutes. Top meat with mustard and sprig of parsley. If preferred, mustard may be combined with glaze. Any leftover teriyaki sauce may be stored in tightly-closed jars and refrigerated. Before using, bring to boil and skim surface of any scum. It will keep a month.

TORI TERIYAKI *grilled chicken with sweet shoyu-seasoned glaze*

6 whole chicken breasts or 12 chicken legs
3 cups teriyaki sauce
1/4 cup teriyaki glaze
4 tsp powdered mustard
12 sprigs fresh parlsey

Bone chicken breasts in following fashion: Hold breast skin side down and bend back until spoon-shaped bone pops up. Pull out and cut breast apart with heavy, sharp knife. One at a time lay each breast, bone side up, on chopping board, with the tapered end away from you. Slip point of sharp boning knife under base of slender single small rib bone attached to rib cage. Press flat knife up against bone and cut flesh away, freeing bone. Hold bone in one hand pulling it gently up toward you, meanwhile scraping away flesh adhering to adjacent ribs. Continue scraping and cutting movement until entire rib cage and adjacent small bones have been detached from meat. Pat boned breast back in shape. Repeat entire process with remaining breasts. Leave skin intact on all breasts. *To bone chicken leg:* Start at drumstick end, using bone as guide, cut meat away from bone in large pieces. Strip meat of all cartilage and gristle, but leave skin intact.

Combine powdered mustard with enough hot water to make thick paste. Set aside 15 minutes. Preheat broiler or light hibachi or charcoal broiler. Dip chicken breasts in teriyaki sauce, coating well, and broil skin side up 3 inches from the heat 2 to 3 minutes, or until golden brown. Dip breast in sauce again. Broil on other side 2 to 3 minutes. Dip third time in sauce and broil skin side up, another 3 to 4 minutes. The finished chicken should be rich golden brown. Broiling takes 7 to 10 minutes. Cut chicken in 2- to 2-1/2-inch pieces and arrange on individual plates. Pour teriyaki glaze evenly over each portion, garnish with a little mustard and sprig of parsley at side of plate.

HIYASHI CHAWAN MUSHI *cold custard soup*

3 eggs	**Kake Jiru:**
3 cups dashi	1 cup dashi
1 tsp salt	1/4 tsp salt
1 tsp shoyu	1/4 tsp shoyu
6 shrimps, uncooked	1/2 tsp mirin
1/2 tsp sake	1 tsp cornstarch
1/2 tsp shoyu	1 tbsp water
6 shiitake	
1/4 cup canned bamboo shoots	

Beat eggs well and mix with dashi, salt and shoyu. Mix well. Avoid making too foamy a mixture. Strain. Peel and devein shrimp. Sprinkle with sake and shoyu. Soak shiitake in warm water to soften. Divide bamboo shoots in 6 parts. Place prepared ingredients in 6 individual bowls. Pour egg mixture over them. Steam 15 minutes over medium flame. When cooked and cooled, store in refrigerator until serving time. For convenience make a day ahead. **Kake Jiru:** Combine dashi, salt, shoyu, mirin and bring to boil. Stir mixture of cornstarch and water in dashi sauce when thickened. Cool and pour Kake Jiru over cooked custard soup before serving.

KATSUO NO SURI NAGASHI JIRU *bonito soup*

3/4 cup bonito fillet
1/2 cup miso
4 cups dashi
1 tofu
2 stalks green onion, chopped

Using medium speed on blender, make 3/4 cup bonito fillet into paste. Add miso, gradually followed by 1 cup dashi. When smooth in texture, place in pot with 3 cups dashi. Stir gently and add cubes of tofu when it boils. Serve with chopped green onion.

GOMOKU HIYASHI CHUKA SOBA *cold Chinese-style noodle with five ingredients*

4 bundles Chinese style noodles
2 breasts of chicken, boned
1/4 lb cooked ham
1/3 lb shrimp
1 tbsp sake
1 tsp salt
2 eggs
1 tsp oil
2 stalks green onion, minced
2 tbsp parsley, minced

Tsuke Jiru:
sesame:
3 tbsp sesame seeds, roasted
    and ground
3 tbsp shoyu
3 tbsp water
3 tsp sugar

ginger:
3 tbsp ginger, finely minced
3 tbsp shoyu
6 tbsp vinegar

mustard:
3 tbsp mustard paste
6 tbsp shoyu

hot chili pepper:
2 tsp hot chili pepper sauce
2 tsp sesame oil
2 tbsp shoyu

Cook noodles . Boil chicken meat and drain, cool and cut in strips. Cut ham in julienne strips. Cook shrimp in boiling water with 1/2 tsp salt added. Cool, shell and cut in bite-size pieces. Sprinkle with sake and 1/4 tsp salt. Beat two eggs, add 1/4 tsp salt. In skillet, heat oil. Pour half beaten eggs into skillet and shake skillet quickly. When surface becomes dry, turn. Repeat with remaining egg. When cool cut into julienne strips. Cut green onion into julienne strips. Soak in cold water to crisp and get rid of bitter taste. Pat dry. Arrange five ingredients on large platter. Mix each of dipping sauces and place in five separate bowls, garnish with minced parsley. Serve five ingredients with dipping sauces and cold noodles.

HIYASHI BACHI *cold chicken with vegetables*

1 lb chicken breast meat
2 squares tofu
2 cucumbers
2 stalks celery

Tsuke Jiru:
1/2 cup miso
1/4 cup sugar
2 tbsp water
1/4 cup vinegar

Slice chicken in bite-size pieces and dip in boiling water. When meat turns white, remove quickly, place in colander and run cold water over to cool. Pat dry. Cut tofu in 1-inch cubes. Dip in boiling water 2 minutes. Remove and let cool. Cut cucumbers in half lengthwise and remove seeds. Cut in strips 3 inches long. Cut celery in thin strips 3 inches long and soak in cold water to crisp. **Tsuke Jiru:** Combine miso, sugar and water in pot and bring to boil, cool and add vinegar, stirring well. Arrange chicken, tofu and vegetables on an ice bed. Serve with Tsuke Jiru.

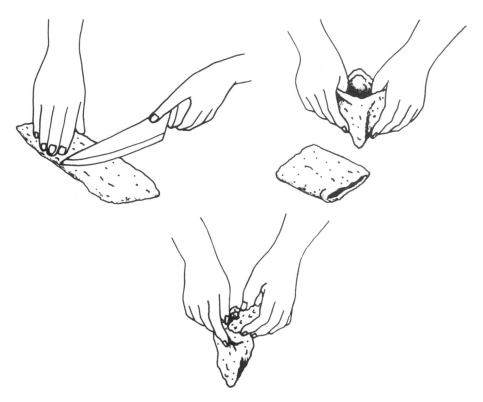

INARI ZUSHI *stuffed fried soybean curd sushi*

3 cups rice
3-1/2 cup water
3 inches konbu
9 aburage

Seasoning for rice:
3-1/2 tbsp vinegar
1-1/2 tbsp sugar
2 tsp salt

Seasoning for aburage:
1-1/2 cup dashi
9 tbsp sugar

4-1/2 tbsp shoyu
1/4 lb fresh ginger
12 tsp salt

Seasoning for pickling ginger:
1 tbsp vinegar
1 tsp sugar
1/2 tbsp water
1/5 tsp salt

Wash and drain rice one hour before cooking. Using heavy metal pot, combine rice, water and konbu. Bring to boil over medium heat. Remove from heat, discarding konbu. Reduce flame to low and cover, cooking until cooking water evaporates. Then bring flame to simmer. Wait 5 minutes and remove hot rice from pot to shallow pan. Pour over seasoning of vinegar, sugar and salt quickly. Fan to cool while mixing. Slap aburage between palms of hands and cut in half lengthwise. Pour boiling water over to remove excess oil. Squeeze. Turn half aburage inside out. Cook in dashi, sugar, shoyu covered 1/2 hour over low flame and let cool. Slice ginger in paper-thin pieces. Dip in boiling water, drain. Sprinkle with salt. Combine vinegar, sugar, water, salt and pickle sliced ginger 1/2 hour before serving. Open cooled aburage and stuff with seasoned rice. You will have nine of each inari zushi, one with outside, one with inside out. Serve with pickled ginger.

Inari Zushi is a welcome addition to picnics.

HOSO MAKI ZUSHI *skinny wrapped sushi*

4 sheets nori	2 cups cooked and seasoned rice
1 cucumber	1 tbsp wasabi paste
1 sack fresh codfish roe	
Special equipment: *sudare*	

Roast nori over low flame to crisp. Cut in half. Slice cucumber lengthwise and divide 6 ways. Slit open codfish roe sack. Gently scrape out pink roe. Divide 4 ways. Place nori on sudare and spread rice flat on nori sheet, leaving 3/4-inch space at edge furthest from you. Arrange roe in center of rice. Take a good grip at front of sudare and roll. Moisten nori edge with vinegar and water mixture to seal. For cucumber wrap, dot with wasabi paste along side cucumber piece placed in rice center instead of roe. Serve hoso maki rolls whole or cut in 3-inch pieces.

Makes very elegant hors d'oeuvres.

SOMEN *cold noodles*

3 bunches somen noodles	**Dipping sauce:**
9 cups cooking water	4 cup dashi
2 lb shrimp	2 cup shoyu
1 tsp salt	1/4 cup sake
18 medium shiitake, dried	2 tbsp lemon peel, grated
1/2 cup dashi	
2 tbsp shoyu	
1-1/2 tsp sugar	

In large pot, bring to boil 6 cups of water. Add loosened somen, bring to second boil, add cold water. Repeat procedure three times, being careful not to overcook. Rinse with cold water, washing off glutinous substance. Drain. Keep refrigerated no more than three hours. Devein and cook shrimp in 3 cups of water and 1 tsp salt. When cool, shell. In warm water soften dried shiitake. Cook in dashi, shoyu, sugar and mirin. Simmer until shiitake absorbs all liquid. Set aside to cool.
Dipping sauce: Combine dashi, shoyu, sake and bring to boil. Cool. Grate lemon peel. Arrange somen, shrimp and seasoned mushrooms in bamboo basket. Place wine glass filled with dashi sauce and lemon peel in container with lots of ice and water. Place in center of table. Diners rinse somen noodles in iced water, and then dip in cold sauce with shrimp and shiitake.   *Continued on next page*

Enjoy a summer evening with iced somen. This is summertime's favorite food. There is an art in choosing somen. In purchasing, one must make certain that the somen color is not white. White somen is recently made, will have a faint odor of oil and is not ready to be eaten. It takes one year or more before the odor of the oil used in making the noodles disappears. Select somen at least two years old or almost yellow in color.

ZARU SOBA *buckwheat noodle served in bamboo basket*

1-1/2 lbs cooked soba

Tare no Moto:
2 tbsp mirin
6 tbsp shoyu
2 tbsp sugar

1-1/2 cups dashi
1/2 cup green onion, minced
1 sheet nori
1 tbsp wasabi paste

In 4-quart pot, bring 2 quarts water to boil. Add soba and stir occasionally. Cook about 7 minutes or until soft. Drain noodles in colander and rinse with cold water. Drain again and place noodles in 6 serving "zaru" or bamboo serving baskets or on a serving plate. Prepare tare no moto according to basic recipe (see index). Add

Continued on next page

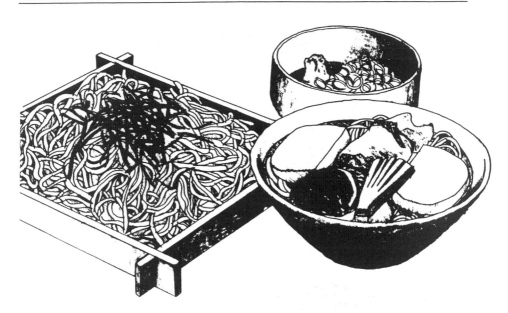

1-1/2 cup dashi. Simmer 5 minutes. Chill. Mince green onion and cut nori into thin strips. Divide soba and arrange in serving containers. Garnish top of the soba with seaweed strips. Arrange minced green onion and wasabi paste in small bowl. Serve dipping sauce in small teacup or small glass cups.

This is another summertime favorite noodle dish. It is served in a box lined with slatted bamboo mats or in a chilled bowl. This recipe will make 4 or 5 generous servings— a delightful summer snack or meal.

TORINIKU NO HIYASHI SOBA *chicken and cold noodles*

1 lb Chinese style noodles	**Kake Jiru:**
2 tbsp oil	2 tbsp white sesame seeds, roasted
2 pieces chicken breast meat	2 tbsp shoyu
1 tbsp salt	2 tbsp vinegar
1 tbsp sake	1 tbsp sesame oil
2 cucumbers	1 tsp hot sauce
1/4 lb cooked ham	5 tbsp dashi
	1 tsp salt

Cook noodles in large pot and when done, place in colander, rinse with cold water and drain. Spread over flat bamboo basket and sprinkle with oil. Place chicken breasts on plate, sprinkle with salt and sake. Using steamer, steam on plate 10 minutes or until tender. Remove and when cool, shred into small strips, retaining any liquid on plate. Cut cucumbers in half lengthwise, remove seeds and slice in thin pieces. Cut and slice ham in same manner. **Kake Jiru:** Coarsely grind sesame seeds and add shoyu, vinegar, sesame oil, hot sauce and dashi, using liquid from steamed chicken, salt. Mix well. On deep serving platter, spread noodles and garnish with cucumbers, ham, and chicken. Pour Kake Jiru over.

TARE NO MOTO

2 tbsp mirin	2 tbsp sugar
6 tbsp shoyu	dashi

Heat mirin in small saucepan. When it boils, ignite a match and burn off alcohol. When flame is gone, add shoyu and sugar and simmer 5 minutes. Add dashi according to needs of particular kind of menrui being prepared. One can double recipe for future use. It can be conveniently refrigerated for as long as 2 months. *People lament that home-made menrui broth is not so good and savory as one finds in a noodle shop.*

HIYASHI KISHIMEN *cold thick Japanese noodles*

3/4 lb kishimen (cold thick Japanese noodles)	2 tbsp sake
	3 tbsp sugar
2 tsp sesame oil	3 pieces fried soybean curd
4-1/2 cup dashi	2 cups beansprouts
5-1/2 tbsp shoyu	

Bring water to boil in large pot and cook noodles until done. Place in colander, rinse with cold water and drain. Mix well with sesame oil and refrigerate. Combine 4 cups dashi, 4 tbsp shoyu, sake, 1 tbsp sugar and bring to boil. Set aside to cool. Pour boiling water over fried soybean curd to remove excess oil. Cut each piece in 4 triangles. Simmer 20 minutes with 1/2 cup dashi, 2 tbsp sugar and 1-1/2 tbsp shoyu. Wash beansprouts. Parboil and rinse with cold water to cool. Refrigerate until serving time. Divide cold noodles in 6 bowls. Cover noodles with cooled seasoned soup topped with seasoned bean curd and beansprouts. Chili pepper powder may be sprinkled over this dish.

HARUSAME NO GOSHOKU MORI *beanthread with five colors*

2 pkgs harusame	4 shiitake
2 cucumbers	5-1/2 tbsp shoyu
4 oz cooked ham	2 tbsp sake
2 eggs, beaten	4 tbsp mirin
dash of salt	1-1/2 tsp sugar
1 tsp cornstarch	3 stalks green onion, minced
1 tbsp water	1-1/2 cup dashi

Bring water to boil and cook harusame 1 minute. Remove pot from heat and let stand until harusame becomes transparent. Rinse in cold water, cut in 3-inch long pieces and drain well. Peel and cut cucumber lengthwise in half. Slice in strips and place in cold water to crisp. Slice and cut cooked ham in strips, similar to cucumber size. Combine eggs, salt, cornstarch, water and mix well. Make 2 thin sheetlike omelets. Cut in small strips. To soften shiitake place in warm water. Bring 2 tbsp shoyu, sake, 2 tbsp mirin and sugar to boil. Add softened shiitake and simmer until liquid is absorbed. Remove from fire and cool. Remove stems and cut in strips. **Dipping sauce:** In small saucepan, bring to boil dashi, 2 tbsp mirin and 3-1/2 tbsp shoyu. Remove from heat and cool. Serve dipping sauce in individual glass containers. Using large serving plate, spread cooked harusame in even layer. Top with cucumber, ham and omelet strips spread fan-shape with minced green onion at center.

NUKAZUKE *rice bran pickle*

Nuka-zuke is usually a warm-weather pickling method because of the abundance of vegetables. Fermentation of rice bran bacteria, rich in vitamin B and minerals, behaves much better in the summertime. Quite frequently, many households allow their rice bran bed, or nuka doko, to have a winter hibernation. I know of families in Japan that kept their nuka doko for generatons, much like that started for making yogurt. For hibernation, nuka doko containers are sealed tight and left in a cool place until late spring. When you realize that Japan tends to have a very humid summer climate, this practice makes great sense.

Nuka zuke treated vegetables do not keep very long. Being kept overnight in the nuka doko and then eating is the best, premium eating time for this form of tsukemono.

Making a nuka doko is the fermentation of yeast bacteria; most often a wide-mouthed ceramic pot, glass container or wooden tub of two- to three-quart capacity is used. Plastic and metal containers are not used since the fermentation process brings out unpleasant chemical tastes.

It is very important to purchase rice bran which is fresh. When first preparing a nuka doko, pickle vegetable peels or the outer wilted leaves of cabbage or daikon daily for a week. Rub peels with salt and keep overnight in the nuka doko. Discard them daily. This practice helps to "ripen" the nuka doko with a good balance of flavor and moisture. To speed maturation, one can also use a starter from a neighbor's nuka doko. Twice a day, one mixes as though "heaven and earth have changed places." Human hands are most desirable for this particular endeavor since one's body temperature helps to ripen the nuka doko.

When the nuka doko becomes too watery, which can happen from the moisture released from the vegetables, add roasted rice bran as needed to try the following: make a dent in nuka doko with your fist and insert a clean sponge. After the sponge has absorbed the excess moisture, remove it.

I must also add that a mature nuka doko exudes a strong, very pungent aroma.

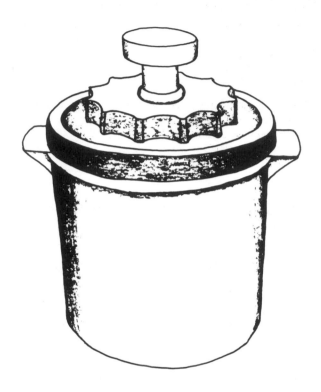

SHIO ZUKE *salt pickle*

Salt pickling in this day is relatively easy. The Japanese have devised a spring form or screw-type device which eliminates the trouble of finding the proper weight stone or wooden barrel for pickling which we call *taru*. The pressure from the modern device or the traditional weight of the stone put on salted vegetables releases its liquid. The liquid then becomes the brine which pickles the ingredients.

NUKA DOKO ZURKURI *making of rice bran bed*

3 lb roasted rice bran
12 oz salt
8-1/2 cup water
2 slices fresh bread
5 cloves garlic, sliced

2 red chili peppers
2 tbsp dashi no moto (essence
  of dashi
10 inches dashi konbu

In pickling container, combine rice bran, salt, sliced garlic, dashi no moto. Add 5 to 6 cups water and mix well. If too dry, add more of the remaining water to make paste. To help with fermentation, tear bread slices into the paste mixture. Add chili peppers and dashi konbu. Cover with a large damp towel. Place a tight lid on nuka doko and put container in a cool place.

Following are instructions for various vegetables which can be pickled in the rice bran bed.

NASU

6 Japanese eggplants
1 tbsp salt

Choose Japanese eggplants slender in shape. Rub eggplant skin with salt. Cut criss-cross into very tip of the eggplant, 1/4-inch deep. Dig a deep enough hole for the eggplant to sit upright. It will be ready for consumption within 24 hours.

KYURI

Cucumber as you need. Cut off both ends of the cucumbers. Rub skin with salt. For the evening meal, pickle cucumber in the morning.

SHIRO URI

Cut in half horizontally. Salt lightly. White melon can be eaten after 4 to 5 hours pickling.

CABBAGE

6 leaves or desired amount. Place nuka paste between each leaf. Form a bowl shape and cover with more paste. Cabbage will take 10 hours before being ready to eat.

NINJIN

Wash well. Pickle carrots whole. It will take 3 days.

CELERY AND BROCCOLI

Celery and broccoli will take 10 to 12 hours before ready.

MITSUMAME *honey beans*

1 stick kanten	1/2 cup kidney beans, cooked
2-1/2 cup water	1 can pineapple 12-1/2 oz
1-1/4 cup sugar	1 cup mandarin oranges
1/4 tsp vanilla, lemon extract or	3 or more kinds of fruit in
mint flavor	season

Soak kanten in water for 30 minutes. Cook with water until kanten melts. Add 3/4 cup sugar and cook on slow flame 15 minutes. Add flavoring and let cool in flat pan until kanten hardens, then cut in cubes. Drain kidney beans from can. Cook with 1/2 cup sugar gently on very low flame, until beans are sweetened. Cool in cooking liquid. Pour in a bowl a can of pineapple with syrup. Add kidney beans, fruit and mandarin oranges. Top with cubed kanten. Chill before serving. Kanten can be colored with 1/2 tbsp any food coloring. This makes jewel-like cubes when serving. Clean and prepare fruit in season. When using bananas, sprinkle slices with lime juice to avoid turning brown.

秋

Autumn

TSUKUMI *Moon Viewing*

The weather was perfectly calm and the moon shone brightly over our heads. In such stillness the party began. We were served sake in *sakazuki* or wine cups, rather large-mouthed, to catch the reflection of the moon. I remember once the clouds passing over the full moon in the small world of the sake cup, a moving experience for a girl in her late teens.

The Japanese celebrate two moon viewings in late summer, *Jugoya* on August 15, and *Jusanaya* in very early fall, on September 13. Determined by the lunar calendar when the moon is full and at its most brilliant, offerings are placed on the altar or *engawa* where the moonlight falls on the prescribed nights. Poems are composed for the occasion and appropriate stories told by moonlight.

It was a thrilling and fulfilling experience to be included in a moon viewing and poetry reading party. I felt so grown up in the moon viewing night setting. On a small, lacquered table on the *engawa*, there would be offerings of fruit, flowers and autumn grasses to the brilliant satellite. I remember an offering of sake and twelve rice cakes, placed in tiers, with gracefully arranged autumn weeds.

While a Westerner might view this growing-up experience as frivolous, or sentimental, it provided me a rich, emotional experience. Traditional Japanese culture gives a high regard to nature and the environment and their beauty. As I remember these things, I realize that in such memories I still am deeply Japanese.

Menu for Moon Viewing Party

Kame no sakamushi *sake-steamed duck*

Tsuki Mi Wan *moon viewing soup*

Karei no arai *chilled flounder sashimi*

Namazake no Teriyaki *teriyaki salmon*

Shinoda Bukuro to Satoimo no Mori Awase *stuffed fried beancurd with taro potatoes.*

Momiji Ae *"maple" salad*

Ebi No Kikka Age *fried shrimp in the shape of chrysanthemum*

Yamaji Gohan *autumn mountain pathway flavored rice*

Bancha *tea*

KAME NO SAKAMUSHI *sake-steamed duck*

2 whole boned duck or chicken breasts with skin
1 tsp sea salt
1 tbsp sake

Place boned duck or chicken breasts, skin side up, on pyrex dish and sprinkle with salt. Wrap tight with plastic wrap. Refrigerate and marinate for at least a half day. Preheat broiler. Meanwhile, pour sake over duck and steam 7 minutes in an oriental style steam basket or steamer substitute. Remove plate of duck from steamer and slide it under broiler 3 inches from heat. Broil 2 minutes or until breasts turn rich, golden brown. Cool to room temperature, then cut in 1/4 inch slices. Serve as appetizer or first course.

TSUKI MI WAN *moon viewing soup*

Egg custard:	**Soup**
2 eggs	4 cups dashi
1-1/2 cup dashi	1 tbsp shoyu
1/2 tsp salt	1/2 tsp salt
2 tsp sugar	alfalfa sprouts
Special equipment: *Nagashi-bako or obento*	

Beat eggs. Combine cooled dashi, salt, sugar with eggs. Strain into rectangular Japanese mold, nagashi bako, Japanese lunchbox, or obento. Steam 20 minutes over medium flame. Cool. Use round 2-inch diameter cutter to cut moon-shaped custards. Combine 4 cups dashi, shoyu, salt and bring to boil. Place moon custard in serving bowl with few sprigs of alfalfa sprouts. Pour hot broth over and serve.

KAREI NO ARAI *chilled flounder sashimi*

1 large flounder, fresh	1 tsp sake
1 cucumber	1 tsp mirin
1 stalk celery	1/2 cup shaved bonito
	chiso leaves or coriander
Tosa joyu sauce:	1 tbsp wasabi paste
6 tbsp shoyu	ice cubes
1/2 tbsp tamari shoyu (thick)	

Clean, remove scales, and cut flounder to gomai oroshi, five-pieced filleting (see illustration). Place skin side down on cutting board. Insert knife between skin and meat on tail and pull skin off. Cut in diagonal bite-size pieces. Place ice cubes and water in deep bowl. Soak skinned flounder in ice water. To hasten chilling, stir vigorously with wooden chop sticks 5 to 7 minutes. When flounder slices are well-chilled and very firm in texture, drain and pat off excess water. Cut cucumber in katsura-muki and cut in sengiri style. Cut celery and chiso leaves also in sengiri style. Soak in iced water to crisp.

continued on next page

Tosa joyu sauce; Combine shoyu, tamari sauce, sake and mirin in pot and bring to boil. Add shaved bonito. When shaved bonito settles down to bottom of pot, strain. Using deep glass bowls and serving on ice cube bed, arrange cucumber chilled flounder, celery and chiso leaves. Serve with large mound of wasabi paste and small individual bowl or tosa joyu sauce.

NAMAZAKE NO TERIYAKI *teriyaki salmon*

6 pieces fresh salmon steaks	**Tare sauce:**
1 tbsp shoyu	3 tbsp shoyu
1 tbsp sake	3 tbsp sake
	3 tbsp mirin
	2 tbsp oil

On salmon steaks sprinkle shoyu and sake. Let stand 15 to 20 minutes. This treatment will remove fishy smell and tighten texture of fish. In a pot over slow flame, combine shoyu, sake and mirin and bring to boil. Cool. Wipe moisture from marinated salmon steaks. Heat skillet with oil. Saute salmon steaks, shaking skillet gently while cooking. Turn when under side is slightly brown. When salmon steaks are 80% done, add half of tare sauce, shaking pan gently. When sauce starts to bubble, turn steaks again and add remaining tare sauce. Serve with pickled turnips or sweetened chestnuts.

SHINODA BUKURO TO SATOIMO NO MORI AWASE *stuffed*
fried beancurd with taro potatoes

1/4 lb kiriboshi daikon	2 tbsp shoyu
4 cups boiling water	2 tbsp mirin
1-1/2 cups dashi	1/2 tsp salt
2 tbsp shoyu	
1/2 lb chicken meat	1 lb satoimo
1-1/2 tsp shoyu	1 tbsp suet
4 aburage	4 cups water
40-inches kanpyo ribbon	2 tbsp kome nuka
4 cups water	1 cup dashi
1/2 tsp salt	1 tbsp sugar
3-1/2 cups dashi	1 tbsp mirin
3 tsp sugar	1 tbsp shoyu

Place kiriboshi daikon in large bowl. After rinsing with cold water, pour over 4 cups water and cover. Let stand until water cools. Stir gently. Rinse again in cold water. In large pot, bring 4 cups water to boil. Cook kiriboshi daikon until tender. Drain and squeeze out water. Simmer cooked kiriboshi daikon in dashi and shoyu and set aside. Cut chicken meat in small strips, marinate in shoyu. Slice aburage in half, pouring boiling water over to remove excess oil. Turn inside

Continued on next page

out. Soak kanpyo in 2 cups water 30 minutes. Drain. Boil in 2 cups salted water until soft. Cut in 8 pieces. Divide seasoned kiriboshi daikon and chicken meat in 8 parts. Stuff in aburage pouch and tie with gourd ribbon. In shallow pot, place stuffed aburage pouches and simmer with dashi, sugar, soy sauce, mirin, salt plus cooking liquid from kiriboshi daikon. Cook until most of liquid has been absorbed by aburage pouches. Peel satoimo and wash with 1 tbsp salt. rubbing between palms of the hands. Bring 4 cups water to a boil with kome nuka. Cook satoimo until easily pierced with a bamboo skewer. Wash in cold water and drain. Combine dashi, sugar, mirin, shoyu and bring to boil. Simmer satoimo in this mixture 20 minutes. Arrange aburage pouches and satoimo in serving dish. Serve hot or cold with any green garnish.

MOMIJI AE *"maple leaf" salad*

2/3 lb radishes	3 eggs
1 small carrot	salt
1/3 lb cucumbers	vinegar
3 shiitake	sugar
1/2 lb prawns, uncooked	

Peel and slice radishes and carrot into 1-1/2-inch strips. Without peeling cucumber, cut in half, lengthwise, remove seeds and slice in same manner. Salt and allow to stand until cucumbers, carrots and radishes become soft. Squeeze out liquid with hands. Soften mushrooms in enough cold water to cover, then slice into thin strips. Mix vegetables and mushrooms with 1-1/2 tsp vinegar. (This is called vinegar wash.) Squeeze gently. Devein shrimp and insert skewers through back to maintain straight shape during boiling. Boil in salted water until tender and cool. Remove skewers and shell. Slice lengthwise. Beat eggs. Add 1 tsp salt and 1 tbsp sugar. Stir while frying to make granulated, finished mixture. Force egg mixture through sieve while hot and allow to cool. Add 2 tbsp vinegar and mix. Add vegetables and shrimp gently to egg mixture. Arrange salad on individual plates in form of maple leaves in a pile. These colors suggest fall coloring of the momiji.

EBI NO KIKKA AGE *fried shrimp, in the shape of chrysanthemum*

1-1/2 oz fresh prawns	**Tentsuyu sauce:**
1 egg white	1-1/2 cup dashi
salt	1/2 cup mirin
1-1/2 tsp cornstarch	1/2 cup shoyu
3 oz harusame	4 tsp daikon, grated fine
frying oil	2 tsp ginger, grated fine

Shell and devein prawns. Wash and wipe dry. Grind and mix with egg white, 2/3 tsp salt, and cornstarch. Make balls 3/4-inch in diameter, Cut harusame into 2-inch lengths. On one side of shrimp balls, allow some cut noodles to stick out, forming a chrysanthemum flower form. Deep fry.

Tentsuyu sauce: Bring dashi, mirin, and shoyu to boil. To serve, place prawns on absorbent paper on dish with small dish of tentsuyu on the side. On 4 individual plates, place 1 tsp daikon and 1/4 tsp ginger.

YAMAJI GOHAN *autumn mountain pathway flavored rice*

3 cups rice	1 tsp mirin
2 cups water	2 tsp shoyu
1/3 lb shimeji or button	1-1/2 cups water
mushrooms	1-1/2 tsp salt
2 carrots	1 tbsp sake
1/2 cup dashi	20 ginkyo nuts, canned
1-1/3 tsp sugar	

Wash rice few times and drain well. Soak in 2 cups of water. Wash, clean mushrooms and cut into desirable size. Peel and slice carrots into 1/8-inch thick pieces. Cut out with maple leaf cutter. In small saucepan, place dashi, carrots and cook 3 to 4 minutes. When carrots are soft, add mushrooms, sugar, mirin and shoyu and cook additional 2 minutes. Drain liquid into measuring cup. Add enough water to make 1-1/2 cups. Combine this with rice soaking in 2 cups water. Add salt and sake. Using a heavy metal pot just for cooking rice as directed in basic rice cooking. While simmering add all ingredients last 5 minutes. Cover tight. Let stand 10 minutes after removing from heat. Toss lightly before serving.

This is a very poetic expression of autumn pathway in mountain, carpeted with scarlet maple leaves, nuts with a surprise discovery of mushrooms behind old tree trunks.

This is a wonderful brunch idea:
> **Aji no Kaori Zuke** *marinated horse mackerel*
> **Hikiniku soboro no Lettuce Tsutsumi** *crumbly meat wrapped in lettuce*
> **Onigiri** *rice balls with pickled plum*

AJI NO KAORI ZUKE *marinated horse mackerel*

2 fillets horse mackerel	**Boiled marinade sauce:**
(approx. 1 lb), fresh	3 tbsp shoyu
1 tbsp ginger juice	2 tbsp vinegar
1 tbsp sake	2 tbsp sugar
1 tbsp shoyu	2 tbsp sake
3 tbsp cornstarch	oil for deep frying
	2 cucumbers, sliced very thin

Clean and make 6 horse mackerel fillets. Marinate in ginger juice, sake, and shoyu 30 minutes. Combine ingredients for marinade sauce. Bring to boil, then cool. Heat cooking oil to 370 degrees F. Dust mackerel fillets with cornstarch and deep-fry 4 to 5 minutes. Marinate in sauce. Soak sliced cucumber in water to crisp then drain. On serving plate, arrange cucumber bed with fish on top. Pour sauce over fish fillet.

Onigiri

ONIGIRI *rice balls with pickled plum*

> 4 umeboshi, pickled plums
> 1 sheet nori
> 5 cups cooked rice
> 1 tbsp black sesame seeds, roasted

Remove seeds from umeboshi and tear into small pieces. Cut nori sheet into 1-inch long ribbon-like strips. Divide rice in half. Using the half of rice, take, 1/4 cup rice per ball, stuff with bits of plum, and make them into oval rice balls. Wrap around with nori strip, like a belt. With remaining half of rice, use 1/4 cup each to make triangular shapes. Stuff with bit of plum, and sprinkle with roasted black sesame seeds.

TORI NO OHARAME *"bundles of firewood" chicken*

> 1/3 lb chicken thigh meat
> 1 tbsp shoyu
> 1 tbsp sake
> 1/2 sheet of Asakura nori
> 1/2 egg white, slightly beaten
> vegetable cooking oil

Remove skin from chicken thigh meat, cutting into strips 2 inch x 1/5 inch. Do not chop chicken meat in little pieces. Let stand 1 hour in shoyu and sake mixture. Cut across width of seaweed to make 1/2-inch width bands. Taking 4 to 5 strips of chicken in one hand, use other hand to dip one side of the seaweed band into eggwhite. Fasten seaweed around center of chicken. Deep fry in vegetable oil. Drain and serve.

In the Kyoto area the Japanese farming women gather fire wood and bundle it with straw rope which they carry on their heads. They walk through the narrow paths of Kyoto selling the wood. These women are called **Oharame,** *because most of them come from the Yasa Ohara village in the Kyoto area. This dish resembles fire wood bundles.*

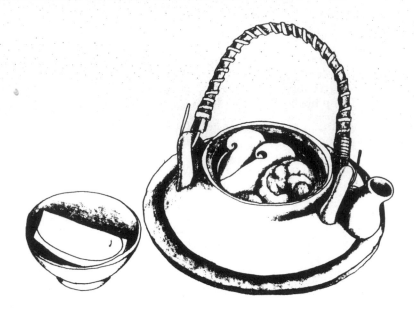

DOBIN MUSHI *clear teapot soup*

3-1/2 cup dashi
1-1/2 tsp salt
1 tsp shoyu
4 mushrooms
4 medium sized prawns,
    uncooked

1/4 lb chicken breast meat
1/2 tsp shoyu
4 sprigs watercress
20 ginkyo nuts (canned)
1 lime

Special equipment: *fireproof teapot, ceramic or metal**

Prepare dashi with salt and shoyu, bring to boil, set aside. Clean mushrooms, cut in half and place in teapot. Devein and shell prawns retaining tails. Cut slit in back center and open prawn. Place on top of mushrooms. Slice chicken breast meat in small thin pieces. Marinate with shoyu. Add to teapot. Wash and clean watercress. Add 1 sprig to teapot. Top all ingredients with 4 or 5 ginkyo nuts. Fill teapot with dashi and cover. Place teapot on very slow burner until contents start to bubble. Remove immediately to avoid bubbling over. Cut lime into quarters. Place one section on cup bottom overturned on the teapot.

Dobin mushi is a very unique and intriguing way of serving clear soup. The soup is so named because of the container used for serving. The container resembles a little teapot with a Japanese wine-sized cup overturned placed ontop the teapot lid. When ready to serve, the cup is turned over and used to drink the soup poured from the teapot. The lime wedge placed on top the cup bottom is squeezed in the soup.

KAREI NO HISUI AGE *jade sanddabs*

5 sanddabs
1 tsp salt
30 ginkyo nuts (1 small can)
2 tbsp cornstarch
1/4 cup flour
5 chrysanthemum leaves
1/2 cup grated daikon
1/4 cup grated carrot

Koromo:
1 cup flour
1 egg
4/5 cup ice water

Tentsuyu:
3/4 cup dashi
3 tbsp shoyu
3 tbsp mirin
oil

Cut sanddabs in 3-piece filleting style. One boneless fillet is cut from each side of fish. The skeleton forms the third piece. Lightly salt. Slice ginkyo nuts into thin pieces and dust with cornstarch. Dust fillets with flour. Heat oil for deep frying. Prepare koromo or batter according to basic tempura recipes. Dip dusted fish in batter. When well coated, cover one side of fillet with ginkyo nuts. Deep-fry until crisp. Coat underside of chrysanthemum leaves with batter and deep fry.

For Tentsuyu: Combine dashi, shoyu, mirin and bring to boil. Serve fish with small mound of momiji oroshi, mixture of grated daikon and carrot. Tentsuyu can be served in a separate small dish.

KABU NO NARUTO MAKI *seaweed shoot and turnip wrap*

2 large turnips
1 tsp salt
Sanbaizu sauce:
7 tbsp vinegar
3 tsp salt
2 tbsp sugar
8 gms wakame
additional salt

Peel and slice turnips in very thin pieces. Sprinkle with 1 tsp salt. Set aside 15 minutes, then squeeze water out of turnip. Combine vinegar, salt and sugar to make sanbaizu. Use 1/3 vinegar sauce to pickle sliced, salted turnip. Soak wakame in water. When soft, drain and pat dry. Pickle wakame in 1/3 vinegar sauce. Place sliced and pickled turnip on cutting board. Form square shapes overlapping each other. Place pickled wakame on top of turnip then repeat. Roll from near end. Slice roll in 1/2-inch pieces. Pour remaining sauce over. Serve cutting side up.

TORI NO LEMON SAUCE KAKE *chicken with lemon sauce*

1-1/2 lb chicken breast meat
1-1/2 tbsp shoyu
1-1/2 tbsp sake
1 tsp ginger, grated
1/2 cup flour
1 egg
2 tbsp water

3/4 cup bread crumbs
3/4 cup water
1/4 cup sugar
2 tsp cornstarch
2 tsp water
2 tbsp lemon juice
1 lemon, thinly sliced

Remove skin from chicken breast meat. Pound, marinate with shoyu, sake, and grated ginger 20 minutes. Dust with flour. Dip in mixture of beaten egg and water. Coat with bread crumbs. Deep fry until golden brown. Bring to boil water and sugar. Add cornstarch mixed with water and lemon juice. Remove from heat. When sauce begins to thicken slightly arrange chicken on serving plate. Spoon sauce over chicken. Garnish with lemon.

KABU TO ABURAGE NO SUNOMONO *turnip and fried soybean curd with vinegar sauce*

6 small turnips
1/2 tsp salt
2 aburage
4 shiitake

Sauce:
1 tbsp vinegar
2-1/2 tsp sugar
1/3 tsp salt
2 tsp shoyu

Wash turnips. Cut in 8 wedges and boil in 1/2 tsp salt and water 5 minutes. Drain and set aside. Place aburage in colander and pour boiling water over to remove excess oil. Squeeze and cut aburage in half lengthwise then cut in 1/2-inch wide strips. Soak shiitake in warm water to soften. Squeeze and cut sengiri style. Combine vinegar, sugar, salt and shoyu. Add cooked turnip, aburage, and shiitake. Toss gently and serve.

RINGO TO KYURI TO KAKI NO OROSHI AE *vinegared apple, cucumber and persimmon with grated daikon*

1 large apple
1 medium sized persimmon, firm and flat in shape
1 cucumber
1 cup daikon, grated
2 tbsp vinegar
2 tbsp sugar
1 tsp salt

Peel and core apple and persimmon, cut in 1/2-inch cubes. Cut cucumbers in 1/2-inch cubes. Squeeze grated daikon gently to remove some of the water. Combine vinegar, sugar and salt. Mix well, add daikon, then add cubed fruit and cucumber. It makes a delightful addition to the autumn dining table.

Note that pointed persimmons are soft and not desirable for this dish.

HANA KYABETSU TO KANI NO SUMISO AE *cauliflower and crabmeat with soybean paste sauce*

1 lb cauliflower	1 oz ginger, fresh, slivered
16 cups water	5 oz miso paste
1 tbsp wheat flour	2 tbsp sugar
1/2 tsp salt	3 tbsp sake
1/2 can crabmeat or	1-1/2 tbsp vinegar
3 oz frozen crabmeat	

Soak cauliflower 1 hour in mixture of 8 cups water and 1/2 tbsp wheat flour. Drain. Combine 8 cups water and 1/2 tbsp wheat flour again. In it boil cauliflower, adding salt. When tender, wash in cold water, drain and slice in bite-size pieces. Break crabmeat apart in small pieces. Blend miso paste, sugar, sake and bring to boil over low flame, stirring continuously. Pour in bowl and chill. Add vinegar. Serve cauliflower and crabmeat in individual bowls. Top with sauce and garnish with ginger slivers.

YASAI NO RINGO ZU AE *vegetables with apple sauce*

2 cucumbers	**Sauce:**
1 tsp salt	1 apple
6 shiitake	3 tbsp vinegar
3 carrots	1/3 tsp salt
	additional salt

Pare cucumbers. Slice thinly, sprinkle with salt and let stand 15 minutes. Soak shiitake in warm water. When soft, squeeze out water. Cut off stem and cut in thin strips. Cut carrots in sengiri style. Boil in salted water until soft. Core apple and halve. sprinkle with salt and grate. Add vinegar and salt and mix well. Combine cucumber, shiitake with apple. Sauce and serve.

BEER DAKI *pork and vegetables with beer broth*

2 bunches harusame	**Sauce A:**
1 bunch spinach	1 tsp parsley, minced
2 cups hot water	1 tsp green onion, minced
8 oz beer	3 tbsp shoyu
1 lb pork fillet	1 tsp lemon peel, minced
	Sauce B:
	1 tbsp ginger, grated
	3 tbsp shoyu

Place harusame in boiling water. Remove from heat and let cool in pot. Remove from pot when transparent. Rinse and cut into 5-inch lengths. Clean, wash spinach and remove stem ends. **Sauce A:** Combine parsley, green onion, shoyu and lemon peel. **Sauce B:** Combine ginger and shoyu. Using shallow electric skillet, boil hot water. Add beer and softened harusame. When boiling add pork and spinach. Serve with either dipping sauce.

HORENSO NO PEANUTS AE *spinach with peanut sauce*

2 lbs spinach	**Sauce:**
salted boiling water	1 cup roasted peanuts
2 tsp shoyu	1-1/2 tbsp sugar
	2 tbsp shoyu

Holding rootends, dip 1/4th spinach into salted, boiling water until soft. Rinse in cold water and drain. Repeat with remaining spinach. Squeeze gently. Cut lengthwise into 2-inch pieces. Sprinkle with shoyu. Let stand while preparing sauce. Grind roasted peanuts into paste with morter or blender. Add sugar, shoyu and mix well. Before serving, squeeze any remaining moisture from spinach. Toss with peanut sauce and serve.

HARUSAME TO KYURI NO SANBAIZU *vinegared bean threads and cucumber*

1 bunch (4 oz) harusame	**Sanbaizu sauce:**
1 cucumber	5 tbsp vinegar
	1-1/2 tsp salt
	1 tbsp sugar

Soak harusame 5 minutes in water until soft. When soft, cook in hot water for 1 minute. Cover until transparent. Wash in cold water, then drain well. Cut into 6 cm in length. Cut cucumber in half lengthwise scooping out cucumber seeds with spoon. Slice and cut in thin strips sengiri style. Soak in cold water to crisp. When cucumber strips are crisp, drain water and pat dry. Combine ingredients to make sanbaizu and mix well. Toss cooked harusame and cucumber. Arrange in serving dish. Pour over sanbaizu before serving.

This makes a delightful evening salad.

GAN MODOKI *deep-fried bean curd balls*

2 medium shiitake	1/2 cup shredded carrots
2 tofu	oil for frying
1 tsp salt	mustard
2 tsp sugar	shoyu
1 egg	

Place shiitake in enough cold water to cover. Squeeze out water and cut in small strips. Wrap tofu in dish towel and drain water by placing between two cutting boards under weight. Then place in bowl and knead until sticky. Add salt, sugar, egg, shiitake and carrots, mix well. Shape in 3-inch diameter balls and deep-fry. Place on wire rack to drain oil. Serve with small dish of mustard and shoyu sauce.

Variations: Add cooked crabmeat or cooked chopped pork, and minced green onions.

KUSHIAGE *deep-fried nibbles on skewers*

10 shrimp	**Batter:**
3 oz scallops	4 eggs
2 tbsp green nori flakes	1 cup milk
2 stalks green onion	1 tbsp sake
3 oz snapper fillet	1 cup flour
2 chiso leaves	1 tsp sugar
1/3 lb pork	1/2 tsp salt
5 small onions	2 cups breadcrumbs to coat
2 inch ginger slices	shoyu
5 brussel sprouts	tonkatsu sauce
1/3 lb beef	ketchup
1/3 lb chicken meat	prepared mustard
1 tbsp shoyu	lemon
1 tbsp sake	salt
1 green pepper	
1/4 lb green pepper	
1/4 lb mushrooms, fresh	
2/3 lb squid	
2 sheets nori	

Shell, devein shrimp and insert skewer. Cut dry scallops and skewer, sprinkle with green nori flakes, alternate with white part of green onion, cut 1 inch in length. Cut snapper fillet into 1-1/2-inch squares. Use 1/4th the chiso leaves to wrap snapper and then skewer. Cut pork into 1-1/2-inch squares. Skewer with combination of small onions, ginger and brussel sprouts. Soak bite-size pieces of pork and beef in shoyu and sake 15 minutes, then skewer with combination of green pepper chunks and/or mushrooms. Remove outer skin of squid. Cut in 2-inch squares, wrap with 1/2 x 2-inch strip of nori. Beat eggs well. Add milk, sake and mix well. Sift in flour, sugar, salt and mix gently. Heat cooking oil to 360 degrees F. Dip skewered ingredients in batter, then coat with breadcrumbs. Shake off excess breadcrumbs and deepfry. Serve as desired with any combination of sauces. *This dish can be cooked by the hostess or guests can make up their own combination of ingredients.*

We were always told that the best kushiage was served in the Osaka area. Unlike tempura, kushiage dough is not transparent; you will be in a constant guessing game as to what is being served. One can create an endless number of combinations on the skewer. This recipe can give you only a few of the possibilities. Use any available seasonal ingredients.

TORI NO TATSUA AGE *fried chicken in cornstarch*

4 pieces chicken thigh meat
1 tbsp shoyu
1 tbsp sake
1/2 tsp sugar
4 tbsp cornstarch

oil for deep frying
1 green pepper, cut in 8 wedges
salt
lemon cut into wedges

Cut chicken in large pieces and marinate in shoyu, sake and sugar 20 minutes. Roll in cornstarch. Heat cooking oil to 360 degrees F. Fry until golden brown. Deep-fry green pepper wedges. Sprinkle with salt. Serve both with lemon wedge.

TORI MOMO NIKU TO KURI NO NIKOMI *chicken leg meat and chestnut simmered dish*

6 chicken legs (thighs and
  drumsticks together)
1 tsp salt
1 tbsp sake
2 medium carrots
4 tbsp sugar
1 cup cooking oil
1 stalk green onion

1 finger fresh ginger
3 tbsp sake or dry sherry
1 tbsp shoyu
2 cups dashi
1 can sweetened chestnuts
  (drain syrup)
1 tbsp sesame oil
additional salt, sake and sugar

Cut into chicken leg with knife until tip touches bone. Sprinkle salt and 1 tbsp sake on each leg. Allow to stand so it will not mush when sauteing. Cut carrots into shapes of flower, using vegetable cutter. Each flower should be 3/4-inch in thickness. Place carrots in small saucepan with enough water to cover. Add 1 tsp sugar and cook over slow flame until water is gone. Wipe prepared legs dry. In large skillet, heat cooking oil. Saute chicken until skin turns brown. Cut green onion in 1-inch pieces. Crush ginger with flat surface of knife. In dutch oven or deep pot, place green onions, ginger, 1 tbsp sugar, sake, shoyu and dashi. Bring to boil. Add chicken legs and cover. Simmer 20 minutes. Turn over chicken legs, add sweetened chestnuts and sesame oil. Simmer another 30 minutes. Arrange on serving dish one piece of chicken leg, a few chestnuts and flower-shaped carrots. Garnish with pine needles.

SAKANA NO SHIO YAKI *salted-broiled horse mackerel*

4 (approx 1-1/2 lbs) horse
  mackerel, fresh
3 tsp salt

Clean fish. Sprinkle both sides with salt. Let stand 30 minutes. Using metal skewers, skewer fish *odori-zushi* style, as though fish is alive and swimming or dancing. Head and tail should be up. Rub salt on fins, opening fins into fan-shape. It is called *kasho*, "make-up salt". Broil both sides with high flame, taking care not to burn skin.

NAMAZAKE NO TSUTSUMI YAKI *wrapped salmon bake*

4 pcs (approx 1-1/2 lb)	3 stalks green onion
fresh salmon fillets	8 shiitake
6 tbsp sake	12 ginkyo nuts, canned
1 tsp salt	4 lemon wedges

Special equipment: *aluminum foil for baking container*

Preheat oven to 450 degrees F. Cut heavy-duty aluminum foil in 4 12-inch squares. Cut salmon fillet in 2 or 3 small pieces and place in center of aluminum foil. Sprinkle with 1 tbsp sake and pinch of salt. Slice green onions in thin strips. Place shiitake in warm water to soften. Squeeze, remove stems and cut thin strips. Arrange 1/4 green onions, shiitake and ginkyo nuts on top of salmon fillets. Sprinkle with 1 tsp sake and dash of salt. Close both edges of foil, overlapping. Gather ends and twist to be air tight. Bake 10 to 12 minutes. Serve on platter with lemon wedges.

HIKINIKU SOBORO NO LETTUCE TSUTSUMI *crumbly meat wrapped in lettuce*

2 medium shiitake	**Miso sauce:**
4 oz canned bamboo shoots,	4 tbsp miso
boiled	3-1/2 tbsp sugar
2 stalk green onion	2 tbsp mirin
1 tbsp oil	1 tbsp sesame oil
1/3 lb ground pork	1/4 tsp red pepper
1/3 lb ground beef	1 head leaf lettuce
1 tbsp sake	
1 tbsp shoyu	
1-1/2 tbsp flour	

Soak skiitake in warm water to soften. When soft, squeeze out water. Remove stems and mince fine. Chop bamboo shoots. Shred 1 stalk of green onion and soak in water to crisp. Mince the other 2 stalks of green onion. Heat skillet with oil. Saute minced green onion, shiitake, and bamboo shoots. Add ground pork and beef and stir until meat is cooked. Add 1 tbsp sake, 1 tbsp shoyu, 1 tsp sugar, 1-1/2 tbsp flour, mix well and set aside. In small saucepan, combine ingredients for miso sauce. Cook over medium heat and stir until mixture becomes smooth in texture. Rinse lettuce well and drain. Serve the loosened lettuce leaves on a plate with shredded green onion on side. Serve meat mixture in bowl, miso sauce in another. Place the meat mixture on 1 or 2 lettuce leaves, spoon miso sauce and shredded onion over. Eat with fingers.

SAKE NO NABE TERIYAKI *skillet salmon teriyaki*

3 pieces fresh salmon, 1-inch thick

Sauce for marinade:

1 tbsp sake	1/2 cup flour
3 tbsp shoyu	1-1/2 tbsp oil
3 tsp sugar	1/2 piece daikon, grated

Split salmon fillet in half and remove center bone. Marinate salmon in sake, shoyu and sugar 1/2 hour. Remove fish and wipe off excess liquid. Dust with flour. Heat skillet. When hot, add oil and place floured salmon in skillet. Brown both sides over slow flame. Pour over remaining marinade to glaze and serve with grated daikon.

GYUUNIKU NO MISO MAKI YAKI *miso-flavored rolled beef*

4 stalks green onion	2 tbsp shoyu
1-1/2 lb beef	3 tbsp sugar
1-1/2 tbsp oil	1 tbsp sake
4 cups miso	2 tbsp sesame seeds, roasted

Cut off roots and clean green onion. Broil without burning. Cut in 3-inch pieces. Set aside. Slice beef fillet thin. Open in 4-inch square or use 2 small pieces of sliced beef to make 4-inch square. Wrap 3 broiled green onions like rolling jelly roll. Heat skillet and add oil. Brown evenly on all sides rolling gently. Remove from skillet and set aside. In small saucepan, combine miso, shoyu, sugar, sake and bring to boil. In skillet place wrapped onion beef rolls. Add miso sauce and stir gently until meat absorbs the sauce. Serve family-style on large platter. Sprinkle with roasted sesame seeds. Serve this with *kikuka-kabu* (vinegared chrysanthemum-shaped turnips). See index.

MIZUTAKI *boiled chicken*

5 lb chicken	1 tbsp grated fresh ginger
1 cup dashi (soup stock)	3 tbsp green onion, minced
5 tbsp shoyu	salt
1 tbsp mirin	pepper
1 tbsp lemon juice	

Chop chicken in 1-1/2 to 2-inch chunks. Bone and skin are left intact. To make seasoning sauce, mix dashi, shoyu and mirin and bring to boil. After chilling add lemon juice. Bring 15 cups water to boil. Drop in cleaned chicken and continue cooking without lid. Skim off fat and residue. Cover and continue simmering 1 hour. When chicken is tender enough to fall apart, remove from heat. Bring pan and heating units to center of table. Arrange pile of grated ginger minced green onion on plate. Have salt and pepper on the table. From these seasonings individuals will adjust sauce to taste. When sauce becomes thin, feel free to spoon chicken soup and drink, or add more seasoning to make new sauce.

NIKU DANGO TO HAKUSAI NO DONABE NI *meatballs with wonbok in clay pot*

1/2 lb ground pork	6 shiitake
1 finger, ginger, minced	2 tbsp oil
1 stalk green onion, minced	4 cups dashi
1/2 tsp salt	4 tbsp shoyu
1 tbsp shoyu	1 tbsp sugar
2 tbsp sake	
oil for deep frying	**Optional:**
1 head wonbok	noodles, mochi

Mix ground pork, minced ginger, minced green onion in large bowl, then add salt, shoyu and sake. Coat palms of hands with oil, divide mixture into six parts, shape into flat oval patties. Heat cooking oil to 365 degrees F and deep-fry patties 5 to 6 minutes until golden brown. Since patties will cook in broth later on, they need not be cooked through at this time. Wash wonbok, cut into bite-size pieces and saute lightly in oil. Soak shiitake in warm water and squeeze out water when soft. Remove from water, cut off stems, cut in half. In clay pot place dashi, shoyu and sugar. Bring to boil. Then place wonbok, shiitake and pork patties in broth and simmer 20 minutes. Add ginkyo nuts and serve in clay pot at table. For added pleasure, noodles and mochi can also be placed in pot during the last 20 minutes.

KAREI NO OROSHI NI *braised flounder with grated radish*

3 flounder, fresh	**Sauce:**
1/2 cup flour	1-1/2 cups dashi
oil for deep-frying	1 tsp sugar
	1 tbsp mirin
	1/4 tsp salt
	2 tbsp shoyu
	1 cup daikon, grated
	2 stalks green onion, sliced thin
	1 tbsp shoga, grated

Cut flounder in half, one half retaining head, other half the tail. Clean and wipe dry. Make shallow slits on skin. Dust with flour. Heat cooking oil to 360 degrees F and fry fish until meat next to bone is cooked. Set aside. Combine dashi, sugar, mirin, salt, shoyu and bring to boil. Add daikon, onion,shoga and mix well. In shallow pan, place deep-fried flounder. Pour over dashi mixture. Simmer 5 minutes and serve while hot.

TOFU NO KAWAI HAMBURGER *tofu patties*

2 squares tofu	1 tbsp cornstarch
3 shiitake	6 oz crabmeat, canned or fresh
1 carrot	frozen
2 oz coriander, fresh	2 tbsp salad oil
1 tsp salt	1/2 cup dashi
1/4 tsp pepper	1/4 cup shoyu
2 eggs	1/4 cup mirin
	1 cup daikon, grated

Wrap tofu with cheesecloth and place weight on it for 30 minutes to squeeze out water. Soak shiitake in warm water to soften. Remove stems and cut in thin strips. Cut carrots in thin strips, sengiri. Rinse coriander leaves. Cut stems 1-inch long. Heat skillet with 1 tbsp oil and saute shiitake and carrot. Add salt and pepper. Using a food processor, combine tofu, egg, cornstarch. Mix one minute or mix with hands. Add crabmeat, cooked vegetables and mix gently. Divide and make ten patties. Heat skillet with 1 tbsp oil and cook tofu patty until golden brown. Make dipping sauce with dashi, shoyu and mirin. Serve with grated daikon on side.

HIKINIKU TO HAKUSAI NO SOUP NI *wonbok and ground meat stew*

3/4 lb ground pork	6 shiitake
3/4 lb ground beef	1/4 lb harusame
1 tbsp ginger, minced	1 square tofu
1 tsp salt	2 tbsp oil
1 tbsp shoyu	4 cups dashi
2 tbsp sake	2 tbsp sugar
oil for deep-frying	4 tbsp shoyu
2-1/2 lb wonbok, Chinese cabbage	

Combine ground pork, ground beef, minced ginger, salt, shoyu, sake in bowl. Knead well with hands until mixture has very smooth texture. Coat palms of hands with oil and divide meat in 6 balls or patties. Heat cooking oil to 365 degrees F and deep-fry 5 to 8 minutes. Drain off oil and set aside. Wash and cut wonbok in six parts lengthwise, then cut horizontally according to wonbok size. Soak shiitake in warm water to soften. Remove stems and cut in half. Soak harusame in warm water to soften. Cut in 4 to 5-inch lengths. Cut tofu in 1-inch cubes. Heat large skillet or wok with oil. Stir fry wonbok and shiitake. Add dashi. Bring to boil then add deep-fried meat balls, sugar and shoyu. Simmer 20 minutes then add beanthreads and tofu. Cook 45 minutes. Transfer to serving pot or bowl. This dish should be served in soup bowls. It will warm you in the crisp autumn weather.

TAKARA MUSHI *treasure chest pumpkin*

1 pumpkin about 5 lbs	1 tsp usukuchi shoyu, substitute
4-1/2 tsp salt	3/4 tsp regular shoyu
4 medium size shiitake	18 small shrimps in their shells
5 tbsp sugar	16 to 20 snow peas
1 tbsp shoyu	1 tbsp mirin
1-3/4 cup niban dashi	30 ginkyo nuts, canned
1/4 cup sake, or dry sherry	

Scrub pumpkin vigorously with stiff brush under cold, running water. Cut off top with large, sharp knife, making lid, and leaving stem intact for use as handle. Scrape seeds and stringy fibers from lid and pumpkin shell. With small spoon or melon-ball cutter scoop out balls of pumpkin meat, but leave a 3/4-inch wall of flesh intact as shell. Set balls aside. Sprinkle flesh side of lid and inside walls of pumpkin evenly with salt. Place pumpkin and its lid in colander with small support. Place colander in pot large enough to enclose it completely for preliminary steaming. Pour water in until it reaches 1 to 1-1/2 inches below colander. Bring water to boil. Cover pot tightly and steam over high heat 10 minutes. Remove colander, its contents and set aside. Place shiitake in enough cold water to cover and set aside 1 hour. Bring to boil in small saucepan, then simmer, uncovered, 15 minutes. Cool to room temperature, strain liquid in bowl and set aside. Remove stem and cut mushrooms in 16 to 20 1/2-inch pieces.

In 1-qt saucepan, combine 1/2 cup mushroom liquid with 1 tbsp sugar and shoyu. Bring to boil over high heat, add mushrooms and stir frequently. Cook briskly, uncovered, 10 to 20 minutes, until all liquid has evaporated. Set aside. In 2-qt saucepan, combine 1 cup niban dashi, 2 tbsp sugar, 3/4 tsp salt and pumpkin balls. Bring to boil. Stir in 1 tsp sake. Boil uncovered 5 minutes, then remove pumpkin balls with slotted spoon and set aside. Reduce liquid in pan by boiling over high heat until liquid becomes thick syrup. Watch for any signs of burning and regulate heat accordingly. When thick, stir in usukuchi shoyu, remove from burner and stir in pumpkin balls.

In 2-qt saucepan, bring 2 cups of salted water to boil. Drop shrimp in and boil 3 to 4 minutes. Drain in colander and run cold water over shrimp to stop cooking. Peel shrimp and slit along backs. Remove vein with tip of knife and cut shrimp in half crosswise. In a 2-qt saucepan, combine 1/2 cup niban dashi, 2 tbsp sake or dry sherry, 2 tbsp sugar and 3/4 tsp salt. Bring to boil, cook down to about half amount and remove from burner. Add shrimp, stirring to moisten them thoroughly and set aside. In 1-qt saucepan, bring 1 cup of salted water to boil. Drop in snow peas, return to boil. In colander, drain and run cold water over immediately to stop cooking and retain color. Combine 1/4 cup niban dashi, 1 tbsp sake or dry sherry, and 1/8 tsp salt in saucepan and bring to boil. Drop in flavored snow peas, boil again, then remove from heat. Cool by placing pan in large bowl of cold water.

In 1-qt pan, combine mirin, 1/8 tsp salt, and ginkyo nuts. Cook over high heat 1 to 2 minutes, shaking pan almost constantly until liquid is gone. Remove from

continued on next page

burner. Cut thin slice from base of pumpkin to prevent it from rocking. Place mushrooms, pumpkin balls, shrimp, snow peas and ginkyo nuts inside pumpkin. Cover pumpkin with pumpkin lid and carefully transfer pumpkin to colander. Return colander to deep pot and fill with water to 1-1/2-inch below colander. Bring water to boil. Cover tightly and steam 5 minutes. Serve at once.

KURI NO SHOKA MUSHI *steamed red rice with pork stuffed with sweet chestnut*

1/2 cup mochi gome	1 can (13 oz) sweet chestnuts in
1/2 tsp red food coloring	heavy syrup
1 lb ground pork	1 tbsp sake or sherry
1 tbsp green onion, minced	shoyu
1/2 tsp ginger, grated	mustard
1 tsp salt	

Wash and soak mochi gome overnight in water with red food coloring. Drain rice and dry with cloth. Spread on plate. Mix well ground pork, minced onion, grated ginger, salt. Divide into 24 equal portions. Drain syrup from canned chestnuts. Cut chestnuts in quarters. Wrap chestnut pieces with seasoned ground pork mixture, shaping in 2-inch diameter balls. Roll balls in red rice, coating evenly. Press rice gently. Spread dish cloth in steamer and place balls inside. Steam 15 to 20 minutes with high steam. Serve hot with mustard and shoyu mixture sauce.

The dish resembles the pine flower.

BUTA HONETSUKI NIKU NO KETCHUP KARAME *country-style pork spareribs with ketchup sauce*

2 lb country-style pork spareribs	4 tbsp Worcestershire sauce
1 tsp salt	2 tbsp ketchup
1 tbsp shoyu	2 tbsp sugar
1 tbsp sake	oil for deep frying
2 cloves garlic, crushed	1 tbsp sesame oil
1/2 cup cornstarch	lettuce leaves

Cut and separate spareribs in small pieces. Marinate 60 minutes in salt, shoyu, sake and garlic. Wipe off excess liquid. Dust with cornstarch. Combine Worcestershire sauce, ketchup and sugar. Mix well and set aside. Heat cooking oil to 365 degrees. Deep-fry marinated pork spareribs. Fry until meat is well cooked, 5 to 7 minutes. Drain. In skillet, heat sesame oil, saute crushed garlic from marinade sauce, add ketchup sauce mixture. When it boils add spareribs. Stir until ribs are well coated with sauce. Serve on lettuce leaves.

SOBO NO TEUCHI SOBA

1 lb soba flour	1/4 cup hot water
1/2 cup hot water	1/2 cup soba flour for dusting
4 oz wheat flour	

Place soba flour in large bowl and pour in hot water. Stir quickly. Then using one's hands, mix well. When mixture becomes crumbly, add wheat flour, hot water and knead well. Make dough in ball shape, cover with wet cheesecloth and let stand 30 minutes or more. Then wrap dough with dishcloth and stamp with feet or pound with hands. Place dough back in bowl. Repeat procedure several times. Transfer soba dough onto a soba-floured board. Flatten with feet or by hand. Quite a bit of pressure is required. Using rolling pin, roll dough out, dusting with soba flour. Roll out dough 2 mm thick, fold in half, then in fourths. Cut in very thin, ribbon-like strips. When cut, soba dough should not be exposed to air. When cut, store in covered container for later use. Soba noodles should stay fresh for 1 week. The amount of hot water needed to add to soba flour differs. Some flour absorbs more moisture, some less, depending on age and nature of flour.

Grandmother never actually taught me how to make soba noodles. I was often her singing companion, however, while she happily mixed the flour. Since I was a ballet student, I had extremely powerful legs and feet and thus a very strong stamp! We sang "Sumida River Song," her favorite melody, she the soprano, the alto my department. I even remember grandmother gave her soba noodles as gifts to her favorite friends. We never told anyone, however, that the noodles had been kneaded by a very special method! Now they know it was foot-kneaded by her dancing granddaughter.

Cooking method for soba: Fill large pot with water. Bring to boil. Shake excess flour off the noodles. Add soba to boiling water and cook. When it boils, stir gently. Cook another minute. Drain. Rinse with cold water. Drain again. Serve either hot or cold. Recipes follow.

KABOCHA NO EBI MISO KAKE *pumpkin with shrimp miso sauce*

2 lb pumpkin squash	1/2 lb shrimp, uncooked
2-1/2 cup dashi	1/2 lb white miso
1 tsp salt	2 tbsp sugar
2 tsp shoyu	2 tbsp sake
1 tsp sugar	1 tbsp water

Select fresh, tender skinned pumpkin squash. Divide in 6 equal pieces. Bring to boil dashi, salt, shoyu, and sugar. Add pumpkin squash and cook over low flame with cover. Cook until squash is tender. Remove from burner and let stand in broth 20 minutes. Shell, devein and mince shrimp. Place shrimp, miso, sugar, sake in water in small pot and cook over low flame, stirring constantly. Place pumpkin squash in serving dish and pour broth over squash. Dress with shrimp miso sauce and serve hot.

KANI IRI TAMAGO DOFU SOMEN SOE *crab-egg custard tofu with* noodles

3 eggs	1/4 lb crab, canned or fresh
1/3 tsp cornstarch	1 bunch coriander
1 tsp water	1 bundle (4 oz) somen noodles
1 cup dashi	1 cup dashi
1/3 tsp salt	1/2 tsp mirin
1/3 tsp shoyu	2 tsp shoyu
1/3 tsp mirin	1/3 tsp salt

Beat 3 eggs. Mix cornstarch with water. Add to dashi, salt, shoyu, mirin and bring to boil. When cool, add beaten eggs. Stir well. Prevent from making too many air bubbles which would cause custard to have holes. Strain through fine sieve. Dip coriander in boiling water and rinse in cold water. Cut in 1/2-inch pieces. In 6-inch square mold, pour three-fourths egg mixture. Steam 3 minutes over medium flame. Reduce flame and steam additional 10 minutes. When surface becomes custard-like in texture, wipe off moisture gently. Scatter crabmeat and cooked coriander over custard surface and pour over remaining one-fourth of egg mixture. Steam over medium flame 5 minutes or more. Remove from steamer and cool. Boil somen noodles in large pot, cooking until tender. (For doneness, a strand tested in cold water should be translucent.) Bring to boil dashi, mirin, shoyu, salt and cool. Cut egg custard in cubes. Divide somen noodles in 6 portions. Serve in individual bowls with sauce over.

IKA NO TOFU ZUME *squid stuffed with tofu*

1 square tofu	1 tsp garlic, finely minced
2 lb squid, fresh or frozen	1 tbsp sesame seeds, roasted
1 tbsp oil	1 tbsp sesame oil
1 tbsp carrot, minced	1/2 tbsp shoyu
2 tbsp onion, finely minced	1/2 tsp salt
1/4 tsp salt	1/4 tsp pepper
1/4 tsp pepper	6 chiso leaves

Wrap tofu with cheesecloth. Place weight on top to remove excess moisture. Remove and discard insides of squid. Chop legs fine. Heat skillet, add oil, saute minced carrot, onion and chopped squid legs. Season with salt and pepper. Place tofu in food processer and/or knead by hand. Add sauteed onion, carrot, squid legs and garlic, sesame seeds, sesame oil, shoyu, salt and pepper and mix. Stuff squid body with tofu mixture. Steam 15 minutes over high flame. Serve on chiso leaves. May be served with dressing of 3 tbsp each vinegar and shoyu.

HIRYOZU NO NIMONO *fried "flying dragonheads"*

4 oz carrot	1 egg
4 oz gobo	2 tsp mirin
2 oz green beans	2 tsp shoyu
1 shiitake	oil for deep frying
6 oz shrimp	3 cups dashi
3 tbsp sesame seeds	2-1/2 tbsp shoyu
2 squares tofu	2-1/2 tbsp sake
6 oz yamaimo	

Peel and cut carrot into short julienne strips. Peel gobo into shaped small hasagaki. Parboil green beans and cut in thin pieces. Place shiitake in warm water to soften. Remove stem and cut in thin strips. Devein, shell shrimp and cut in 1/2-inch pieces. Roast sesame seeds and set aside. Wrap tofu in cheesecloth and squeeze out water. Peel and grate yamaimo or use food processor to make puree. Combine with tofu. Blend well until very smooth and creamy in texture. Add egg, mirin, shoyu and mix well. Add carrots, gobo, green beans, shiitake, shrimp, sesame seeds and stir. Make 20 to 24 balls. Heat cooking oil to 365 degrees F. Place 5 balls at a time in oil and cook 6 to 8 minutes, turning gently. When golden in color, remove and drain. In pot, combine dashi, shoyu and sake. Add deep-fried "flying dragonheads" and simmer 20 minutes. Serve when cold.

Why is this recipe called "flying dragonheads?" Our ancestors somehow felt that the tofu balls resembled the silhouette of the dragon's head. Perhaps your imagination can create another name.

TORI GOHAN *chicken and rice with mushrooms*

1 whole chicken breast, about 1/2 lb, skinned and boned	4 tsp mirin
	1 tsp salt
4 medium sized shiitake	1 tsp shoyu
4 cups white pearl rice, washed, and soaked in enough water to cover 3 hours	2 oz gobo about 4 inches, washed and thinly slivered
	1 tbsp finely chopped parsley
4 cups niban dashi, fresh or canned	

Cut chicken breast into shreds 1-inch long and 1/8-inch wide. Steam shiitake 1 minute in oriental or improvised steamer. Remove from pot and shred mushrooms as finely as possible while still hot. Drain rice and combine with dashi, mirin, salt and shoyu in 3 or 4 qt pot. Add gobo, shiitake, then chicken. Bring to boil over high heat, stir once or twice and cover tightly. Reduce heat to moderate and cook 3 minutes, then lower heat and continue simmering 4 minutes. Turn off heat and let tori gohan rest covered 2 minutes before serving. Divide equally, garnish each portion with sprinkling of chopped parsley. Serve as luncheon dish, accompanied by miso soup. For variation, shredded uncooked shrimp, clams, or lobster may be substituted for chicken, and cooked the same way.

KINOKO GOHAN *mushroom in flavored rice*

3 cup rice
3-1/3 cup dashi
1/2 lb mushrooms

3 tbsp shoyu
4 tbsp sake
1 tbsp lime juice

Wash rice and drain well after final rinsing. Place washed rice in heavy metal pot. Add dashi and let stand 30 minutes to one hour before cooking. Clean, wash mushrooms and cut in fourths. Place in flat-bottomed bowl and sprinkle mushrooms with shoyu, sake, let stand 10 minutes. Drain liquid in rice pot. Bring to boil and add mushrooms, stirring from the bottom. Cover, turn heat to medium and cook until dashi is absorbed. Add lime juice and cover 15 minutes. Toss rice before serving.

DAIZU GOHAN *soybeans with flavored rice*

1/4 cup dried soybeans
3 cups rice
3 cups dashi
1/3 lb chicken meat
4 oz carrot
4 oz green beans

Seasoning for vegetables:
1-1/2 tbsp shoyu
1 tbsp sake
1-1/2 tbsp sugar

Seasoning:
1-1/2 tbsp shoyu
1 tbsp sake
2 tbsp mirin
2 tbsp salt

Wash and soak dried soybeans in water 3 hours and drain. Using large enough pot filled with boiling water, place beans in pot. Cover and let stand 30 minutes. Drain and fill again with boiling water simmering 20 minutes. Wash rice several times and drain. In heavy metal pot, combine rice and dashi. Soak 30 minutes one hour before cooking. Cut chicken meat in small bite-size pieces. Peel and cut carrots into fan shape. Remove strings from beans. Parboil and julienne. Combine cooked beans, chicken meat, carrots with shoyu, sake and sugar. Bring to boil and simmer 3 to 4 minutes. Drain cooking liquid into measuring cup, adding enough water to measure 1/4 cup. Add liquid to rice cooking pot and bring to boil. When cooking liquid starts to recede, add seasoned ingredients, except green beans. Simmer 15 minutes then add green beans. Toss lightly before serving.

SAKE GOHAN *salmon in flavored rice*

3 cups rice
3-1/2 cups water
5 inch dashi knobu
1-1/2 tbsp sake

1-1/2 tsp salt
1/3 lb fresh salted salmon
4 shiitake
20 ginkyo nuts, canned

Wash rice several times and drain well. Place water in heavy rice cooking pot. Add dashi konbu, sake, salt and washed rice. Let stand 30 minutes to one hour before cooking. Broil salted salmon without any burn marks. When cooked, skin and debone. Shred broiled fillets into small pieces. Soak shiitake in warm water to soften. Squeeze and cut in thin strips. Bring rice cooking pot to boil. Add ingredients, cover tight and simmer 15 minutes. Toss before serving.

KURI GOHAN *chestnuts in flavored rice*

1 lb (1-1/2 cups) chestnuts, raw or canned	1/2 cup sweet rice
1-1/2 cups water	3-3/4 cups water
2 tsp sugar	5 inch konbu
1 tsp mirin	3 tbsp sake
1/4 tsp salt	1 tsp salt
3 cups rice	1-1/3 tbsp shoyu

Cook chestnuts in boiling water 3 minutes and dip in cold water. Peel off outer shell and inner skin. Wash peeled chestnuts in cold water. In saucepan, place chestnuts, 1-1/2 cups water, sugar, mirin, salt and cook 3-4 minutes. Reduce to simmer, cooking until chestnuts become tender. Combine rice and sweet rice, wash, rinse well and drain. In large, metal rice cooking pot, combine rice, water, konbu, sake, salt, shoyu and let stand 30 minutes to one hour. Remove konbu before cooking. Bring to boil and add seasoned chestnuts. Reduce to medium flame until moisture is all absorbed. Remove from fire and let stand 15 minutes. Remove cover, toss and serve.

Among flavored rices, chestnut rice is my favorite. Whenever chestnut rice was served in October and November, it was always in my honor. Mushroom rice was in honor of my little brother... I was always willing to help peel the chestnuts which is a painstaking and tedious job.

KIKU MESHI *chrysanthemum rice*

3 cups rice	1 tsp salt
3-1/3 cups water	3 tsp vinegar
3 tbsp sake	4 oz yellow chrysanthemum petals
3 cups water	2 tsp salt

Wash rice well and drain. In heavy metal pot, combine water, sake and washed rice. Let stand 30 minutes to one hour before cooking. In pot, bring 3 cups water, 1 tsp salt and vinegar to boil. Cook chrysanthemum petals 30 to 40 seconds, keeping petals down in boiling water. Drain in basket. Rinse and soak in cold water 10 to 20 minutes for "aku-nuki," removal of bitterness. Squeeze moisture out and mix with 2 tsp salt. Cook basic recipe rice. When rice is done and still very hot, sprinkle with yellow flower petals and toss lightly in cutting motion with spatula.

Imagine eating flowers! Flower-eating people? Yes, it is a must for elegant fall dining in Japan. The contrast between yellow chrysanthemum petals and pearly white rice is striking. Among all the chrysanthemums, yellow ones are the most fragrant and do not possess the bitter taste of other colors. Take the petals off the flower base. With large mums you will have enough with two flowers.

KINOKO ZUSHI *soft rice stew with mushrooms*

3-1/2 cups dashi
1/4 cup miso
1 tbsp sake
2 cups cooked rice
1/4 lb mushrooms
2 oz coriander, chopped

Bring to boil dashi with miso and sake. Add rice, bring to boil, then simmer 5 minutes. Wash mushrooms, cut in half, add to simmering pot, bring to boil and simmer 3 minutes. Sprinkle chopped coriander over.

OYAKO DONBURI *chicken and egg on rice*

2/3 lb chicken breast meat	1/4 cup shoyu
1 tsp sake	1/4 cup mirin
1 tsp shoyu	1 tsp sugar
5 large shiitake	5 eggs
1/2 lb onion	4 cups cooked rice
3/4 cup dashi	1 sheet nori

Cut chicken meat in small pieces, the size of an almond. Sprinkle with sake and shoyu. Marinate 10 minutes. Soak shiitake in warm water to soften. Remove stems and cut in thin strips. Cut onion in half and slice very thin. In small pot, combine dashi, shoyu, mirin and sugar. Bring to boil to make cooking sauce. Divide ingredients in 5 equal parts. Fill 5 large, individual bowls with rice and cover with lids. In oyako nabe, put 1/5th cooking sauce and 1/5 th onion, dashi, shoyu, mirin and sugar. When tender, reduce flame to low and add 1 beaten egg, being careful not to stir like scrambled egg since a velvety texture is desired. When egg is almost cooked, remove and place on top of rice. Sprinkle with bits of nori. Cover and serve.

"Oyako" literally means "mother and child" referring to the relationship of the chicken and the egg. This is a very popular lunchtime favorite in restaurants throughout Japan. I often serve oyako donburi for unexpected lunch guests. It is an easy, quick and delicious dish to prepare.

SHINAGAWA DONBURI *shrimp and onion with egg over rice*

1/2 lb shelled shrimp	1/4 cup shoyu
1-1/2 tsp sake	1/4 cup mirin
1-1/2 tsp shoyu	1 tsp sugar
1 medium onion	5 eggs
1 bunch coriander, chopped	1 nori, roasted
3/4 cup dashi	4 cups cooked rice

Sprinkle shelled and deveined shrimp with sake and shoyu. Set aside. Cut onion in half and slice very thin. Cut coriander in 1/2-inch lengths. Bring to boil, dashi, shoyu, mirin and sugar to make cooking sauce. Divide ingredients in 5 equal parts. In small skillet or oyako nabe, put 1/5th cooking sauce and 1/5th shrimp and onion. When mixture boils, turn flame to low and cook 2 minutes. Add chopped coriander, one beaten egg. Be careful not to stir like scrambled egs since a velvety texture is desired. When egg is almost cooked, remove from fire, slide on top a bowl of rice. Roast nori over fire and crumble inside paper bag. Sprinkle with bits of nori over eggs. Cover and serve.

Shinagawa Donburi is a delightful lunch. Shinagawa used to be a seaport and shrimp was something that was harvested there. I am sure the name of this recipe comes from that source.

OKONOMI YAKI *as-you-like-pancakes*

1/2 lb chopped beef	2-1/2 cups flour
1/3 tsp salt	1 tbsp oil
1/3 tsp salt	1 tbsp oil
dash of pepper	
2 cabbage leaves	**Yakumi sauce:**
1 pkg frozen mixed vegetables	1 tbsp green onion, minced
1 stalk green onion, minced	2 tbsp shoyu
4 oz sakura ebi, or small shrimp	1 tsp salad oil
	2 tbsp tomato ketchup
Batter:	1 tbsp Worcestershire sauce
2 eggs	
1-1/2 cups water	

Saute chopped beef. When brown, add salt and dash of pepper. Set aside. Shred cabbage very fine. Thaw frozen vegetables. Slice onion in very thin rings. Combine minced green onion, shoyu and salad oil for sauce. Arrange cooked beef, shrimp, mixed vegetables, cabbage and onion on large platter. Beat eggs, add water and stir. Mix in flour and salt. Heat skillet or iron griddle hot enough to cook pancakes — a drop of water will bounce rapidly — and coat with oiled cotton pad. Using 1/2 cup batter per pancake, adding whatever one wants in their pancake to the batter, pour batter onto grill. When pancake edges start to dry, turn over. Serve brushed with yakumi sauce, ketchup or Worcestershire sauce. Substitue any pre-cooked meat or fish.

For a weekend brunch, have fun serving Japanese pancakes.

As a child of eight or nine, my shortcut to get home from school passed through a district garden of shrines. Whenever I passed in midafternoon, there was always the tantalizing aroma of burning shoyu.

One day I decided to explore and locate the origin of the aroma. Following the scent, I discovered an *okonomi-yaki-ya-san* or portable cart on wheels, which had little wooden benches built on the sides of the pust cart. The operator, a woman with a hunched back, stood behind a portable brick burner with iron sheets for a grill. She was surrounded by many young customers. As though she were a magician, the children watched every move she made.

From a small pitcher, she mixed a pancake-like dough, adding shrimp, shredded cabbage and pickled red ginger as it was ordered by her little customer sitting across from her. She poured the mixture onto the greased iron sheets. Soon, bubbles appeared, the edges began to cook, and then she would flip the little pancake.

It was magic to my childhood eyes. I noticed she next would brush shoyu from a small container on the pancake top. I said to myself, "That's it! That's the aroma I recognize!"

With a smile the child received the pancake wrapped in a small sheet of paper. Obviously not everyone was ordering pancakes. The other children were looking at her customer with great envy, I among them! My fascination with *okonomi-yaki* started at that moment.

EBI NO GOMOKU OKONOMI YAKI *shrimp pancakes*

Ingredients for 6 pancakes:

2 cups flour	2 oz fresh squid, chopped
1-1/2 cups water	2 oz clams, fresh or canned,
6 eggs	chopped
1 tsp salt	1 oz bonito flakes
4 oz cabbage, shredded fine	1/2 oz nori flakes
2 oz sakura shrimp	1 tbsp oil
2 oz green onion,	2 tbsp shoyu
shredded fine	1 tbsp ketchup

In large bowl combine flour, water, eggs, salt and mix. Add shredded cabbage, shrimp, green onion, squid and clams. Stir until ingredients are well-mixed. Heat skillet and coat with oil. wiping off excess oil. Pour 1/6th batter and sprinkle 1/6th bonito and nori flakes on top. When pancake becomes dry, turn over. Cook 3 minutes until slightly brown. Brush with shoyu or ketchup and serve while hot.

TSUKEMONO *pickled things*

The Japanese take special pride in preserving, predominantly by pickling, assorted vegetables and fruits. Sometimes mild, sometimes pungent in aroma, they are very often called aromatic things, *ko-no-mono*. Many households have a special family recipe passed down through generations. This often is called "flavor of mother", *ofukuro-no-aji*.

The different kinds of tsukemono are:

nuka-zuke, rice-bran pickle

shio-zuke salt pickle

miso-zuke soybean paste pickle

kazu-zuke (a byproduct of making sake) fermented rice pickle

About my proficiency in making *tsuke-mono,* I must make a confession. I cannot really say I know everything there is to know about it through my own experience. The making of *tsukemono* was mostly supervised by my mother, grandmother and the various household help in Japan. When I moved to Hawaii and was doing my own cooking, there was not enough time left for me to do pickling.

Fortunately, through a mutual friend, I was lucky to meet Mrs. Ann Iawasaki. She is Nisei, second generation Japanese-American (which usually means born in the United States) from Reedley, Califonia who grew up in Watsonville. Conversing with her, I discovered she has acquired an incredibly wide knowledge about making *tsukemono* using available American produce. What is more surprising is that Mrs Iwasaki did not learn how to make *tsuke mono* as a young person. In her adult years, she felt a strong desire to learn how she could preserve the abundant produce available where she lived. Hit-and-miss trials gave Mrs. Iwasaki an enormous repertoire and competency in *tsukemono.* She has used raisins in making *tsukemono* to provide a mild sweetness and lovely aroma. This touch is definitly a California influence I find very delicious!

Mrs. Iwasaki is now retired, but makes *tsukemono* the year around, distributing her delectable delights to her lucky friends. She has so generously honored me by consenting to let me present her California *tsukemono* in this section.

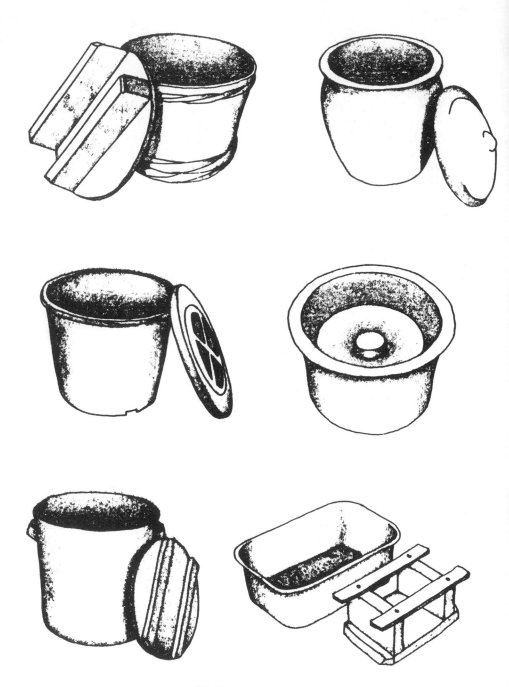

Pickling containers

HARI HARI ZUKE *pickled sun-dried daikon*

3/4 cup vinegar	1 carrot
1/4 cup water	3 inch dashi konbu
1/3 cup shoyu	1 tbsp tangerine peel
1 tbsp sake	2 red peppers, remove seeds
1 tbsp mirin	slice very thin
2-1/2 tbsp sugar	2 tbsp black sesame seeds,
1/3 lb kiriboshi daikon (sun-	roasted
dried shredded radish)	

Combine vinegar, water, shoyu, sake, mirin and sugar in saucepan. Bring to boil, add red peppers. Set aside to cool. Wash and rinse kiriboshi daikon until rinsing water becomes clear. Soak in water 5 or 6 minutes to soften. Shred carrots and konbu. Also shred tangerine peel and soak in water 10 minutes to blanch. Drain. Combine all ingredients, let stand 1 hour. Sprinkle with black sesame seeds. This keeps one week without refrigeration and is a delightful accompaniment to one-pot dishes and simmering rice.

FUKUJIN ZUKE *vegetable pickle Japanese style*

3 lb Japanese white uni or	6 chiso leaves shredded
American cucumber	1/2 cup sesame seeds, roasted
2 lb Japanese eggplant	1 cup shoyu
2 lb daikon	1-1/2 cup sugar
1 tsp salt	1/2 cup vinegar

Cut uni or cucumber, Japanese eggplant and daikon crosswise into 1/4-inch thick slices. In large container, combine sliced vegetables sprinkled with salt. Place weight* twice that of ingredients on top and let stand overnight. After 8 to 10 hours, drain all water from container. Bring to boil shoyu, sugar and vinegar. Add pressed vegetables and bring to boiling point. Remove from fire. Separate cooking liquid and vegetables immediately and cool individually. Repeat cooking in this manner for 2 more times. Add shredded chiso leaves and roasted sesame seeds. Place in hot sterilized jars and cover with new lids. If properly sealed pickles wil keep for years.

For a weight, I use a teapot filled with water.

This recipe came from Mrs. Ann Iwasaki.

DAIKON PICKLE *Japanese white radish pickle*

        5 lb daikon   1-1/3 cups pineapple juice
        1 tbsp salt   1 cup vinegar
        2 cups water   1/4 cup salt
        2 cups sugar

Cut daikon crosswise in 1/4-inch slices. In large container, combine radish slices, salt and mix well. Place weight twice that of ingredients on top and let stand overnight 8 to 10 hours. Drain all liquid. Place pressed daikon on paper towel, or cheesecloth, and blot moisture. Bring to boil water, sugar, pineapple juice, vinegar and salt. Let cool. Fill jar with pressed daikon. Pour cooled liquid over. Sealing with very tight cover. This pickle can also be stored in small jars.

This too is from the collection of Mrs. Ann Iwasaki.

KARASHI NA NO SHIO ZUKE *salt pickle of mustard greens*

        2 lb mustard greens
        2 tbsp salt

Remove brown parts from stem ends. Wash, rinse well and drain. Fill large pot with water and bring to boil. Hold top end of greens with hand and dip bottom end into boiling water. Hold 1 minute. Then dip entire greens in and out of boiling water. Spread mustard greens on a flat basket. Cool quickly. Sprinkle 1/4th salt on bottom of pickling container. Add cooled mustard greens. Sprinkle with another 1/4th salt. Repeat this. Place weight three times that of ingredients on top and pickle for 3 days. This pickle will keep two weeks.

OSAKA ZUKE *Osaka style pickle*

        1-1/2 lb daikon
        1/2 lb daikon stems and leaf tips
        3 tsp salt

Peel daikon. Cut in 2-inch x 1-inch x 1/4-inch pieces. Bring to boil 2 qt water with 1 tsp salt. Dip daikon stems and leaf tips in and out of boiling water. Rinse quickly in cold water. Squeeze dry and cut in 1/2-inch pieces. Combine daikon with stems and leaf tips in pickling container and sprinkle with 2 tsp salt. Place weight twice that of ingredients on top. Press 4 to 5 hours before serving at table.

HASAMI ZUKE

1/4 salted Chinese cabbage	1 yellow chrysanthemum
2 cups water	1 bunch parsley
1 tsp vinegar	

For cabbage, use salted variety from your pickling. Bring to boil water and vinegar. Cook chrysanthemum petals for one minute, drain and rinse with cold water. Squeeze petals gently between hands to remove moisture. Rinse pickled cabbage and squeeze out water. Between cabbage leaves, stuff chrysanthemum petals and sprig of parsley. Reshape to original cabbage form. Place under pressure 1 hour. Slice. Serve cut side up with shoyu. It's a lovely addition when entertaining.

NASU NO KARASHI ZUKE *pickled eggplant with mustard flavor*

2 lb Japanese eggplant	3 tbsp shoyu
2 tbsp salt	2 tbsp mirin
1 cup water	1 tbsp mustard paste

Cut eggplant in small Kangiri, diagonal half cubes. Sun-dry 3 hours. Turn, dry another 2 hours. Rinse sun-dried eggplant, pat dry. Combine salt and water in pickling container. Press lightly with cover 3 to 4 hours and drain. Squeeze water from pressed eggplant. Mix well shoyu, mirin, mustard. Combine with pressed eggplant. Serve without washing.

NASHI TO MUSCATS NO SHIRA AE *pear and muscat grapes with white dressing*

1 pear	**Dressing**
1/4 lemon	6 oz tofu
1/2 tsp salt	4 tbsp white sesame seeds
6 oz muscat grapes	2 tbsp sugar
	1 tsp salt

Peel pear and cut in cubes, the size of muscats. Salt. Slice lemon in thin pieces and mix well together. Peel muscats and discard skins. Make Shira ae dressing, (see index) with listed ingredients. Toss gently but mix well. Serve slightly chilled.

Kangiku-no-Gyoen *Chrysanthemum Party*

Kangiku no Gyoen literally means "To view Chrysanthemum Party." In November of every year it is a widespread practice in Japan. *Kangiku no Gyoen* also has provided, like *Hyaku-nin-Isshu* or 100 Poem Game, an opportunity for young persons to meet each other. Here, however, it is usually through the skillful arrangements of an *omie*, or "go-between." This matchmaker traditionally is a person of equal social rank who helps negotiations along for proper marriages. A hobby for most of them, the social status and rank is necessary because often meetings between the young people and their parents might occur in the matchmaker's home! Also, if anything goes wrong with the marriage, the matchmaker, or *omie*, has to be consulted as a third party or arbiter! And when it really goes wrong, the *omie* is blamed!

I myself remember meeting such a young man on such an occasion when I was about 20 and my family was keen on my getting married. It was all very elaborately casual. Both of us had at least two other companions, middle-aged, so you can imagine just how casual and informal it all was! Actually, each social occasion of the year was an opportunity to expose marriageable young women to prospective bridegrooms.

About this same time one *Kangiku-no-Gyoen* stands out in my memory. I was asked to accompany my grandmother to the *Kangiku no Gyoen* at the Shinjuku Imperial Gardens located outside the moat of the Japanese Imperial Palace in Tokyo. I was to represent my family along with my grandmother. *Kangiku no Gyoen* is an occasion for inviting officials, foreign dignitaries and various people to meet the Emperor and Empress. Everyone comes in their best, formal dress or uniform, very distinguished looking and not particularly young. Accompanying my grandmother to whom it was "a big thing," I found this one experience very intimidating.

A special kimono was ordered for me for this occasion with *furi so de* sleeves, the variety which go all the way to the floor. I remember the color was amber with *momiji* or autumn-hued maple leaves mingling with the warm yellow-brown tones of amber.

Like most older women in Japan traditionally reared, my grandmother was dressed in a kimono of muted tones — this time in mauve. The family crest, or *mon,* appeared on each sleeve and on the back. The only other decoration was at the bottom, a practice we call *susomoyo.* The kimono itself we called *homongi,* or one to greet people.

The invitation duly arrived from the Japanese Government. We were driven to the Shinjuku Gardens by car where we walked along a path of pebbles in felt-soled *zori*. I had been instructed not to say anything, but to be ready to bow as deeply as I could on cue.

The chrysanthemums on display were all the labor of master gardeners and growers, some in tubs on the ground, but many in pots on stands erected especially to display the autumn blossoms. Like so many practices in Japan, chrysanthemums and their viewing had started in China. This particular one dates back to the Han dynasty, and was introduced into Japanese life at the same time that Chinese calligraphy and Buddhism became a part of our culture. The practice became an annual affair during the Heian Period. As you might guess, some of the most popular varieties we enjoy today in Japan came from China during our Nara period and the route of their arrival lay through Korea.

One thing I remember particularly was that some of the master gardeners had trained their plants with wire to droop in a graceful cascade of blossoms, like a waterfall.

The Emperor appeared in a silk top hat and a morning coat. The entourage around him was dressed the same way, but the Empress Nagako wore a long and beautiful kimono.

Sake was passed after the Emperor arrived and the guests were served finger food. As we left, each guest was given a small, bamboo-lined obento box containing *khako no mochi.*

My principal memory of the affair was walking behind my grandmother like a piece of bonito, stiff and scared. I think I was the only person in her twenties there at that particular *Kangiku no Gyoen.*

APPENDIX

Glossary

Abura, oil

Aburage, soybean curd, fried; golden and leathery in appearance when prepared; highly perishable and needs refrigeration if not used immediately

Ae, to mix, toss

Ae mono, salads

Age, to fry

Age mono, foods, deep-fried

Aji, flavor

Ajinomoto, Japanese monosodium glutamate (MSG)

Aji shio, lemon and salt dip, commonly served with tempura Mixture is 3 parts salt, 2 parts of aji no moto, garnished with a few lemon wedges

Aka, the color red

Aka jiso, leaf of the beef steak plant

Aki, autumn

Amai, sweet

Amazu, vinegar, sweet and sour

Anago, sea-eel

Ankake, food with sauce; a thick used over ingredients

Anko, a paste of beans

Anzu, apricot

Ao nori, sea vegetable flakes, green in color and sold in cans or glass bottles; used to garnish rice, udon and Okonomiyaki

Anakura nori, sea vegetation, dried in rectangular frames to form thin, crisp sheets of dark color; used to wrap sushi and other rice dishes; the name Asakasa comes from the Tokyo area, since Tokyo Bay was the traditional place to collect seaweed

Asari, clam

Atsui, thick; also means hot

Awabi, abalone

Azuki, beans, red in color, used for Sekihan and Zenzai

Azuki an, paste made from red beans used for Japanese sweet things

Beni-shoga, ginger, red and pickled

Bento or *Obento,* lunch or lunch box

Bo, stick

Bocho, knife, when modified, designating specific kind of knife

Budo, spear play (**Naginata** for girls, *Yari* for boys)

Bofu, a variety of parsnip

Buta, pork, pig

Buta niku, pig meat

Calpis, brand name for syrupy drink

Chikuwa, fish cake, steamed and broiled

Chimaki, traditional Boys' Day food, glutinous rice wrapped bamboo leaf; eaten with soybean flour mixed with sugar and a bit of salt

Chuka soba, noodles, Chinese style

Chirashi, to scatter

Chirashi-zushi, rice, vinagared with small scattered ingredients

Daikon, radish, white; the Japanese harvest daikon the year around; the entire daikon is edible; used in garnish, pickling, soup making, cooking of all sizes and shapes, a most versatile vegetable and rich in Vitamin C

Daizu, soybeans, fried; in Japan often called "beefsteak of the field"

Dango, dumpling, ball

Dashi, soup stock; made from konbu, katsuobushi, kelp and bonito shavings, clear in color (discussed under Basic Ingredients)

Dashi no moto, soup stock essence; powdered or freeze-dried

Deba bocho, cleaver
Dengaku, vegetables and meat, simmered; served with dipping sauce
Donburi, large bowl
Donabe, earthenware pot

Ebi, shrimp (prawn, lobster)
Eda-mame, soybeans, fresh
Endo-mame, snow peas

Enoki-dake, mushroom, white straw-like

Fuki, vegetables, spring; similar to rhubarb
Furai, to fry
Futo-maki, to roll thick or fat
Fu, wheat gluten, croutons
Fude-shoga, ginger, young, pencil-like and pickled
Fuyu, Winter

Gari, vinegared ginger, popular side dish with *sushi.*
Genmai-cha, tea with roasted barley
Gan-modaki, soybean curd, fried
Gin-gami, foil made of soil
Gin-nan, nut from ginko tree, harvested in the fall
Giri, to cut
Gobo, root of burdock
Gochi-so-sama, said after a meal; liteeral translation: "Thank you for the feast" and the form is honorific
Gohan, meal; also means rice
Goma, sesame seeds
Goma-abura, sesame oil
Gomai-oroshi, fish, 5-piece filleted
Goma-shio, sesame seeds with salt
Gomoku, 5 different things, assorted
Gyu, beef; also means cow
Gyu niku, "cow meat"

Haji-kami-suzuki, ginger shoots, pickled
Hakusai, Chinese cabbage
Hana, flower
Hana-gata, cutter, flower-shaped
Hana Matsuri, popular name for Cherry Blossom Festival
Handai, wooden tub for mixing rice with seasonings
Han-getsu-giri, to cut in half-moon shape
Hanpen, fish cake

Haru, Spring
Hashi, chop sticks
Hasu, lotus root
Harusame, noodles made from mung beans; thin and transparent when soaked in water
Hibachi, firebox, an open grill used for cooking and for heating in a traditional Japanese home
Hijiki, sea vegetable, black in color
Hitashi, vegetable in sauce
Hiyashi, cold or chilled
Hocho, knife, singular the kangi character does not change
Hokkaido, northernmost large island in the Japanese chain of islands
Hone, bone
Hune-nuke, to remove bone
Hone-nuki, de-boning tweezers
Hoshi-ebi, shrimp, dried

Ichi, one; also *dai-ichi,* literal translation: number one
Ika, squid, or cuttle fish
Inari, food prepared with fried bean curd
Ingen, string beans
Iri, to put or place in; also roasted, whether pan or dry
Iri-nuka, rice bran, dry and roasted
Iri-tamago, egg, scrambled
Itadaki-masu, to eat now with respect; polite invitation to a meal
Itame-ni, to saute

Jiru, soup
Jo-shin-ko, fine rice flour for pastries
Ju, box filled with rice (referred to in section on *Oshogatsu*)
Jubako, box used in serving foods
Junsai, vegetable, slippery

Kabayaki, eel, grilled
Kabocha, pumpkin, squash
    Kaiseki-Ryori, cooking, formal; an elegant or formal dinner
Kaki, oyster, persimmon
Kamaboko, fish cake
Kaminari-giri, to cut, curlicue style
Kani, crab

Kanpyo, ribbons of dried gourd — gourd is shaved in long strips which are then sun-dried; used in sishu and as ties for other vegetable dishes

Kanro, syrup, sweet

Kansai, Kyoto, Osaka region West of Gate Ausaka

Kanten, agar-agar, sea gelatin; made of sea vegetable called "Tengusa" or heavenly grass; jells without refrigeration; comes either in brittle sticks or powder form

Kanto, plain of Tokyo, Yokohama region East of Gate Ausaka

Kappa-maki, rolled sushi with cucumber; outside is wrapped with nori

Kappogi, apron; literal translation: cooking wear; designed to be worn over kimono to prevent its getting soiled; covers sleeves generously and has elasticized wrists; traditional kind is always white

Kara-age, to deep fry until crisp

Karai, spicy, salty

Karami, spice which usually is grated green radish or ginger.

Karashi, mustard

Katakuri-ko, arrowroot, cornstarch

Katei-Ryori, cooking, family or home style

Katsuo, bonito

Katsuo-bushi, bonito, dried

Katsura-muki, a cutting style for garnish; thin and wide peel

Kayaku, ingredients, assorted, mixed with rice or noodles

Katsu, cutlet

Ken, shredded vegetable and crisped in bowl of ice water. When drained it is served as decoration for sashima. Made from cucumber, daikon, cabbage, celery, etc.

Kikurage, mushroom, wood-tree-ear

Kimi, yolk of egg

Kimono, traditional Japanese garment for men and women

Kinako, soy flour; fine and pale yellow in color; used to coat sweet things for dessert

Kinome, leaf of ash tree; aromatic and used for garnishing soup, salad meat and fish dishes

Kinugoshi-dofu, Japanese style tofu, soft and finer in texture than regular tofu.

Kiri, to cut

Kiri-boshi-daikon, radish, shredded and sun-dried

Kirimi, fillet, slice

Ko, flour; meaning varies according to the *kanji* — flour, bread crumbs, flakes, powder, also means child.

Ko-haku, red and white, colors of felicity

Kona sansho, pepper, powdered, Japanese style

Konbu, kelp used for making dashi; looks like dark, dusty leather but gives dashi sweetness

Konnyaku, food made from tuberous root; pearly-dried gelatinous cake

Kori, ice

Kosho, Japanese pepper

Kotatsu, heating system used under the table in a traditional Japanese home

Kuchi, mouth; also means taste

Kuri, chestnut

Kuri-no-kanro-ni, chestnuts, cooked, in sweet syrup

Kuro-goma, sesame seeds, black

Kurumi, walnuts

Kushi, skewer, stick, comb

Kushi-gata, to cut in comb-like fashion

Kuwai, arrowhead; water chestnut-like
textured vegetable

Kyu-Do, Archery

Kyuri, cucumber

Maguro, tuna fish

Maki, roll, to roll

Mame, bean

Maru, whole or round

Matsuba, to cut in pine needle fashion

Matsuri, festival or holiday

Matsudake, mushroom

Meshi, rice
Mijin-giri, to cut in mincing fashion
Mikan, mandarin orange
Mirin, wine, sweet rice variety
Miso, soybean paste
Miso shiru, soup thickened with fermented bean paste
Mitsu, syrup
Mitsuba, trefoil, a 3-leaf vegetable with slender stalk
Mizore-ae, sauce for salad, mixed with grated radish
Mizu, water
Mizuame, millet jelly
Mochi, cake made from glutinous rice
Mochi-gome, rice, glutinous variety
Mochi-ko, flour made from glutinous rice
Momiji-oroshi, grated radish and carrot in form of autumn maple leaves
Mono, thing; also refers to food; 'thing' is literal translation
Moritsuke, an arrangement, a presentation
Moyashi, bean sprouts
Mugi-cha, tea made of barley
Muki, to peel or hull
Mushi, steamed
Mushi-mono, steamed foods; literal translation: steamed things

Nabe, pot
Nabe-mono, food cooked at the table; literal translation: pot thing
Nagashi-bako, rectangular mold made of metal
Nama-age, soybean curd, half fried
Na-kiri-bocho, knife for vegetables
Nameko, mushroom, slippery
Nara-zuke, pickle from Nara
Naruto, fish cake, steamed
Nasu, eggplant
Natsu, summer
Natto, soybeans, fermented
Negi, onion, leek, scallion
Ni, to braise, simmer
Niboshi, dried sardines, used for making *dashi*
Nigiri, to compress

Nihon shu, generic name for Japanese wine, *sake*
Niku, meat
Nimono, food, braised or simmered; literal translation: braised thing
Ninjin, carrot
Nira, chive
Noren, parted curtains to frame kitchen or restaurant entrance
Nori, sheets of seaweed; also called *laver*
Nori-maki, sushi fried with gourd wrapped in sheets of seaweed
Nuka, rice bran powder
Nuka-zuke, rice bran pickles

O, when added to a word implies the honorific or polite form
Okome, rice in its raw state
Ocha, green tea
Ohitashi, see *hitashi*
Okara, by product of tofu, a soy pulp
Okayu, porridge
Omochi, see *mochi*
Oroshi-gane, daikon grater
Oshinko, pickles
Oshogatsu, Osechi, New Year's
Osushi, rice dishes made of vinegared rice
Otoshi-buta, drop lid for cooking; see section on Cooking Utensils
Oya, parent
Oyako-nabe, cooking pan; literal translation: chicken and egg pot
Okayo-donburi, chicken and egg dish over rice

Ramen, noodles, Chinese style, served in soup; sold in the U.S. in small individual packets with seasoning
Ran-giri, to cut in oblique fashion
Reigi-saho, etiquette
Renkon, lotus root; see *hasu*
Robata-yaki, cooking in open-hearth style
Ryori, cooking or food; see description of Japanese cooking styles

Saba, mackerel
Sado, Way of Tea, also known as *Cha-No-Yu*

Saikyo miso, light bean paste, a brand and regional name

Sakana, fish

Sakazuki, wine cup

Sake, wine made from rice

San, three (3)

San-mai-oroshi, 3-piece fillet

Sansho, Japanese pepper

Sapporo, principal city in Hokkaido, northernmost large island in Japan; also brand name of Japanese beer

Sarashi, cotton cloth

Sasagaki, cutting in bamboo leaf style

Sasage mame, red beans, small and dried

Sashimi, raw fish, sliced

Sashimi-bocho, knife used for slicing fish and meat

Sashimizu, water adding technique in cooking *udon* and beans

Sato-imo, potato or taro

Satsuma, a variety of plum; also an area in the island of Kyushu, historically very important; form of noted enamel ware

Satsuma-imo, sweet potato or yam

Satsuma-age, fish cake, fried

Saya-endo, snow peas

Sazae, shellfish, turbot

Sazae-no-tsubu-yaki, shellfish broiled shell, usually turbot shellfish

Sendai-miso, soybean paste, dark; both a regional and a brand name

Sendai, a city on the northeastern coast of Honshu, the main island of Japan

Seki-han, rice with Azuki beans

Senbei, Japanese style rice crackers

Sen-giri, slicing, julienne style

Shake, salmon; also spelled *sake*

Shakuji-dohi-ho reigi-saho, time of eating, etiquette of eating

Shamoji, wooden spoon, shaped like a paddle

Shi, four (4)

Shichi-mi, pepper, 7-spice hot

Shiitake, mushroom, black; available fresh or dried; also sold in "tree" form to grow at home

Shimofuri, frosted

Shim mai, new rice

Shinshu ichi miso, medium bean paste; also regional and brand name

Shio, salt

Shirataki, konnyaku cut into strips; literal translation: white waterfall

Shirata konbu, kelp, pale green, broad

Shiratamako, flour used in making Japanese pastries

Shira-tama-ko, misture of rice flour glutinous rice flour

Shiro, white

Soba, noodles made of buckwheat

Soboro, crumbs, fine

Somen, noodles, thin

Su, Japanese rice vinegar, also known as yonezu

Sudare, mat made of bamboo and used for rolling sushi

Subasu, lotus root sweet and sour

Suehiro, cutting in fan shape

Sugata, whole body shape

Suimono, soup, clear

Su-joyu, sauce made of vinegar and soy

Sukiyaki, beef and vegetables, sauteed

Sukiyaki nabe, skillet of wrought iron for cooking *sukiyaki*

Sunomono, anything prepared with vinegar or vinegar marinade

Suribachi and *surikogi-bo,* mortar and pestle, Japanese style; *surikogi-bo* is pestle stick

Sushi, rice, prepared with vinegar

Sushi-oke, tub made of wood, used to mix rice for *sushi*

Sushi su, vinegar, seasoned for *sushi* making

Take no kawa, bamboo bark

Takenoko, bamboo shoots

Taku-an, radish, yellow and pickled

Tamago, egg

Tamago-yaki-nabe. pan for omelets, rectangular shaped

Tanabata, Star Festival, seventh day of seventh month

Tare, Glazing sauce

Tazuna. cutting in style of braid or rope

Tekka, tuna, raw; also refers to the firing process of iron

Tekkyu, stand to hold skewers

Tempura, food thin batter-dipped and deep fried

Tempura-ko, flour for making thin batter

Tempura-nabe, pan for deep frying

Tengusa, seaweed; literal translation: heavenly grass

Tentsuyu, dipping sauce for tempura; literal translation: heavenly dew

Teppan, iron griddle

Teri, to glaze

Teri-yaki, to glaze and grill

Te-uchi, made by hand

Te uchi senyo komugiko, flour made especially for making thick white noodles

Tofu, curd of soy bean, sold packed in water

Togarashi, pepper, red hot!

Tonkatsu, pork cutlet

Tonkatsu-sosu, pork cutlet sauce, dark in color

Tori, chicken

Tori-niku, chicken meat

Tororo-konbu, seaweed; literal translation: melt in mouth seaweed

Tosa joyu, dipping sauce for sashimi

Tsukemono, pickle

Tsuma, garnish which is medicinal in nature and used to enhance flavor of fish and provide pleasing contrast in color. Aids digestion. Usually chiso leaves, chiso flowers or Hanakyuri, flower of miniature cucumber.

Tsutsumi, small hand drum, used in Japanese classical theatre, tiny version in hands of doll musician

Tsuya, to shine

Tsuyu, liquid

Uchiwa, fan made of paper

Udon, thick noodle

Umeboshi, pickled plum

Ume-shu, wine made from plums

Unagi, eel

Unagi no Kabayaki, eel, glazed and broiled

Uragoshi, sieve

Uroko, fish scales

Uni, sea urchin

Uroko tori, scaler for cleaning fish

Usu, thin; also wooden tub used to pound *mochi*

Usu guchu shoyu, thin or light soy sauce

Wakame, young seaweed shoots

Wakegi, scallion

Wan, a bowl

Warabi, fern sprouts

Wari-bashi, wooden chopsticks, disposable

Wasabi, horseradish, green and special to Japanese cooking

Yaki, to grill or broil

Yaki-mono, food broiled or grilled

Yamaimo, yams which are glutinous

Yonezu, Japanese rice vinegar; also known as su Yori udo, curlicued vegetable peels

Yuba, by product of tofu which forms a film, a part of soy milk and high in protein. Often sold in dry form, by-product of making *tofu*

Yukimi, snow viewing party

Yurine, Tiger Lily bulb

Yuzu, green lemon

Zaru, colander or strainer; usually made of woven bamboo

Zaru-soba, buckwheat noodles in a basket

Zen-mai, mountain-grown vegetable

Metric Conversion Tables

Volume

¼ tsp = 1.25 ml (milliliters)
½ tsp = 2.5 ml
¾ tsp = 3.75 ml
1 tsp = 5 ml
¼ tbsp = 3.75 ml
½ tbsp = 7.5 ml
¾ tbsp = 11.25 ml
1 tbsp = 15 ml

½ pt = 236 ml
1 pt = 473 ml
1 qt = 946.3 ml
1 gal = 3785 ml

¼ cup = 59 ml (milliliters)
¹/₃ cup = 78 ml
½ cup = 118 ml
²/₃ cup = 157 ml
¾ cup = 177 ml
1 cup = 236 ml

Fluid Ounces

¼ oz = 7.5 ml
½ oz = 15 ml
¾ oz = 22.5 ml
1 oz = 30 ml

Weight

¼ oz = 7.1 g (grams)
½ oz = 14.17 g
¾ oz = 21.27 g
1 oz = 28.35 g
¼ lb = .113 kg (kilograms)
½ lb = .227 kg
¾ lb = .340 kg
1 lb = .454 kg
2.205 lbs = 1 kg

Temperature

200°F = 94°C	325°F = 164°C
225°F = 108°C	350°F = 178°C
250°F = 122°C	375°F = 192°C
275°F = 136°C	400°F = 206°C
300°F = 150°C	425°F = 220°C
	450°F = 234°C

The recipes give all temperatures
in degrees Fahrenheit (°F). To convert
to degrees Celsius (°C), subtract
32 and multiply by .56. To change
Celsius to Fahrenheit, multiply by
1.8 and add 32.

Editors Note:

There is no set rule for hyphens in Japanese words. The hyphen is used, usually, to indicate that the phrase or word is all one thing. For example, the name *Sogetsu Kai* refers to a club. *Kai* is the word for club. Some Japanese like to hyphenate it, like *Sogetsu-Kai,* but like Japanese newspapers, we have eliminated the hyphen except in the Introductory material.

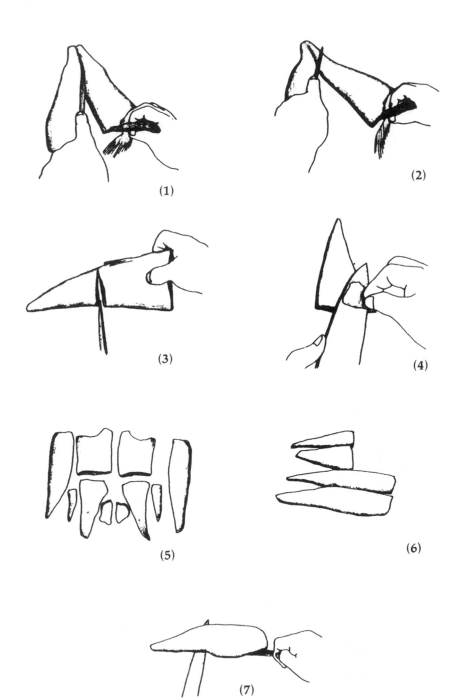

Cutting fish for sashimi

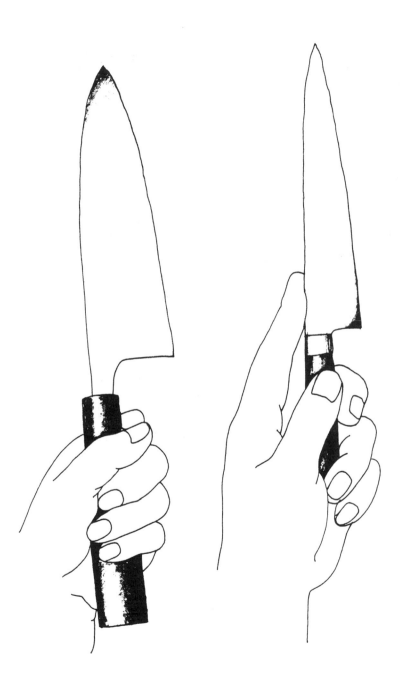

How to hold Japanese knives

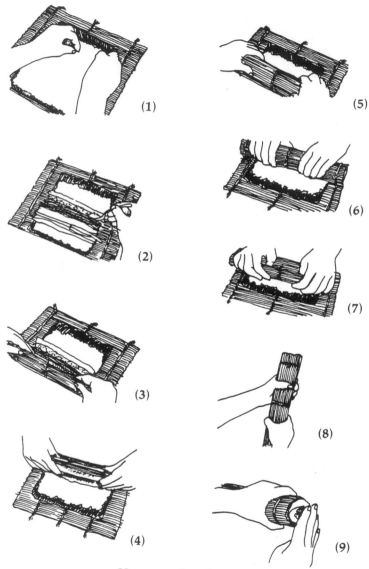

How to roll sushi

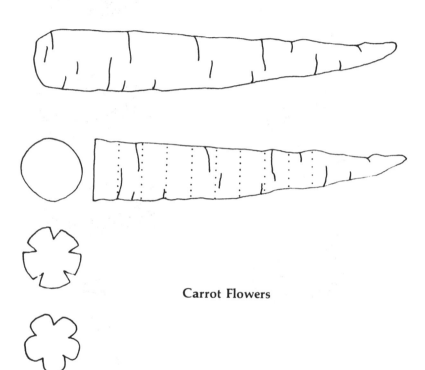

Carrot Flowers

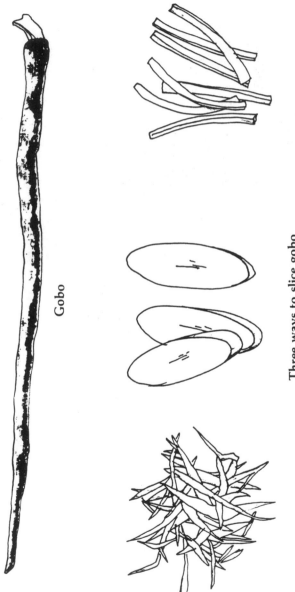

Gobo

Three ways to slice gobo

Decorative containers made from fruits and vegetables — limes, lemons, oranges, tangerines, turnips, cucumbers, etc.

Turnip Cup

Aburage Treasure Bags

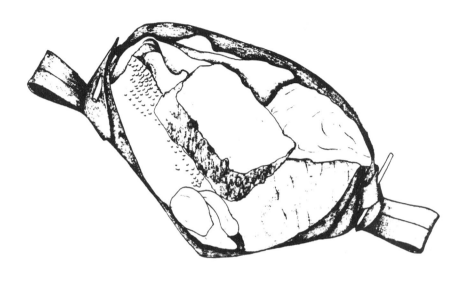

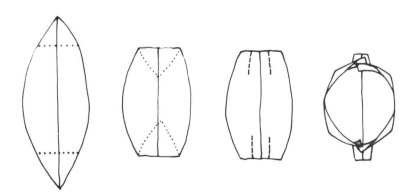

How to make a leaf basket

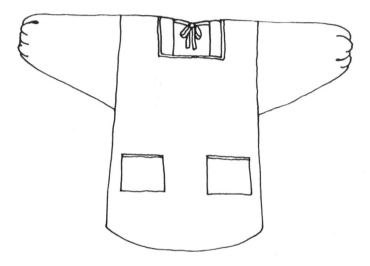

Japanese Apron

Chronology

Continued on next page

Dates	Mediterranean/Europe	India/Southeast Asia	China/Korea	Japan
200 B.C.		Ajanta Caves; Funan Kingdom, Cambodia		
100 B.C.				
0	Augustus			
100 A.D.	Baalbek	Beginnings, Ghandhara Sculpture		
200 A.D.	Roman Pantheon	Amaravati in India, Ceylon, Java, Cambodia; Dvaravati, Siam *Natyasastra*, Sanskrit Theatre/Dance Manual written down		
300 A.D.	Theodosius I Suppression of non-Christians	Gupta era, 320	Eastern Chin Dynasty	
400 A.D.		Ajanta Caves 16-17	Northern Wei Dynasty 389 Buddhist cave temples, Tun-Huang	
500 A.D.	Justinian at Byzantium, Hagia Sophia, Ravenna	Kalidasa, India author of Sanskrit classic drama, *Shakuntala*	Sui Dynasty, 581	Buddhism to Japan, 552 Empress Suiko, 593-628
600 A.D.	Arab-Muslim Empire	Ellura, Elephants	Tang Dynasty, 618	
700 A.D.	Baghdad, 754	Bengal; Palas Ellura, Kailasa Temple Borobudor, Java		Early Nara Period, 645-707 Tempyo Period, 708-811 Todaiji Heian Period, 782-888

Chronology (continued)

Dates	Mediterranean/Europe	India/Southeast Asia	China/Korea	Japan
700 A.D.				Kobo Daishi, Shingon & Tendai Sects; Kyoto, capital of Japan, 794; Gagaku est. in Imperial Court; 701, official court function in 810
800 A.D. 900 A.D.	Charlemagne	Old Pagan, Burma; Khajuraho, N. India; Chola, S. India; Angkor I, Cambodia	Northern Sung Dynasty, 960-1125; Koryo Dynasty, 918-1392 Korea	
1000 A.D.	Crusades; Battle of Hastings, 1066 A.D. William of Normandy conquers England	Rajput States		Fujiwara, beginning of Shugunate; Murasaki, Shikibu-Tale of Genji, 1007-1001
1100 A.D.		Chola Dynasty, South India; Muslim Conquest, North India, 1192-16; Rajput States; Pagan, Burma	Southern Sung, 1126-1271	Kamakura Period, 1186-1335; Zen Buddhism
1200 A.D.	Magna Carta, Runnymede, 1215; Notre Dame, Paris; Cologne Cathedral; Dante, 1265-1321	Deogiri, Deccan	Yuan Dynasty, 1271-1368	
1300 A.D.	Giotto; The Alhambra, Spain; Black Death in Europe, 1347-1350	Muslim Conquest, Deccan, South 1306-26; Vijayanagar, 1336	Ming dynasty, 1368-1644; Yi Dynasty, 1392-1910, Korea	Ashikaga Period, 1338-1565; Zeami, 1363-1443

1400 A.D.	Donatello, Fra Angelico, Botticelli, Leonardo da Vinci	Lodi Mosque, 1494 beginnings of Indian miniature paintings Ankor taken by Siamese		Sesshu, 1420-1506 Monotobu 1476-1559
1400 A.D.	Columbus to West Indies, 1492 Vasco de Gama to India, 1498 War of Roses, England, 1455-85 Magellan, 1480-1506			
1500 A.D.	Michelangelo, Rafael, Durer, Holbain Titian, Correggio	——— St. Francis Xavier 1506-1622 ——— Chidambaram, 1520 Rajput paintings Fatehpur Sikri, 1573-80	Portuguese settle Macao, 1557 Korea invaded by Hideyoshi, 1592	Portuguese sailors reach Japan, 1542 Momoyama Period, 1576-1603
	Elizabeth I, England 1533-1603 Shakespeare, 1564-1616 El Greco			Women's Kabuki, 1603-1629 Korean potters taken to Japan, 1597-1598 Tokugawa Period, 1603-1867
1600 A.D.	Rubens, Frans Hall Van Dyck	Taj Mahal, 1630-48	Ching Dynasty, 1644-1911	Edo, 1613 Nikko Chikamatsu Monzaemon, 1653-1725
	Jamestown settlement, Virginia, 1608	Rajasthani Painting Udaipur Palaces, 1628 Hawkins reaches Surat, meets Jehangir at Agra, 1608		Dutch traders confined to Deshima Island, Nagasaki, 1641 Korin, 1658-1716
	Pilgrims at Plymouth Rock, 1620			

Continued on next page

Chronology (continued)

Dates	Mediterranean/Europe/U.S.	India/Southeast Asia	China/Korea	Japan
1600 A.D.	Louis XIV, France, 1638-1715 Peter I "The Great" of Russia, 1682-1725			
1700 A.D.	Wars of Spanish Succession, 1701-14 Watteau, Hogarth Napoleon Bonaparte, 1769-1821	Jaipur founded, 1728 Guler painting, 1738		Utamaro, 1753-1806
1750 A.D.	Tiepolo Reynolds, Gainsborough Declaration of Independence, 1776 Constitution, 1787 French Revolution, 1789	Kandro Painting Aythia destroyed by Burmese, 1757		Chushingura first performed in puppet theatre, Osaka 1748, in Tokyo, 1749
1800 A.D.	Goya, Constable, Delaxcrois, Turner Louisiana Purchase, 1803 Crimean War, 1853-1856	Chakri dynasty, 1782 Thailand Golden Temple, Amritsar British Annex Oudh, 1856 Sepoy Rebellion, 1857	First Opium War, 1839-1842	
1850 A.D.	Manet, Renouir, Monet, Whistler Rodin, Dega, Cezanne Van Gogh, Gauguin			Townsend Harris, U.S. Consul, 1855-1861 Meiji Restoration, 1868-1912

1850 A.D. Munch, Toulouse-Lautrec
American Civil War-
1861-1865
Suez Canal, 1869
Boer War, South
Africa, 1899-1902
Russo-Japanese War,
1904-1905

Sino-Japanese
Jose Rizal
Exectued, 1898
Battle of Manila
Bay, 1898

Sino-Japanese War, 1894

1900 A.D. World War I, 1914-1918

Republic of China, 1912

Russo-Japanese War,
1904-1905
Kanto Earthquake, 1923

1910-Chosen
Sino-Japanese War, 1937-
1945 Period, Korea,
Japanese Occupation

1941-1945
World War II

INDEX

Index